Casebook of Management for Nonprofit Organizations

Entrepreneurship and Organizational Change in the Human Services

About the Author

Dennis R. Young is Professor at the W. Averell Harriman College for Policy Analysis and Public Management at the State University of New York at Stony Brook, and is a member of the Visiting Faculty of the Program on Non-Profit Organizations, at the Institution for Social and Policy Studies, Yale University.

Casebook of Management for Nonprofit Organizations

Entrepreneurship and Organizational Change in the Human Services

Dennis R. Young

The Haworth Press
New York

Casebook of Management for Nonprofit Organizations: Entrepreneurship and Organizational Change in the Human Services is a monographic supplement to the journal *Administration in Social Work*, Volume 8 (1984). It is not supplied as part of the subscription to the journal, but is available from the Publisher at an additional charge.

Administration in Social Work is a quarterly journal devoted to the theory and practice of management and administration in social work and related human service fields.

The Haworth Press, Inc., 28 East 22 Street, New York, NY 10010

Library of Congress Cataloging in Publication Data

Young, Dennis R., 1943–
    Casebook of management for nonprofit organizations.

    "A monographic supplement to Administration in social work, volume 8, 1984."
    Includes bibliographical references.
    1. Social work administration—United States—Case studies. 2. Child welfare—United States—Management—Case studies. I. Administration in social work. V. 8, 1984 (Supplement) II. Title.
HV91.Y68   1984   361.3'068   84-9040
ISBN 0-86656-324-5
ISBN 0-86656-352-0 (pbk.)

In memory of my beloved father, Dr. Nathan Young, an accomplished educator whose dedication, high standards, and keen wit will ever remain an inspiration.

CONTENTS

NONPROFIT SECTOR VENTURES: CASE STUDIES

NEW ORGANIZATIONS FOUNDED FROM SCRATCH

NEW ORGANIZATIONS PARENTED BY EXISTING AGENCIES

NEW INITIATIVES BY EXISTING ORGANIZATIONS

PUBLIC SECTOR VENTURES: CASE STUDIES

Foreword

The use of original case studies for teaching and learning has a long history. Some institutions base a substantial part of their curricula on the case method. In the social services too, case analysis has occupied a key position in preparing practitioners to assume professional responsibilities in social agencies. Paradoxically, the professional literature is largely barren of useful cases. Student recording of organizational experiences, on the other hand, is almost universally required.

In this volume, a serious and informed observer has undertaken the task of preparing detailed and pointed but concise case studies. A sophisticated social scientist, he conducted a series of interviews and observations with leading management actors in a variety of human service organizations, and distilled the most relevant behaviors in order to cast light on the inner workings of organizational leadership. Dr. Young has here moved successfully between the shoals of too great brevity and too elaborate detail, with a view to making each case situation available for ready discussion and analysis.

While stressing entrepreneurship, these studies deal with a variety of aspects of organizational life and touch upon a number of social policy issues. They provide vivid material on innovation, change and organizational growth, detailing constraints and opportunities grasped by creative and skilled executives. The settings of the studies differ in a number of ways. Those who have an interest in understanding the problems of serving children will find a rich lode of professional insight. Others will recognize problems and dilemmas faced by their organizations. Students will find rich material for reflection and study, for here are live, "real" people, many known widely in the field.

The individual studies concentrate on a special aspect of executive leadership—the entrepreneurial spirit, exploring and seizing opportunities for establishing and extending human services. In this sense they deal with particular ways of engineering organizational change.

Teachers will welcome these recorded experiences for use in the human service classroom. Administrators will find an abundance of illustration of principles of management practice.

This volume is an important contribution to the social organizational literature. One hopes it will stimulate others to pursue the example here provided.

Simon Slavin
Editor, Administration in Social Work
Professor of Social Administration
and Founding Dean Emeritus
Temple University

Preface

Case studies have long been a mainstay of education for management of organizations in the commercial sector of the economy. Theory and methods courses are essential too, but the idea behind case studies is that the overall complexity and richness of management problems and life in organizations can best be appreciated and understood by experiencing them—if not directly then at least through the eyes of others as related through case material.

In the area of human services, case material has not, to this point in time, been commonly available or commonly used. One reason for this is that education for human services has put much less emphasis on management and administration than has education for business, or education for government for that matter. The human services, largely concentrated in the nonprofit sector of the economy, are administered by specialized professionals, highly trained in the treatment or technical methodologies of their disciplines—social work, health care, education, the arts—with normally just a smattering of management training added in.

This is changing. Human service organizations in the current economy of scarce resources and efficiency-minded funding sources have come to realize the importance of good management. And education programs for the human services are beginning to put greater emphasis on rigorous managerial training. Indeed, health administration, arts administration, and other areas of human services administration have begun to develop into important and self-contained specialties in their own right.

Which brings us back to case studies. Those who are now being educated for administration in the human services require case materials drawn from these service areas, as existing materials from the business or government sectors can be stretched only so far in order to portray the kinds of experiences human services administrators will face. The collection of cases presented in this volume is intended to address the present lacuna.

These cases are addressed to particular aspects of human services management—the processes of new program development and the management of organizational change. There is particular emphasis here on entrepreneurial activity, that is, enterprising behavior by administrators and other leaders of human service organizations. Thus, just as in the commercial sector, entrepreneurs or enterprising individuals are seen as linchpins or catalytic agents that help set important organizational changes and program developments in motion, and are largely responsible for their successful implementation. This too, is a view that has been neglected in the education of human service administrators, heretofore, and which needs to become a part of such curricula in the future.

The cases here are not widely spread over all areas of human services. Indeed they are concentrated largely on developments in child welfare, though this is broadly construed to encompass not only foster care but also management information systems, mental health care, education, preventive and community-based services, management consulting, diagnostic service programs, programs for runaway youth, and general youth programming. Generically, however, the cases deal with a wide array of types of organizational change, ranging from development of new programs to the birth of new organizations, the merger of organizations, and the expansion and diversification of the service offerings of various agencies. Moreover, the cases touch on many other intrinsic aspects of organizational administration including management of professionals and other staff, working with trustees, financing of programs through government and private sources, coping with governmental regulatory processes, and managing relationships with organizational clients and constituent groups. The cases also cut across sector lines; while most of the cases are based in the nonprofit sector, three cases are drawn from the governmental sector, as well. Thus, the cases are believed to have a very wide band of application for human service administrators not only in social services, but in other professional services areas as well.

The cases were originally developed as part of a research project on entrepreneurship in nonprofit organizations, under sponsorship of the Program on Non-Profit Organizations in the Institution for Social and Policy Studies of Yale University. The cases contributed to a theory of nonprofit organizational behavior[1] and have since been refined as teaching material, successfully tested in courses in nonprofit organizational management at the State University of New York at Stony Brook and at Yale University. As they are written in nontechnical, easy-to-read language, students enjoy them and digest them quickly. They seem to be most effectively used as the basis of open seminar-style discussions of particular issues or lessons the instructor may wish to draw from a given case. As the introductory chapter indicates, the possible choices for such topics are manifold, and thus the cases quite flexibly inserted into the menus of management courses in a variety of ways. However, there is also great value in allowing the cases to speak for themselves. Having read the cases, students often come up with their own interpretations and ideas on what might have happened or what should have been done in the

---

[1]Young, D. R. (1983) *If not for profit, for what?* Lexington, MA: Lexington Books.

circumstances described. As a teacher, I have often found that the most interesting way to use the cases is to keep my own preconceived notions in check, and to allow the interchange among intelligent graduate students to take its own course.

Dennis R. Young

Acknowledgments

I owe a very special thanks to John G. Simon for his guidance and unwavering support throughout this project. I would also like to thank Richard R. Nelson and Harry Weiner for their particular suggestions and general encouragement. Joseph B. Gavrin, who has since passed away, gave me unique assistance and insights for which I am especially grateful. Barbara Blum and Susan Della Sala provided valued help, as well.

Many other people, too numerous to mention, at Yale and Stony Brook, and within the child care and nonprofit areas at large also gave generously of their time. I am especially grateful to those entrepreneurs and officials documented in the cases of this book, and in other cases that did not make it into this volume, who freely opened themselves to my inquiries. I hope the contents presented here are faithful to their trust.

I also want to give special thanks to Si Slavin and Bill Cohen for their confidence in me, their suggestions for the style and format of the book, and for their editorial guidance.

Writing books like this is especially difficult without competent secretarial support. In this instance, the work involved transcription of tapes as well as typing of voluminous manuscripts. Thus I would like to acknowledge Ella Selmquist, Andrea Compton, Marilyn Mandell, and Patricia Schlee, and give a very special thank you to Sandy Nuhn whose talents, dedication, and organizational skills kept my head above water during the initial period of transcription and writing.

This work has been supported by the Program on Non-Profit Organizations, Institution for Social and Policy Studies, Yale University.

Dennis R. Young
September, 1983

Introduction

Since 'tis Nature's law to change,
  Constancy alone is strange

—*John Wilmot, Earl of Rochester (17th Century)*

An important strand of the theory and literature on organizations and bureaucracy centers on the notion that formal organizations permit society to carry out its ongoing functions more efficiently by structuring work into programmed tasks and sequences. By extension, the management of such organizations can be viewed as a routine control and support function—pushing the right buttons, making the right corrections, providing regular supervision and administrative services, and so on, so that organizations continue to operate smoothly and reliably in a steady state. No doubt, mastery of the routine aspects of administration are essential to successful organizational management. But routine administration is by no means the most interesting nor even the most important part of effective organizational management, in the human services or elsewhere in the economy.

It is perhaps trite to indicate that human service agencies, like organizations in other industries, are dynamic entities. They must adapt to changes in their social and economic environments and they must respond to the advance of professional knowledge and scientific technology. To stand still in a changing world is to invite organizational disaster. Thus a key to successful management, especially in the long run, is the understanding of how and why organizations undertake change and how changes in programs and organizational structure can be effectively developed and administered. Indeed, the appropriate image of a successful manager may be less that of controller and facilitator of routine services, than that of leader and entrepreneur—a person who can chart a clear and confidence-inspiring course for his organization and pull together the various elements needed to implement such plans successfully. In the human services particularly, the entrepreneurial role has not been well understood. Narrowly interpreted, the term "entrepreneur" conjures up images of profit making and wheeling and dealing for purposes of self-interest. But as the cases in this volume graphically illustrate, there is much more to it than this. Entrepreneuring in the human services involves a wide variety of motivations—selfish and unselfish—and it is a function that is essential to the ability of human service organizations to carry out their acknowledged, legitimate societal missions.

It is worth a note of clarification to mention that while entrepreneurship is central to managing an organization's successful adaptation to change, entrepreneurship is not precisely congruent with the responsibilities of executive leadership. Entrepreneurship entails identifying a new concept or idea, e.g., a new service to be offered or a new way of providing an existing service, garnering resources and support, planning and advocating, and overseeing implementation of a venture—in short, doing whatever is necessary to move a project from concept to reality. Executive leadership, in contrast, entails a much more general set of responsibilities, for organizational change, as well as for organizational maintenance and stability.

To expand on this point, various routine or day-to-day aspects of organizational life must be tended to by executives—much of this routine activity legitimately characterized as leadership. For instance, a top executive must serve as a good role model for his subordinates, personifying enthusiasm, proper work habits, and style so as to maintain employees' morale through exhortation and example, and to convey the organization's values and ideology (what recent writers on corporate management have called superordinate goals).

To the contrary, entrepreneurship, a nonroutine function, while it clearly involves leadership behavior, can to an extent be delegated by executives to other staff members by granting them sufficient autonomy and resources. Board members or trustees may also involve themselves in enterprising activity on behalf of the organization. Some staff may even specialize in entrepreneurial projects rather than routine administrative responsibilities, just as some executives may farm out as much routine administration as possible so as to concentrate on enterprising. (See the GLIE and Sanctuary cases for contrasting examples.)

In short, entrepreneurship and executive leadership are not full coincident: Entrepreneurs in an organization may not be executives, though they are leaders in a general sense, and executives may not be entrepreneurs. However, as an empirical matter, the correlation between the two roles is strong. And one thing seems certain—successful executive management of human service organizations in a dynamic world requires that the entrepreneurial function be adequately provided for, one way or another. Such provision may entail direct and intensive executive involvement in enterprising activity, as in the cases of Greer and GLIE presented here, or it may involve, as in the Huntington Sanctuary case, establishing an effective organizational regime within which the executive can encourage, nurture, control, and otherwise facilitate new ventures undertaken by staff.

How then can the management of entrepreneurship and organizational change be learned? Probably not very well through textbooks or even case studies. Experience is always the best teacher. However, as an initial exposure, case studies do have the distinct advantage of relating the actual experiences of real administrators and managers and other leaders who have been responsible for carrying out important projects that have altered the faces of organizations, brought new organizations into existence, and have had significant effects and implications for the industries in which they have taken place. Learning the lessons embedded in these cases should help aspiring managers and even those with some managerial experience to embark on their own ventures with some confidence and awareness of the principles they should apply, the factors they should be aware of, and the pitfalls and opportunities that may lie ahead. Perhaps such study will reduce some of the "trial" in the unavoidably trial-and-error process of mastering this subject, and will help to minimize the prospects of failure, either failure by commission of strategic errors, or failure to recognize or exploit circumstances where enterprising activity is appropriate or opportune.

Before fleshing out some of the perspectives and management lessons on which instructors may wish to have their students focus their attentions and discussions, a few words on the selection and structure of the cases themselves is in order. Since the human services are delivered primarily through public and private nonprofit organizations, and because the objective of this volume is to provide educational material illuminating the management of change in primarily professional rather than commercial contexts, the cases here are confined to public and nonprofit enterprise. Moreover, the balance of cases take place in the private, nonprofit sector where the dearth of managerial case studies has been particularly acute. It should be noted, however, that all but one of the private, nonprofit cases involve considerable interaction with government, and that virtually all of the cases reflect the importance of the government–voluntary sector relationships that pervade delivery of human services in the U.S.—relationships that human service managers must deal with, no matter what the sector to which their organizations formally belong.

The cases are grouped into four categories and subcategories according to the type of venture, and the particular sector of the economy within which a case takes place. Most of the cases (11 in all) take place in the private, nonprofit sector and within this collection cases involve three different types of activity: the founding of new organizations from scratch; the founding of new organizations under the wing of existing or parent agencies; and the development of major new programs or expansion of activities by existing organizations.

Three cases of human service ventures in the government sector are also presented. These provide some perspective on differences in incentives, constraints, motivations, problems, and opportunities, between government and the private, nonprofit sector. One of the public sector cases concerns the establishment of a new organization (youth bureau); the other two focus on the development of new programs within the context of existing organizations. As indicated in the Preface, all the cases cluster in the general field of child welfare but range very widely in terms of particular services and programs within this field. Moreover, as elaborated below, the cases concentrate on generic management problems and aspects of organizational change that apply to a very wide spectrum of organizations dealing with professional or human services.

A comment on the methodology of construction of the cases is in order at this point. As noted in the Preface, the cases originally contributed to a theoretical study of behavior of nonprofit organizations.[1] In that context, a variety of different types of ventures, along the lines noted above, were sought. Through various types of (formal and informal) inquiry, organizations which had exhibited each variety of venture (establishing a new organization, developing a new program, etc.) within recent memory were identified. The rationale was that cases that had transpired recently would offer better access to the principal actors involved, greater accuracy of memory of these actors, and greater availability of written documentation.

Ultimately twenty-one cases were identified in organizations whose decision-makers agreed to cooperate. (All of these cases were written up. Three took place in the proprietary sector. Fourteen of the remaining eighteen cases were selected for this volume.) In each case, as many of the principal actors as possible were interviewed extensively by the author. Interviews were tape-recorded and later transcribed. Available written materials such as annual reports, minutes, proposals and other documents were studied as well, and, where possible, outside observers were also consulted. The cases were each written up in draft form and circulated to those interviewed to check accuracy, and subsequently revised and edited. As presented here, the cases provide the available facts, the views of the principal actors, and the author's suggested interpretation and explanation of events.

In order to facilitate comparative discussion and analysis of the cases, they are all structured into a uniform format. Each case is divided into nine sections, each of which describes a particular dimension to the case, as follows:

Précis. This is a short overview summarizing what the venture is, when and where it took place, and a brief glimpse of its character.

The Entrepreneur(s). This section briefly introduces the key participants and indicates some of the history, skills, philosophy, and motivations of these individuals.

The Organization(s). Here an overview is given of the organizational context in which the venture takes place. This includes characterization of the parent organization(s)—if the venture is a new internal program,

---

[1]Young, D. R. (1983) *If not for profit, for what?* Lexington, MA: Lexington Books.

spin-off, or a merger—and if applicable, a description of the new organization.

Chronology of Events. This is simply a list in chronological order of the key events leading to and culminating in the implementation of the venture at issue. This section is intended to serve as a convenient reference for the reader, to guide him in tracking the sequence of events.

Context. This section discusses the social context in which the venture takes place. This includes demographic, economic, and social trends, as well as developments in the professional disciplines that served as stimulative and long-run determining factors influencing the case.

Choices. This section describes the strategic choices facing the managers and entrepreneurs in the case, the alternatives they considered, and the reasons they selected particular courses of action.

Risks and Constraints. Here the professional, personal, organizational, and financial risks facing decision-makers are described and assessed, and the financial, regulatory, bureaucratic, political, and other constraining factors that inhibited the venture's implementation or affected its form, are identified and discussed.

Outcomes. This section tells what ultimately came of the venture, as of a given cutoff date (approximately mid-1979) when documentation was completed. Some sense of the ultimate success or failure of the venture can be gleaned from this presentation.

Analysis. This is a brief discussion that brings together various aspects of the case and suggests a way to crystallize and summarize why the venture took place in its particular form and circumstances. A sense of the overall "chemistry" required to carry off the venture is indicated here.

LESSONS AND PERSPECTIVES

What is the student of management and administration in the human services to learn from these cases? To answer this question, let us begin with the premise previously stated that successfully managing a human service organization requires the ability to guide and inspire programmatic and organizational change, not only the ability to ride out storms and trends in the organizational environment but perhaps more importantly to anticipate requirements for change and to lead an organization through constructive adaptations in advance of debilitating crises. This ability in turn requires that the manager have: (1) a good understanding of how and why major changes in organizations take place and what factors shape the outcomes of efforts to change, and (2) a mastery of strategies and techniques and a knowledge of the prerequisites for successfully implementing and managing change. In the following few pages, an overview of the perspectives and lessons that can be drawn from the cases will be presented. The intent here is to identify some of the important points instructors may wish to emphasize and have discussed by their students. There is no claim of comprehensiveness here, however. Each case is sufficiently rich in detail that instructors or students are likely to draw many other perspectives, interpretations, and management lessons of general value on the subject of change or on other managerial questions such as management styles, organizational relationships, and so on. Indeed this flexibility represents much of the educational value of case studies per se. The cases are meant to be provocative and to challenge the reader, but neither the following discussion nor even the analyses presented in each of the cases constitute the last word. Rather, this material is meant to be suggestive, and perhaps a good jumping off point from which further discussion can take place.

General Perspectives on How and Why Change Takes Place

At least four different lessons may be drawn from the cases here on the subject of why and when major changes take place in human service organizations. These lessons repeat themselves throughout the cases, but here we shall highlight only a few important instances.

The first important perspective is that changes often occur as part of a process of solving an important internal organizational problem. The second perspective is that changes are driven by entrepreneurs who are in the right place at the right time and devote great amounts of energy to the project, for a variety of strong personal motives. The third perspective is that changes at the organization level usually reflect trends and long-term developments in the social, economic, and technological environment of the organization. Fourth, change often reflects the crystallization of some important, new idea.

Problem Solving

A pessimist could survey the cases in this book and observe that organizational crises are the seedbed of change and that unfortunately organizational managers and trustees tend not to see far enough ahead to head off such crises with reforms earlier on. An optimist on the other hand, would note that severe crises often allow organizations to change in ways that make them much stronger and healthier in the end. Both perspectives seem to have strong elements of truth. Financial crises and related difficulties with the quality and workload of organizational services are prominent among the cases and seem often to be at the root of impending change. For example, Seabury Barn, a residential program for runaway youth sponsored by the Smith Haven Ministries (SHM), was a compromise component of a package proposal to a state funding agency designed to shore up the Ministries financial condition and allow it to honor its serious debt obligations.

Sometimes financial problems are tied closely to workload problems. Characteristic of many charitable organizations, Smith Haven Ministries and the Group Child Care Consultant Services (GCCCS) were overextended in terms of the services they wanted to provide their needy clientele, compared to the resources that were available to provide these services. A new program and a reorganization followed from these circumstances, respectively. The Harlem-Dowling program sponsored by the Spence-Chapin organization was also inspired in part by an economic overburden the agency faced with its foster care program, and a desire to avoid having its foster care program overwhelm the main agenda of adoption and research and demonstration programs that Spence-Chapin considered its principal mission.

Quality problems sometimes couple with financial difficulties to inspire change. The two spectacular examples of the Florida Sheriffs Youth Fund and Greer-Woodycrest Children's Services illustrate how the greatest successes in organizational growth, development, modernization, and efficiency, can follow from the depths of physical plant and service deterioration and management stagnation. Greer and Florida Sheriffs are classic "turnaround" situations.

Finally, serious "image" problems that impair and threaten an organization's relationships with its supporters and constituents may be seen to inspire change. In the case of Greer, the perception of low quality by state regulators was a serious blow and impetus to reform. In the case of Florida Sheriffs, it was the poor public image of the sheriffs as law-enforcement officials that prompted their organization to get into the business of helping troubled youth. And in the case of the Pleasantville Diagnostic Center of the Jewish Child Care Association (JCCA), the perceptions of New York City officials and others in the child care community, that JCCA, especially its Pleasantville campus, was an institution only for well-behaved, white Jewish children, stung at a time when the social priorities required service to troubled minority children. In all these instances, the image problem contributed to an impetus to do something to reverse those outside perceptions, perceptions which represented a serious long run threat to the viability of the organizations involved.

Entrepreneurs

It is impossible to read the cases here without realizing that the energies, drives, and skills of entrepreneuring managers or other leaders are crucial to the formulation, launching, implementation, and nurturing of new programs and organizations. It is clear in many of the cases that the particular organizational changes might never have occurred without the right entrepreneurial characters in place at the particular time. For example, the Group Live-In Experience (GLIE) in the South Bronx, the Sagamore outpatient program, and the Melville House on Long Island, are special and unusual programs that are uniquely associated with particular social entrepreneurs and seem unlikely to have come into existence without them. There seems to be no inevitability surrounding such innovations, and without their entrepreneurial roots there seems to be no reason to believe that something like them would have sprung up in a proximate time and place.

In other cases, where alternate ventures might have filled in the vacant market niches, the entrepreneurs clearly put their individual stamps on the character of the programs they inspired, and at the least could be credited with ventures their organizations would not otherwise have undertaken or succeeded in. Greer, for example, or Florida Sheriffs Youth Fund, might not have survived at all, much less develop into the organizational pathbreakers they eventually became, were it not for the fortuitous employment of Harry Weaver and Ian Morrison, respectively, at crucial times in the histories of these organizations. While in cases such as the Child Welfare Information Service, the Sanctuary Program of the Huntington Youth Bureau, and the Brookhaven Youth Bureau, it seems clear that some programs like these would eventually have come along (with other leaders at the helm), the expediency with which they did develop, and the particular form they took, derived much of their substance from the ideas and energies of the entrepreneurial characters, Joe Gavrin, Andy Casazza, and Tom Williams, respectively.

Finally, it is of interest to note that the opportunity to make money or to gain other material rewards is *not* necessarily the essential or even most common motivation underlying enterprising behavior in the human services. Contrary to the stereotypical concept of the entrepreneur, financial return is not the sole engine of venture even in the profit-making sector, and certainly not in the not-for-profit parts of the economy. A perusal of the cases here reveals that motivations vary widely. They include: artistic-like urges to build and create; the seeking of status or inner satisfaction from professional achievement and accomplishment; a psychological need to test oneself and prove that one is capable of carrying off a major project or program; pursuit of innate desires to help, teach, or serve the less fortunate members of society; intellectual satisfaction from shaping and implementing new ideas; the achievement of personal recognition, power, and social status; the urge to control people and events; the fulfillment of strong social or religious beliefs or causes; a desire for autonomy and independence (to be one's own boss); maternal-like satisfactions of parenting an enterprise and seeing it grow; and material security and gain. Thus the entrepreneurs encountered in the cases here are quite a diverse group, ranging from the grandiose builders like Bert Beck, Jay Goldsmith, and Ian Morrison to the outspoken and unencumbered firebrand Lorraine Reilly, to the soft-spoken, behind-the-scenes facilitators like Joe Gavrin and Peter Ryan, to the persistent idealists like Tom Williams and

Ken Goldman, to the highly professional achievers Jane Edwards, Andy Casazza, and Mary Hagamen, to the very businesslike Harry Weaver, to the almost reluctant enterpriser and devoted educator in the person of Alan Keith-Lucas. But this diversity of motives and styles belies certain strong common traits that bind these entrepreneurial characters together—the intense energies and commitments they have exhibited in pursuing their objectives in clear, single-minded, and opportune fashion.

The Environment

While each venture is impressive and somewhat unique in its own right, each case may also been seen as a current or eddy in a stream of social, economic, and technological change. No organization changes in a vacuum, and most organizational changes signal larger changes taking place in the environment. Thus, while individual ventures and program developments may not be inevitable manifestations of environmental trends, at the very least these ventures tend to blossom when developments in that environment signal that "their time has come."

Technological change, for example, is reflected in the case of the Child Welfare Information Service (CWIS) where the advent of the computer makes inevitable improved information processing for management of child care agencies in the New York City system, and prompts the agencies to take initiative in this direction. Or, in the case of the Sagamore Outpatient Clinic, new professional knowledge of mental retardation and autism in children influenced the development of new, noninstitutional services.

Changes in the economic environment also have a strong influence in prompting enterprising behavior. In the instance of Harlem-Dowling, for example, the New York City fiscal crisis severely depressed the per diem rates which the City could pay for child care, at first delaying the possibility of launching this new agency, but eventually creating such strains on the parent agency (Spence-Chapin) that cutting the new agency loose became imperative.

Demographic trends may be seen to underlie much of the economic pressure that influences the development of new ventures in the human services. In the case of the Jewish Board of Family and Children's Services (JBFCS), a merger of two Jewish agencies in New York City reflected the need for services consolidation in a region where the Jewish population was declining. By contrast, the case of Florida Sheriffs Youth Fund illustrates how a venture can ride a demographic trend to prosperity, in this instance, the growing elderly population in Florida which generated a strong element of voluntary contributions through estate planning.

Demographic change may be observed to have a much more pervasive influence on enterprise in human services than just what is felt through direct economic effects. The increase in the youth population in Brookhaven Town, for example, was a major justification for the establishment of the Youth Bureau in that location while that same trend in nearby Huntington Town and surrounding Suffolk County underlay the developments of the Sanctuary program in Huntington and Smith Haven Ministries' Seabury Barn, respectively. Similarly the turnover of youth and family populations in New York City, featuring a large influx of racial minorities, played a large part in stimulating the program developments of Greer-Woodycrest Children's Services, Pleasantville Diagnostic Center, Harlem-Dowling, and other cases in this volume.

Other kinds of social changes also influence organizational enterprise in important ways. The growing phenomenon of runaway youth in the 1960s and 1970s, for example, was a direct antecedent of the programs presented in the GLIE, Sanctuary, and Seabury Barn case studies. And the deterioration of urban centers such as the South Bronx or the Lower East Side of New York helped inspire the GLIE and Lower East Side Family Union (LESFU) projects. Finally, important shifts in the role and character of government social services policies overtime underlie a number of the changes described in the case studies. Demands for greater accountability in the public sector, for example, directly influenced the development of projects like CWIS which would provide better information to monitor child care agencies under contract to government, while the deinstitutionalization movements in mental health and retardation, social services, and criminal justice, which deemphasized residential care in favor of services delivered in the community, underwrote elements of the GLIE, Sagamore, and LESFU cases.

In short, it is almost always necessary to ask where an individual venture fits into the "big picture" of social, economic, and technical change, in order to obtain a comprehensive understanding of why a given enterprise developed in the particular time, place, and form that it did. Even where particular ventures seem to buck the trends, such as the Florida Sheriffs Youth Fund case, which grew solely on private, philanthropic funding at a time when dependence of social service agencies on government funds was generally dramatically increasing, they can be understood by studying the local context, in this case, the growing elderly population and the political conservatism of Florida.

Ideas

It is striking how often the strength of simple but profound new ideas or concepts serve to inspire and crystallize program developments. Such ideas may capture the essential purpose or character of ventures, hence their articulation gives the participating parties the vision they need to push the enterprise forward and rally its supporters. A few examples will suffice to illustrate this phenomenon. In the Child Welfare Information

Service case, the idea that "information is power" played an important motivating role, and the desire for shared control over such information underlay much of the energy for the child care agencies to develop a management information system of their own before the government developed one in which they would have little part. In the Huntington Sanctuary, Brookhaven Youth Bureau, LESFU, and JBFCS cases, the "model" of a comprehensive mental health or social service delivery system that coordinates various kinds of services from different sources or divisions provided the essential design principle by which these enterprises were developed. In the case of LESFU and Harlem-Dowling, the concept of social service agencies having to be firmly rooted into the local communities and populations they service also played a central inspirational role.

Professional concepts, reflecting current disciplinary thinking in social work, mental health, and related fields provide the intellectual cores around which various other programmatic developments grow. For example, the idea of comprehensive problem diagnosis prior to foster care placement formed the conceptual foundation for the Pleasantville venture, while the concepts of deinstitutionalization and preventive services clearly influenced the Sagamore and LESFU developments.

Reform strategies also may constitute the central idea. In the case of Sagamore Children's Center, Mary Hagamen devised the "inside/out" notion to convert the center from inpatient to outpatient emphasis over time, while in the Pleasantville case, Jake Trobe saw the diagnostic center as a "foot in the door" that would eventually turn the program emphasis of the whole agency around. In both these cases, the entrepreneurs worked with an explicit concept of incremental or evolutionary reform, envisioning how their initial projects would set in motion a long-term sequence of constructive change.

In short, the context of organizational problems, the presence of entrepreneurial energies, skills, and motivation; trends in the social, economic, and technological environment; and the conception and articulation of key ideas seem to constitute much of the basic chemistry leading to important organizational changes and program developments. For the human services manager it is well to be able to recognize these circumstances and prerequisites if one is to be capable of fostering change by planting the seeds of reform into fertile soil. But what of the nurturing of these seeds and resultant seedlings? What lessons can we draw from the cases, for the successful *management* of change? We turn to this question next.

Principles of Managing Change

There are of course no cookbook solutions to successfully carrying off the development of a major programmatic or organizational enterprise. Every venture is different and of necessity a large degree of adaptation and "learning while doing" must take place, even for seasoned managers and leaders in longstanding organizations. But a perusal of the cases here reveals a surprising number of common principles and lessons that seem to underlie success, and these seem worth fleshing out for consideration:

(1) Styles of administration must be adapted to fit the circumstances. Most managers and leaders have their own personal styles of administration. Some prefer tight centralized control and others put more emphasis on delegation of responsibilities and decentralized control. Some prefer expansion and development of large organizations, and others lean to spinning off new programs as autonomous units, and so on. Similarly, organizations develop their own cultures, policies, and styles of administration over time, which may reflect their size, diversity, age, sources of support, and programmatic objectives. Certainly a wide variety of organizational structures and administrative styles is reflected in the fourteen cases presented here.

It is interesting, however, that the form in which new program developments are administered is not always consistent either with the intrinsic preferences of the guiding entrepreneur nor with the historical style of the organization in which the developments take place. Rather, the styles and strategies for new developments often seem to follow an internal logic dictated by the intrinsic concepts and environmental circumstances in which they are built.

There are several noteworthy examples of this in the cases here. Harlem-Dowling was an embryonic program in the Spence-Chapin agency whose executive style was tight central control. Yet the logic of the program, its ability to function as an indigenous agency to the Harlem community, required a loosening of such control and eventually a letting go entirely. It took discipline on the part of the guiding executive, Jane Edwards, to allow this to happen. A similar case in point is LESFU, a program also built on the concept of indigenous local operation and on the principle of coordinating packages of social services from a number of different local social service organizations. Yet LESFU started out as a program within the Henry Street Settlement under direction of Bert Beck whose intrinsic preferences were to maintain and expand the repertoire of programs under his direct jurisdiction. However, the logic of the program and the cooperation of other local agencies dictated otherwise. Again, Beck had the insight and discipline to let go.

In various other cases, there is more harmony between the logic and requirements of the fledgling program and the intrinsic preferences of the entrepreneur or the style of the parent agency. Joe Gavrin, for example, was perfectly happy to move the CWIS program outside of his Council on Voluntary Child Care Agencies (COVCCA) both as a logical step in its development and as a way of keeping COVCCA in the small and informal style he preferred. And Jay Goldsmith was content, even enthusiastic, to decentralize the JBFCS in order to make management of this very large new agency more viable. So too, the expansive style of Ian Morrison fit the strategy of expansion through merger on which his agency was embarked. In still other cases, however, the reluctance of the entrepreneur to adapt his or her management style to what the program change appeared to require seemed to cause problems. Alan Keith-Lucas's reluctance to get too heavily involved in administration may have held back the needed formalization of GCCCS, for example, when that agency was growing quickly and running into substantial financial and other management difficulties. And, while the fierce, antibureaucratic rebellious style of Mary Hagamen served her well when her program was in vogue and outside funding was available, it may have come back to haunt her when the circumstances changed and the bureaucrats were back in the driver's seat.

A relevant aside here is that the complex and multifaceted requirements for management and entrepreneurial leadership may sometimes be divided into subspecialities, allowing the skills and styles of alternative officers to better match the requirements of the job to be done. In several cases here, this takes the form of having a "Mr. Outside" and a "Mr. Inside." For example, in the Pleasantville case, Jake Trobe is the dominant figure in dealing with the outside world and with his agency's overall governance and administration, but Paul Steinfeld is given the responsibility for implementing the project itself and running it on a day-to-day basis. Similarly, in the Harlem-Dowling case, Jane Edwards is the head honcho but Joe Smith is given responsibility for laying the groundwork in the Harlem community, and initially implementing and running the program. In these cases and others, the chief executives were able to organize themselves in a manner which met the projects' requirements without cramping their personal administrative styles. In the case of LESFU, on the other hand, finding an adequate Mr. Inside proved to be a problem.

In short, entrepreneurs may be able to pick and choose their ventures, and organize their agencies, in a manner consistent with their administrative and leadership styles, but sometimes the intrinsic concepts behind the innovation being implemented, or particular stages in the development of those projects, require adaptation and rethinking of administrative strategies to ensure continued success.

(2) Managing change requires sensitivity to staff, trustees, and constituents.

> Change is not made without inconvenience, even from worse to better.

> —*Richard Hooker, in the "English Dictionary"*
> *(16th Century)*

Change is, by definition, disruptive. In human service organizations it affects the welfare of a number of important groups of participants—

staff, trustees, clients, and the like. Given that successful implementation of change usually requires (at least the passive) cooperation of these participants, an important tenet in the management of change is to deal sensitively with them—bringing them along in partnership, or at least making them aware of why certain painful adjustments or compromises need to be made; giving credit for their support and sacrifice; distributing benefits and costs in a manner that is perceived as fair and reasonable; and respecting existing loyalties, sentimentalities, and personal principles where possible.

Certain of the cases present examples of such sensitive behavior in clear terms. The JBFCS case involved the merger of two agencies with long traditions, loyal staff and boards members, and ties to their client communities. Most of the energy in carrying out the merger was spent on working out arrrangements that would minimize the dislocations and relieve the anxieties of those involved, while still accomplishing the consolidation objectives. Meetings, discussions, training sessions, protocols for allocating positions on the board and staff, "massaging personalities," and paying meticulous attention to the language employed to describe what was being done—for example emphasizing the concept of a "marriage of equals"—dominated the proceedings. Even so, the proposed merger almost failed because of sensitive feelings on both sides of the aisle.

The case of the Brookhaven Youth Bureau provides another good example of sensitive management. Here, because the program was to be implemented in the local public sector, the entrepreneur Tom Williams was meticulous in his efforts to build bipartisan support in order to minimize the risks facing the council members he had gotten behind the effort. He was careful to give credit for the successes, however, and to propose service patterns that benefitted alternative local jurisdictions in a balanced way. The Pleasantville case provides another such example, where an explicit incremental change strategy was adopted in part to bring anxious staff members along slowly, rather than to try to impose a sudden radical shift in clientele upon them.

The Harlem-Dowling case is even more intriguing in this respect. Anxieties of staff members understandably nervous about breaking away from the parent agency were here balanced against the growing impatience of would-be board members of the new agency whose autonomy had been delayed. Here management had to stroke two different groups whose interests were at odds with one another.

In other cases, an inadequate degree of sensitivity may have accounted for problems in implementing or maintaining the venture at issue. In the LESFU case, tensions between research- and demonstration-oriented management and service-oriented staff members were not very well ameliorated. And in the Sagamore case, inattention to the sagging morale of the staff of the contracting inpatient department may have contributed to conditions that eventually became unstable.

Clearly, sensitivity to affected groups cannot dominate the scenarios of change, else too often nothing would be done. Too many have vested interests in the status quo. Hard decisions need to be made, such as in the Greer case where longstanding staff members had to be let go. But the realization that changes will be painful and that successful change can depend on ameliorating that discomfort seems to be a key element in the successful management of major change.

(3) Being creative. Just as problem solving often forms the basis of enterprising behavior, creative solutions to problems frequently seem to spell the difference between the successful implementation of a venture and its stagnation or failure. In a number of the cases, stubborn operational difficulties threatened the viability of whole initiatives and efforts to develop and implement new programs. At the same time, creative thinking—formulating new alternatives or new ways of approaching the problem—saved the day. These creative solutions, though modest in concept, had the common characteristic of being out of the ordinary, demonstrating the need for enterprisers to avoid the mental rut of always going by the book, but rather thinking things out afresh when conventional ways of doing things do not work.

A few examples from the cases will suffice to illustrate the point. In the instance of GLIE, the ordinary procedures for certifying the new agency had led to stalemate. Someone (Barbara Blum of the State Board of Social Welfare) came up with the bright idea of putting the new program under the wing of an existing agency. The solution was obvious, but only in retrospect. Similarly, in the Florida Sheriffs experience, a restrictive trust stood in the way of plans to diversify and expand beyond programs for boys. Harry Weaver conceived the bright idea of setting up multiple corporations at least as a way of circumventing the restrictions in the short run, and as a way of demonstrating to the courts later on that the restrictions had to be lifted. It was not a conventional solution, but it worked. In the Jewish Board of Family and Children's Services case, there was a problem of who would become the board president of the newly merged agency. A Solomon-like arrangement was developed whereby the board presidency would go to the current board president of one of the merging agencies, but then shift to his counterpart in the other agency for a longer term after a given period of time. Unusual, but it was accepted.

The managerial lesson in all of this is straightforward enough, if not so easy to carry out in practice: explore all the angles and don't be confined by the conventional ways of doing things. A simple solution to a knotty operational problem may mean the difference between success and failure.

(4) Enterprise requires risk-taking. Classically, commercial entrepreneurship is commonly associated with risk-taking of a financial nature. There is some of this kind of risk-taking in the public and nonprofit human services as well. In cases such as Melville House or the Brookhaven Youth Bureau, the entrepreneurs faced personal financial sacrifice, at least in the short run, and put their future incomes at risk.

Still, if the cases here are at all typical, financial risk-taking does not seem to be the primary gamble for those who guide new ventures and undertake major programmatic change in the human services. Rather such individuals appear to go out on a limb in other ways, perhaps more courageous ways than simply financial peril. Specifically, these leaders often put their professional and managerial reputations on the line, and risk the security of their jobs, by undertaking bold initiatives whose consequences cannot be fully anticipated. Moreover, the process of organizational change and the success of major new ventures seems to depend importantly on the willingness of entrepreneurs to assume such risks.

In several of the cases, the ventures involved controversial new programs, which if they failed would invite the disdain of professional peers. In the Harlem-Dowling case, for example, there were more than enough naysayers who thought it was foolish to try to establish a new human services agency in the rocky social soil of Harlem. As a fledgling executive director, Mrs. Edwards faced potential ridicule from fellow social workers and loss of effectiveness as an administrator if the venture had backfired. Similarly, Jake Trobe and Paul Steinfeld perceived themselves as playing with fire in their effort to establish a diagnostic center for potentially violent and disruptive children on their campus at Pleasantville. One serious incident might have jeopardized the project and the long-term reform strategy it spearheaded, and would have put the future personal effectiveness of these administrators in doubt as well. The case of the Huntington Sanctuary program is similar. One serious incident associated with the overnight placement of a runaway youth might have undermined the program and had serious implications for the youth bureau itself.

In other cases, the new ventures threatened to mar the reputations and effectiveness of the organizations and increase the managerial burdens of executives, because they introduced complexity into existing administration arrangements. In the case of Seabury Barn, an additional program in an area where the organization had no experience (residential care) was being grafted onto an organization (SHM) which already was straining to hold itself together. Yet this new program promised financial salvation and necessitated the risk. In the Florida Sheriffs case, Harry Weaver set up multiple corporations for his different campus programs, gambling that the courts would strike down the restrictive trust on his Boys Ranch and allow him ultimately to consolidate the organization's operations into a manageable administrative structure. Had he lost this gamble, he would have been saddled with a highly cumbersome and unwieldy managerial arrangement. But had he not tried, he would have been unable to undertake the subsequent expansion and growth of the Youth Fund enterprise.

Finally, in the case of the Jewish Board of Family and Children's Services, two agencies of manageable size and individually respected reputations were merged into a new, very large agency whose future shape and prospects were theorized but largely unknown. Moreover, these agencies were coaxed along into consolidation by the executive directors of each, one of whom, Jay Goldsmith, would have to administer the new arrangement. Not only could Goldsmith be blamed for whatever failure or loss of reputation the new agency might incur, but he faced a potentially overwhelming managerial burden had he not been able to reorganize in a manner that would ease the responsibilities of the top man.

Finally, entrepreneurs in these human services case studies sometimes exhibited an explicit willingness to stick their necks out by taking actions that were unauthorized but which seemed necessary to keep their ventures on track. Most often this brand of risk-taking involved refusal to wait for official government approvals prior to opening new facilities for business. In the cases of GLIE and Seabury Barn such actions were taken both for economic reasons and to prod the bureaucracy into faster action, but they were gambles nonetheless.

Any consideration of risk-taking must of course take into account both sides of the coin—i.e., what were the risks of doing something versus *not* doing it. In several cases, especially those where the venture represented a solution to an important and pressing organizational problem, the risks of not undertaking the proposed project or program were clearly high as well. This applies, for example, to the Seabury Barn case and the early stages of the Greer and Florida Sheriffs experiences, where not undertaking the initiatives might have meant the financial failures of the agencies involved. In other instances, however, the dangers of inaction were not necessarily imminent and the risks were taken by those who could foresee potential long-term benefits from their short term gambles and sacrifices.

(5) Successful enterprise requires persistence. While the entrepreneurial characters encountered in the cases here are a very dynamic and sometimes fervent, hot-blooded group of personalities, they all exhibit unusual degrees of patience and what is called in the slang "stick-to-itiveness." Constraints and complications pepper these cases as they would all significant ventures involving major change, yet the entrepreneurs refused to be defeated by these roadblocks and indeed took them on as personal challenges. This behavior comes out most clearly where these enterprising individuals had to deal with government to obtain certifications, approvals or funding, and where they had to overcome skepticism, political reservations, and bureaucratic inertia and inconsistency.

This is nowhere better illustrated than in the case of Melville House, where obtaining certification from the state bureaucracy to open the facility dragged on interminably and threatened to sink the venture at various points, but where the resolve of the entrepreneurs eventually won out. Similarly, in the GLIE case a charter for the new agency had to be fought for, and interim governance arrangements accepted, before the city's regulatory machinery allowed the program to officially open. And in the case of Sagamore Children's Center, the persistence of the entrepreneur is illustrated by her incredible energy and effort in coping with the state civil service system in order to hire suitable staff for her outpatient program.

Persistence and patience is required not only with the bureaucracy but with the overriding political system as well. Thus, in the Seabury Barn case, Peter Ryan spent endless hours in negotiation with county legislators as well as state officials over funding and governance arrangements acceptable to these interests. Andy Casazza and his staff repeatedly resubmitted their grant proposals for Sanctuary until it was funded. And Tom Williams waited patiently through changes in the town's administration until a receptive town supervisor and councilmen were in place; then he persisted in his efforts to document needs, garner support, and ultimately gain appointment as the Brookhaven Youth Bureau director.

Of course many other facets of enterprise require similar persistence, including pursuit of internal agency matters. Thus, Jane Edwards had to keep up the pressure over a long period of time in order to avoid any tendency of staff members comfortable with present arrangements to slow the emancipation of the Harlem-Dowling project. And Jay Goldsmith had to anticipate months of meetings and negotiations not only to prepare personnel for the JBFCS consolidation, but to deal with setbacks, and to ease the implementation and smooth the transition once the merger had officially taken place.

Overall, the lesson seems to be that the guiding entrepreneurs and managers must be clear-minded about what is to be accomplished, but must also expect that accomplishment to take a long time and to encounter many problems along the way. Ventures can thus fail either because the leaders can lose their senses of direction in the midst of the numerous barriers to implementation, or because they may lack the fortitude to keep plugging in the face of resistance, distraction, and delay.

(6) Beware the dilemmas of funding. One of the trickiest problems the entrepreneurs in these cases seem to encounter is balancing the programmatic and organizational implications of accepting various sources of funds against the benefits of that support. Often, the implications are subtle and even deceiving. In other instances, the implications are fully understood and anticipated, and either funds are rejected or accepted with awareness of the consequences.

In various cases, concessions are made as a necessity of essential funding. In the GLIE case, an onerous oversight arrangement is accepted as a way of qualifying for foster case funding. Even more dramatically, GLIE is forced to separate from its advocacy activities as a condition of funding for its services. The Seabury Barn case also exhibits an example where undesired oversight arrangements are accepted in exchange for funding eligibility. For GCCCS, concessions in autonomy were also the price extracted for overhead support from the university in which the organization is housed.

Alternatively, agencies are sometimes forced to make service program concessions in exchange for funding. Thus, Seabury Barn was itself a project taken on by the Smith Haven Ministries in exchange for funding support of SHM's other programs. And in the LESFU case, spinning-off the project from the Henry Street Settlement was a partial consequence of securing a grant from the state.

In other instances, funding sources were specifically rejected because of the programmatic implications they contained. Thus GLIE rejected various juvenile justice and drug program monies in order to avoid the labelling of its clients that this would entail. And more spectacularly, the Florida Sheriffs organization scrupulously avoided government money of any sort in order to preserve its autonomy and avoid any entanglements that might interfere with its program objectives.

In various cases, the leaders and managers devised strategies to free themselves somewhat from the oppressive consequences of receiving funds from particular sources. Diversification is one strategy, employed by GLIE for example in its later stages of development, and sought by the designers of the JBFCS merger that combined agencies with primary dependence on different public and private funding sources. The federal grant for the Sagamore outpatient project was another instance where diversification permitted escaping the requirements of the state's regular (inpatient-oriented) funding system.

Another strategy is deliberate ambiguity in proposal writing for grant funds. This was an idea used in the LESFU case as a way of maximizing the chances of funding from different sources as well as allowing flexibility in implementation. A third strategy, for the private agencies at least, was to build up endowment or reserve funds that could ultimately generate income in the form of returns on investment, free of external conditions and restraints. This was the objective of Harry Weaver in the Florida Sheriffs case.

But these strategies, even if they worked, were not without problems and unanticipated consequences. For LESFU, ambiguity in the proposal stage translated into uncertainties and tensions when it came to detailed program design and implementation. And in the case of Florida Sheriffs, the strategy of building up reserves meant putting great emphasis on fund-raising activity and particularly the solicitation of donations from conservative elderly contributors, which in turn seemed to dull the aggressiveness and shunt the planning for the agency's primary objective—services to predelinquent youth.

Other dilemmas are also raised by decisions on funding. What was to be the future of the outpatient program at Sagamore when the special grant ran out, given that the state's regular funding programs were designed for inpatient care? Was permanence ever possible in this regime? And what about the dangers of false security once comfortable endowment funds are put into place, as they were in the instance of the Greer agency prior to its deterioration? No easy answers appear to exist. The lesson for management then is to be aware enough to look gift horses in the mouth and to anticipate and be prepared for it when they buck.

The Chemistry of Success

A final perspective that seems worth imparting to the student of management in the human services is that purposeful organizational and program change cannot be taken for granted. Rather it requires explicit management attention, adherence to strategies and principles of the kind indicated in the previous section, and an appreciation of the conditions conducive to change and the elements prerequisite to it. More than this, it is useful to recognize that change is fragile and that successful change requires that unstable elements be brought together at the same time and place in order for the necessary interactions to take place, i.e., the chemistry of change to be effected. The case studies are, by and large, studies of ventures that were successful, at least for a period of time. Instances where ventures were nipped in the bud, or were foregone for lack of the proper combination of factors, would of course be much harder to find and to document. But the number of these would no doubt overwhelm the number of successes that can be identified.

Even the case studies of success, however, contain with them substantial evidence of how fragile, even serendipitous, successful implementation of change can be. Case after case belies the unique combinations of factors, or the critical timing, or the fortuitous catalytic element responsible for action and progress where there might have been none. For example, it is hard to imagine development of the GLIE program without the unique personality of Lorraine Reilly. Indeed, in many cases, GLIE, LESFU and GCCCS among them, leadership was a critical commodity, and where it floundered, so did the enterprise. The GLIE experience also illustrates how a fortuitous suggestion that a parent agency be found to overcome the barriers to having GLIE enter the child care system can make the difference between action and stagnation. The Pleasantville case too demonstrates the role of fortuitous circumstances—the fact that a building fund drive just happened to be going on that could supply renovation funds for a new program facility, and the unanticipated bright idea that Medicaid rates could be adjusted to cover the operating costs. These elements allowed the project to ignite and takeoff when it might otherwise have gone by the boards. Well-timed, sometimes unexpected grant opportunities, such as those that arose in the cases of Sagamore, Sanctuary, and Seabury Barn, also attest to the fortunate confluence of events that often seems to underlie the successful launching of important ventures. And usually the window of opportunity is quite narrow once the necessary elements appear to be in place. The JBFCS merger, for example, had to exploit the retirement of Shep Sherman and be effected before his agency would begin to look for a replacement for him. Moreover, the timing between the agreement to merge and effecting of the agreement itself seemed quite critical. A long enough period was needed to explore the implications, but too long a time period would allow people to have second thoughts and opponents to gather strength. Similarly in the case of Harlem-Dowling, the timing of emancipation of the program from the parent agency Spence-Chapin was critical—too early and the new agency would fall on its face, too late and internal resistance would grow and the motivations to effect the separation would be diffused. And in the instance of Melville House, much further delays in certification by the state would surely have led to an aborted enterprise.

All this is not to suggest that a programmatic organizational change is simply a happenstance affair. A good bit of luck does seem to be involved. But the real managerial lesson here is that circumstances favorable to the successful launching and growth of an enterprising activity do not last forever, and must be recognized and exploited when they do occur. The successful manager of change in the human services field is not unlike a tightrope walker, who needs to master the skills, assess the climactic conditions, map a strategy, make the necessary adjustments in his machinery, resolve to carry on and to assume the risks, understand the potential consequences, and finally when conditions are favorable, make the narrow passage over dangerous territory to hopefully stable ground on the other side.

NONPROFIT SECTOR VENTURES:
CASE STUDIES

NEW ORGANIZATIONS FOUNDED FROM SCRATCH

Melville House

PRÉCIS

Melville House is a small institutional program for troubled teenage boys—the homeless, dependent and neglected, and status offenders. It is located in Suffolk County on Long Island, and was opened in September, 1972, after two years of groundwork by a core group of entrepreneurs who were affiliated with a state children's psychiatric facility.

THE ENTREPRENEURS

Five people functioned essentially as a "team" in the effort to establish Melville House: Ken Goldman, who exerted a subtle leadership for the group and ultimately became Melville's executive director, was Director of Social Services of Sagamore Children's Center at the time discussions began in 1970; Jack DiSantis, a close friend of Ken Goldman's and a social work supervisor at Sagamore, functioned in a fund-raising and public relations capacity for the group but left Melville House shortly after its establishment; Jill Winter was a social worker at Sagamore who ultimately became Director of Social Services for Melville House; Ed Goldman, Ken Goldman's father, is a businessman in real estate and insurance, who facilitated the venture with his business savvy and his encouragement that "it could be done"; Phyllis Marks was a housewife who ran a project for the National Association of Jewish Women on a volunteer basis at Sagamore, and was groomed by Ed Goldman to become Business Manager for Melville House.

Although the core group was small, its members were loosely specialized in their activities. The idea for Melville House seems to have originated in lunch hour conversations of Ken Goldman, Jack DiSantis, and Jill Winter. Ed Goldman was quickly involved when discussions began to center on the feasibility of establishing a residential facility. Phyllis was brought in later, as it became clear that substantial secretarial and bookkeeping work was required. While Ed Goldman served as Business Manager on a part-time basis as the effort got underway, his intent from the beginning was to groom Phyllis Marks for the job over the long run. In the formative period, Ed Goldman served two essential functions. He provided expertise on the business aspects, and he was a stimulant and

27

catalyst who energized the others into action and revived them when they became discouraged. Ed Goldman also provided financial backing for the venture and gave the others (especially his son, Ken) much more confidence than they might otherwise have had.

Jack DiSantis took on the role of developing local community support and raising funds for the proposed venture by speaking before various community groups and organizations. Initially it was conceived that he would take on more of a program development role, and become Program Director for Melville House. But things didn't work out that way. In early 1972 the group had to submit its personnel plans as part of the licensing application. And plans had to take account of the fact that the budget of the new agency would not initially be able to support all four staff-members-to-be (Ken, Jill, Jack and Phyllis). Thus Jill and Phyllis (whose salaries and requirements were more modest) were designated as full time. Jack and Ken would be part time (retaining their current positions part time at Sagamore) until the agency was fully implemented.

Jill Winter and Ken Goldman functioned as a sub-team within the group, focusing on the institutional problems of licensing, program design, and facility preparation. As Jill describes it: "Ken and I worked as a team and obviously we still do. . . . Together [we] dealt with the State Board of Social Welfare people . . . also . . . with the county officials, [i.e.], the Department of Social Services people, in terms of getting commitments from them . . . to use . . . the program. . . . I guess my role . . . was really . . . working with Ken in . . . approaching public agencies, because . . . that had been my background. . . . Ken and Jack's experience was . . . within the confines of the state and working within that system. Mine was outside of that system. . . . So, I think my feelings at the time were [that] it is not the simplistic thing that you think it is. Just because you say you want to open it, and you're going to get licensed, it just doesn't work [that] easily. I know what I went through to open a simple day program for post-hospitalized patients. It took me two years before I could get the community to even consider allowing us. . . ." As described later, the process of dealing with the public bureaucracy proved to be the biggest stumbling block to Melville's establishment.

There may be some exceptions, but most every organized effort has a leader—one who worries about all aspects of the venture and takes ultimate responsibility. In the case of Melville House, Ed Goldman, Jack DiSantis, Jill Winter, and Ken Goldman assumed various parts of the entrepreneurial function—organizing, fund-raising, encouraging others, etc.—but Ken Goldman was recognized as the leader. His leadership style is subtle and low-key, but he is the one the others looked to for direction. As Jill Winter puts it: "[He is a leader] in a very subtle way. He's sometimes kidded about it. The absent-minded professor kind of . . . concept. I think he doesn't come off as being the dynamic executive director.

But he's like the Rock of Gibraltar. It's that quiet kind of strength. . . . In his quiet little way he goes around and gets things done. . . ."

The members of the core group showed a mixture of motives for engaging in the Melville House venture. For Ed Goldman it may largely have been the satisfaction of a parent in being able to help and encourage his son and son's contemporaries, but also the challenge of helping create something worthwhile from nothing.

For Ken Goldman, Jack DiSantis and Jill Winter, the professional motives were more important. Ken explains: "[We] were in a situation [at Sagamore] where we basically could sit on our behinds and make a good salary and move up. We just felt we couldn't see spending the next 20 years of our lives collecting a paycheck for doing a very limited amount of creative things that wouldn't really meet people's needs."

Jill Winter gives more emphasis to her personal involvement with the children served: ". . . Where somebody can get tremendous pleasure . . . out of looking at [a] budget and seeing that it balances, I could care less. But my pleasure comes from a long distance phone call from Greenland, from one of the boys who left three years ago . . . to tell me he's getting married and everything's going great. . . . Because I think if I don't have that, I couldn't sit behind this desk. . . ."

Trying to establish the new agency was a challenge and an adventure for the core group; It was an exercise in creativity and it promised opportunities for more rewarding professional work and autonomy in designing programs and services. In no case was it viewed as a way to get rich. For Ken Goldman, the Melville House venture came partly out of a sense of frustration with the opportunity structure within the state framework in which he worked at Sagamore: ". . . I came out of graduate school [in] the boom era for social programs and was able to move very rapidly to a high-level position. At a very young age [for a social services director] I said, 'Well, where am I going to go from here?' I looked around at the existing jobs and nothing really seemed very exciting or creative. . . . Everything was kind of penned in by all kinds of structures and red tape."

Until recently, the opportunity structure for nonmedical personnel in the state mental health system was limited. Had it changed earlier Ken Goldman might have stayed. A more wide-open career ladder in the state system would have appealed to him. He was always an achiever, and a richer opportunity structure might have given him the goals he needed, and the chance to prove himself early in his career.

THE ORGANIZATION

Melville House was started from scratch, and grew modestly during its first six years of operation. Until Melville House opened in 1972, the core group functioned in a basically cooperative, informal mode, with a specialization of function as described in the previous section. For purposes of licensing application, organizational titles were designated but actual responsibilities evolved quickly as operations began. Ken Goldman was envisioned as Executive Director from the beginning. Jack DiSantis was initially designated for Program Director but this job devolved to Jill Winter (who was originally listed as "social worker"), while DiSantis became Administrative Director, a position that was eliminated after DiSantis left the organization. Phyllis Marks was trained as Business Director by Ed Goldman, who maintained an informal consulting relationship with the agency. By 1978 Melville House had opened a nonsecure detention facility on its small campus, administered by a new Program Manager, and had grown approximately fourfold in terms of budget and clientele. This growth required greater formality of administration, but the organization retained the same basic compact administrative structure that it had at the beginning, with basically the same group of people at the helm.

From the beginning Melville House maintained a dual advisory structure. The board of directors is composed largely of businessmen and other community representatives. As Goldman describes it: "Basically, this organization was started by professional people who got board members because they were legally required. . . . It was part of the licensing process. . . . The board of directors were primarily people whom we knew . . . would be interested in supporting this kind of thing . . . [and] who played a secondary role initially. . . . Now they play more of a role because . . . fund raising and so forth is of paramount importance."

The second advisory component is an advisory committee composed of professionals: judges, doctors, educators, etc. As Goldman indicates, ". . . people . . . whom we need . . . but [who might have] a professional conflict if they were on the managing board."

As executive director of Melville House, Ken Goldman participates in various outside committees, task forces, and associations concerning child care and juvenile delinquency. But Melville House essentially operates autonomously, as a small (30 to 40 boys), single campus institution for older boys.

CHRONOLOGY OF EVENTS

The following is a brief, approximate timetable of events surrounding the establishment of Melville House:

Late 1970—Discussions begin at Sagamore between Ken Goldman, Jack DiSantis, and Jill Winter.

Late 1971—Phyllis Marks joins the group.

Early 1971–September 1972—period of organizational activity by

K. Goldman, Winters, DiSantis, and Ed Goldman. Phyllis Marks provides administrative support.

July 1972—A provisional (one year) certification is granted by the New York State Board of Social Welfare (BSW).

September 1972—Melville House opens its doors to its first clients.

October 1973—Melville receives another provisional certification from the BSW.

CONTEXT

Objectively, there appeared to be a need for a facility like Melville House on Long Island, and Ken Goldman and his colleagues at Sagamore were in a good position to see this: ". . . We . . . felt that many of the adolescent population were just not being serviced, many of them being sent to mental hospitals or state training schools when . . . they were not necessarily psychiatric . . . or correctional material. But . . . there were no resources for them in the local community. Some were lucky enough to go to private residential facilities upstate, but they were often far removed from their families. . . . they'd come back from way upstate after a year and a half, and not having dealt with the problems that they had to return to.

" . . There was really no residential program like this. There were a few small group homes but . . . no program that offered a comprehensive service to straighten out the confused, messed up, deprived, abused older adolescent. Almost all the programs that existed were for little children. . . . One of the reasons there were really no programs for the older adolescent . . . was because adolescents were very difficult to deal with. . . . Adolescents [who] would come to a residential program had been through . . . years of probation. . . . They had many more disabilities and problems.

"For the older adolescent [boys] there are a few group homes [on Long Island], but many of the kids we get have bombed out of these programs because they don't have the comprehensive service. . . . We have a long-term program basically geared toward preparing youngsters for independent living. . . . We become many of these kids' families . . . maybe a third of our kids are our 'orphans.' They've been through five, ten foster homes and they really don't have anybody but us."

If there was a need in 1970, Goldman also saw that there was an opportunity then, which in 1978 no longer existed: ". . . Five years ago there was much more sympathy for kids. . . . Now . . . little kids are still innocent victims but teenagers . . . should be locked up, put in jail, whatever. . . . There should be no sympathy for those kids because they're like junior adults and they should be punished. So you see, right now [there's], a definite getting away from trying to help kids. . . . At the time we started there was, I think, just as much sympathy for all kids, up to maybe 18 years of age."

Economically, times were also better in the early 1970s on Long Island. As Goldman notes: ". . . There was more money in the community. . . . You could go to top people in corporations and get $1,000 . . . or $3,000." Equally important, while there was a dearth of services for the adolescent, the professional community recognized this problem and was supportive of the Melville proposal. Goldman, for example, had no trouble getting support letters for the application process required in setting up the agency. Indeed, foster care services for older children, especially those involved with the courts or with mental hospitals, had become a serious problem for the whole state of New York, and particularly for nearby New York City. Several stinging reports were issued by state agencies on this subject. On Long Island, with a growing young population but a lagging social service base, few agencies were attempting to deal with the problem. Melville House seemed to fill part of the vacuum.

CHOICES

It seems fair to conclude that from the very beginning of discussions among the core group members, there was a consensus on several aspects of the proposed venture—that it should address the needs of older adolescent boys who were highly troubled but not requiring hospitalization or incarceration in a correctional facility; and that it should be a residential facility that could provide a wide array of supportive and therapeutic services. Within this framework, there was a preference for a small, high quality program, and one that could be selective of its clientele. These preferences were tempered, however, by pragmatic (economic) considerations. Ken Goldman recalls:

". . . We basically wanted to have a somewhat smaller program. . . . we felt that . . . this age group needed much more tender loving care. They also needed educational services, recreation, psychiatric, psychological . . . social . . . vocational [but] you couldn't provide these [for] too small a number because the program couldn't support economically the complete bag of services. . . . since we operate on a per diem [system of reimbursement], our overall income increases as we increase our size. We never really wanted to be this big but . . . the economics have squeezed things more and more. . . . We are committed to not going beyond a certain size, so we've had to put more emphasis into . . . fund-raising."

Jill Winter elaborates: ". . . We kind of had an oath between us . . . that it would be quality over quantity. We knew that we would be in a better financial position . . . if we opened with 20 kids. . . . we were going to be getting as a per diem from the referring agencies . . . $33 a day [which] was absolutely ludicrous. . . . We knew it was going to cost much more to implement that kind of program. . . . We had to make a value judgement. The judgement was very simply, which was probably bad business practice, [that] we would start out with 10 boys and we would go up very, very slowly. And that's exactly what we did up to a point. We went from 10 to 12 . . . to 17. . . . When we got to 20 . . . we didn't want to go to 25, but we recognized that financially we had no choice . . . that there were expenditures that we didn't count on. . . . So suddenly you're a bigger program than you ever had envisioned. . . . I have always felt sorry that we grew to be as large as we did."

Similar pragmatism was necessary in terms of admissions policy. Ken Goldman explains: ". . . We knew from the very beginning, the major bulk of funding is always going to come from government . . . [but] . . . when you're a new organization they don't want to send you kids until you've proved yourself. . . . We had to convince the powers that be, that . . . we were professionally competent . . . to start caring for those kids. Basically, the initial kids that were sent to us . . . they had no other place to send. That was how they tested us out. Some of them were the worst kids, kids who were just roaming the streets. . . . We had to prove our reputation with the first kids. We had to work very hard because they were really not a proper group . . . in terms of the kind of kids that came later."

Flexibility in program design was not totally forced upon the founders of Melville House. Their basic concern was to establish their own agency, and not to have it duplicate mistakes of other programs. As Ken Goldman explains: ". . . We tried not to start this place with a lot of pre-conceived notions about . . . the kids' needs . . . even though we had all worked in the helping professions and with adolescents. We basically opened our doors with . . . just a very loose concept. . . . We felt many programs are wrong because . . . the clients walk into the door and they have to fit into the program whether it meets their needs or not. . . ."

In terms of financing, the founders of Melville House are especially proud of their ability to start up on relatively little cash. But this required some financial gymnastics in view of cash-flow problems associated with the per diem system of payment. Ken Goldman explains: ". . . The problem is you bill at the end of the month for the service rendered and don't get paid for another 30 days, so we had to have 60 days [stock of] money. We had to have all kinds of strategies . . . people holding their pay-checks, getting 60-day credit, . . . arrangement of credit relationships and so forth. Everybody wants to lend you money after you've established . . . credit, not when you're a new organization. So we had to do quite a bit in this area."

For initial start-up, and for continuing operations, Melville depends on a margin of private funding to supplement public revenues. As noted earlier, the founders put up some of their own personal venture capital, in the form of loans. In addition, other choices were made to pursue certain sources of external support. Goldman recalls: "During the first year we had the possibility of . . . a large federal grant which we . . . turned down because we felt that . . . during our very formative stages the entire program would have to be focused around . . . the requirements of the grant rather than meeting the needs of the kids. . . . We felt we would rather be a starving, struggling organization and build something really worthwhile, than ending up being another . . . bureaucratic program . . . geared around federal guidelines and regulations. . . . We feel we took the right course . . . because we had the freedom and flexibility to do what we wanted to do as an organization. . . ."

Large foundation grants were perceived to have similar drawbacks: "We basically stayed away from large foundation grants. . . . the strategy was primarily to get community people and businesses involved. . . . We found that [grant seeking has] become a whole art and science in itself and we were always in the conflict of who devotes their time. . . . Getting major grants . . . involves a lot of staff time and a lot of meetings, a lot of writing. . . . This is something we're more into now. . . ."

Overall, financing choices were made to preserve organizational flexibility and conserve staff resources, and to achieve a start-up under a government system of delayed cash flow, from which the major portion of operating revenues was anticipated.

The organizational format for Melville House offered less selection and was tied to the financial realities as well as core group objectives. The group knew from the start, that a *new* organization was to be set up. Goldman says: ". . . We never ever conceived [working within an existing agency] because we all had worked in . . . these organizations . . . and felt that would stop us from . . . having the freedom to do what we needed to do."

The group also assumed that the new organization would have to be nonprofit. Goldman notes: "It couldn't be . . . a profit-making thing because in New York State in order to get child welfare per diem funding you have to be a nonprofit organization. . . . There are private [proprietary] schools for kids with problems . . . but they cannot . . . get placement of kids through the Department of Social Services [except through] a whole procedure [as] an absolute course of last resort. . . . I don't know that . . . we didn't want to. We just knew from the beginning [that] if we are going to run a residential program it had to be a nonprofit organization. I think also, the reality is obviously [that] if you're nonprofit you can do more with fund-raising. . . ."

"I think if we felt we could have done it within the government . . . we would have stayed and done it, because it would have been much more advantageous . . . personally . . . but our feeling was that you could not do it that way."

In short, financial opportunities and government requirements channelled the core group's organizational and financing choices. Within
these areas of discretion, choices were made to preserve flexibility and
autonomy and ensure economic stability.

RISKS AND CONSTRAINTS

Melville House did not have an easy birth. Its midwives, the core
group, took risks and overcame institutional barriers about which they
still bitterly complain.

The material risks were not inordinate. Ken Goldman, Jack DiSantis,
and especially Ed Goldman stood to lose their personal venture capital—the loans to Melville House. Jill Winter would have had to find another job had Melville House failed early in its operations. Jack DiSantis
and Ken Goldman hedged against job loss by retaining their positions at
Sagamore during the first six months of Melville's existence.

The risks taken were calculated risks. These were not impetuous decision makers. Ken Goldman himself was characteristically a planner, not
prone to impulsive behavior: "There was risk, but I think I was young
enough and idealistic enough to try. . . . I never intend to do things im
pulsively without thinking through Sometimes you have to trust your
own judgement and go on a hunch, but also the reality was that I was not
irresponsibly putting my family or my life in jeopardy. . . ."

The most painful potential costs of failure were not financial, but the
frustration of being thwarted by institutional road blocks strewn in the
path of Melville House's establishment, by the state, county, and localities. The problems of licensure by the state were, according to Ken Goldman, ". . . absolutely horrendous. It was almost as if . . . we were trying
to provide a new service and the state did everything they could to dis-
courage you. . . . It seemed like they put [up] every possible roadblock.
. . . Rules and regulations that were unrealistic and impossible to conform
to, constant changes in [state] personnel . . . which is even a worse problem . . . because one person . . . interprets the regulation one way, the
next person . . . another way, and a mere interpretation could cost your
organization $100,000. . . . The lack of [state] personnel to come down
and meet with you . . . you would prepare something . . . they say . . .
has to be done in two days and then there would be nobody to review it
with you or to approve it; it's kind of hurry up and wait!

"We had problems—getting certain architectural things approved. . . .
One of the delays was four months just to get the state architect . . . to
simply look at what had already been used as a nursing home. . . . You
know . . . if a kid's room is one square foot short, it can't be used. . . .
The space that you might have for your own kid at home, they don't allow. They are very inflexible regulations which result in huge costs.

". . . Our effort almost collapsed at one point, about six months before we opened because they suddenly came in and told us we have to rip out all the doors and put in $25,000 worth of fire doors. . . . We had to get another $25,000. . . . Many people thought it was ridiculous because they required steel doors . . . however, one of our board members at the time was a high-level fire department official. . . . We had oak doors and he said that those doors were better than steel doors because they were fire resistant. . . . But this is the kind of thing we're talking about . . . no thought to the fact that we're a brand new organization and couldn't afford to spend $25,000 . . . plus we had to involve major construction work which delayed and delayed [us]. If we hadn't been in a [vacated] facility . . . owned by the church . . . we probably would have lost the property. . . . Nobody's going to tie up a piece of property and let it go on like that."

Problems also abounded at the local level, particularly with respect to securing an appropriate facility. According to Jill Winter: "That was not easy because we knew we would meet with . . . community disapproval. So we purposely looked on the fringes. . . . We spent many, many mornings just looking at various places. . . . Working out a leasing agreement . . . also took forever, because again we didn't have any money. . . ."

Ken Goldman elaborates: "We had great difficulty finding a piece of property; we were very lucky to find this [one] because . . . there were some big problems with the zoning. This was being vacated; at the same time we looked at hundreds of pieces of property and this was the only one we found. Fortunately, this was originally built as an orphanage and then became an old-age home, so we were able to get the kind of zoning approval that we needed."

In the end, the constraints became the challenge. Members of the core group dug in their heels and refused to be defeated. Jill Winter puts it this way: ". . . A few times we talked about giving up the project. . . . We were all working full time. But . . . I think our egos got involved . . . and [we] said, 'We have got to do this.' There were . . . feelings of despair but I think what happened is . . . that we took the opposite approach. I think it was a kind of 'damn it, we're going to do it.' So every stumbling block then became . . . a challenge, a game of wits—who was going to outsmart whom. . . . A small group of people who were going to be buried by the state . . . had made up its mind, we weren't going to allow it."

OUTCOMES

In six years, since opening in 1972, Melville House became a stable if not prospering operation. It began with an operating budget of under $200,000 per year and an initial caseload of 10 boys, and grew to serve approximately 40 boys on a budget of nearly $700,000, plus a small nonsecure detention facility in addition to its regular long-term residential program. Staff increased from less than a dozen full time employees to more than 40. In view of the original goals, growth is probably not the best indicator of success, but it is clear that Melville House has gained community acceptance and financial stability. Problems with the state have also eased. The long-term commitment of most of the core group, under Ken Goldman, contributed heavily to Melville House's survival.

ANALYSIS

The establishment of Melville House was basically an exercise in emancipation by a small group of social work professionals in a state system who felt hemmed in by limited opportunities to advance themselves or to pursue new programmatic ideas. To a considerable degree, it was also an exercise in commitment to an idea—that a certain group of children were being improperly and inadequately served by the existing array of state services.

The fact that Melville House emerged as an independent organization was substantially an outgrowth of the core group's objectives. Organizational autonomy, and the freedom to determine its own program, was inherent in the venture from the start. The lack of opportunity to engage in such activity, especially within the state bureaucracy, simply reinforced this predilection.

The fact that Melville was organized on a nonprofit basis was essentially a response to existing regulatory constraints and financial opportunities. The state social services system of per diem payments for residential care was viewed as the most viable option for financial support, and this required nonprofit incorporation.

The birth of Melville House also illustrates other important strategic considerations generic to management of nonprofit organizations in the social services field. For example, creating a board of directors appeared to be as much a headache to satisfy government regulations as it was a positive contribution to successful program implementation. However, the board's role grew in value over time, as a vehicle for fund-raising and securing community support. Moreover, the device of an advisory committee, separate from the board, is of managerial interest; that committee served as a means to engage the participation, advice, and support of key practitioners (educators, judges, and so on) who were potential referrers of clients, without posing conflict of interest problems.

One of the most important early strategy decisions for Melville House was its choice of avenues for fund-raising, particularly for start-up capital. Start-up grants from government or foundations were explicitly rejected in order to preserve early flexibility in defining the organization's mission. This strategy succeeded, but the projected source of operating funds, governmental per diem reimbursement funds, still posed a Catch-22 dilemma. In particular, Melville's program had to be off and running—meeting costly regulatory standards and serving clients—before any such funds would be received. This was but one of the severe official obstacles, the founders of Melville House had to overcome.

Melville House expanded considerably in its first six years of operation, but not very far beyond its original conception. Economic considerations seem to have dictated this expansion, to spread the overhead of facility maintenance and specialized and administrative staff. The operation seemed not to be inherently expansionist. Indeed, the growth has been viewed with some dismay by members of the core group who have grappled with the trade-off between program quality and small size on the one hand, and the economic imperatives for larger numbers of clients, on the other hand.

It is worth contemplating that although the need for services proposed by the founders of Melville House was generally recognized to be valid, there were no facilitating structures to bring these services into being. Overwhelming demand (by government) was not the progenitor of Melville House. Indeed, government seemed to smother the effort. The establishment of Melville House was an exception more than the rule, and its experience helps explain why more such efforts do not emerge. The founding is more easily explained by the internal motivations of the founders than by the receptivity of the environment into which Melville House was rooted.

Group Live-In Experience, Inc. (GLIE)

PRÉCIS

GLIE is a child care agency for older children, established in the South Bronx in 1972. It grew out of the Claremont League for Urban Betterment (CLUB), an advocacy group developed under auspices of Our Lady of Victory Roman Catholic Church on behalf of distressed families in the Webster Butler housing projects. Under the dynamic leadership of Sister Lorraine Reilly, GLIE developed three group homes for adolescents, an emergency placement unit for runaway youth, an innovative long-term apartment-living program for older adolescents, and special residential programs for multiply handicapped and autistic youth.

THE ENTREPRENEUR

Several individuals contributed substantially to the successful establishment and growth of GLIE. The early protagonists such as Gary Waldron, Carmen Goytia, Ellen Garcia, Father Joseph Fitzpatrick, and Father Tim Collins were all active in the South Bronx community, mostly through Our Lady of Victory Roman Catholic Church and the associated Claremont League for Urban Betterment. But the central character was Sister Lorraine Reilly, a teacher in the Lady of Victory Parish and an active participant and organizer in the Claremont League at the time GLIE began to emerge. Sister Lorraine is a native and lifelong resident of the South Bronx, a fact which has shaped her single-minded dedication to the renewal of this area.

Sister Lorraine's dynamic personality and humanistic orientation combine themselves into an unusual managerial style. She is feisty and independent, and not afraid to call the shots as she sees them. She can also be very demanding of staff, if she sees a discrepancy between their interests and that of the kids. But, as tough as she can be, Lorraine Reilly is not comfortable as an administrator and in fact she disdains this role and sees herself as a creator, catalyst, and enterpriser. For example, she is quick to turn over program responsibilities to people under her and to delegate authority.

Moreover, Sister Lorraine expresses a basic preference for keeping GLIE small, and spinning-off new programs. This orientation is based partly on Sister Reilly's distrust of large bureaucratic organizations and her belief that a service organization should be close to the community it serves. But it is also a matter of her personal style and motives. She is "a fast mover" and lack of encumbrance and freedom of action are essential to her way of doing things.

Gary Waldron calls Sister Lorraine a "'charismatic advocate.' People tend to want to follow her as a leader. . . . I think she is an advocate of the first order. She believes that the only way the system will change . . . is to make a lot of noise. . . . That is what she does."

A strong motivating factor in Sister Lorraine's calculus is indeed community involvement and social activism. She sees herself primarily as a social work organizer, with the South Bronx as her universe. Her career exhibits a consistent activist orientation. The Claremont League, and the beginnings of GLIE, are examples.

Caring about people, especially kids, and about the neighborhoods she grew up in, and being talented and able to do something to organize and help them—especially in view of the dramatic deterioration of the Bronx—is a great energizer for Lorraine Reilly. She says she plans to continue to devote her efforts to this particular corner of the world, and she means it.

THE ORGANIZATIONS

GLIE was born out of the Claremont League for Urban Betterment (CLUB), grew under the wing of St. Dominic's child care agency in its first three years, and has since evolved as an independent, but still changing, child care agency in its own right.

The relationship of GLIE to St. Dominic's Children's Home from 1972–1975 was a short-lived convenience that enabled GLIE to begin operations before it could secure official status as an independent child care agency. Essentially, St. Dominic's, a chartered foster care institution affiliated with the Catholic Church and the Dominican Order of Sisters to which Sister Reilly belongs, acted as the fiscal agent through which GLIE could be reimbursed for services by the New York City Department of Social Services. Aside from administrative hassles, however, there was little substantive interaction of St. Dominic's with GLIE. (See Choices below.)

If St. Dominic's was a temporary foster parent to GLIE, the Claremont League for Urban Betterment was GLIE's true lineage. CLUB developed as a community action of Our Lady of Victory Church and Parish in the Crotona Park area of the South Bronx. According to Sister Lorraine: ". . . It really starts in '65 (when we didn't [even] have a name) within Our

Lady of Victory Parish . . . working with gangs and being with kids [from the] city [housing projects]. . . . In 1967, through Catholic Charities, we got a grant of $5,000 to develop an advocacy [program] to work with families having difficulty. . . . We incorporated as CLUB [in 1968] and [began] doing tenant organizing. By '68 [with support of Catholic Charities and foundations—including United Fund] we had two storefronts. One was totally for adolescents—an after school tutorial program, an evening rap session program [with] gang members, teenagers . . . whatever. And the other one was an advocacy storefront. . . . From '68 to '72 we worked so much with gangs . . . setting them up in abandoned buildings [etc.] that we got into the whole syndrome and we decided to try to apply . . . [for child care agency status]."

The founders of CLUB were people active in the Church parish. The parish priest was a key figure, along with Gary Waldron, an IBM manager who grew up in the South Bronx and was active in youth recreation programs, parishioners Carmen Goytia, Ellen Garcia, Sister Joan, and Sister Lorraine. It was both a service organization and advocacy group, which according to Gary Waldron: ". . . Attempted to service community people, youth, people with welfare problems, outreach services, and all that." It was basically an informal, volunteer operation, with only three paid staff.

As an informal organization, with no steady means of support and no hard-and-fast mandate, CLUB depended on the commitment of a few people. It is not surprising, therefore, that the Claremont League dissolved shortly after the GLIE program began in 1972. Sister Reilly's energies were devoted to GLIE, and, according to Waldron, "When she spun off from CLUB, several things happened. . . . The local pastor left the priesthood and [CLUB] began to become less and less effective because there was no driving force behind it. There wasn't anybody available every day. There were some people working, but they weren't doing very much, and if I were to look back, I think that GLIE was the thing that was beginning to grow on its own, and Lorraine was really off doing her own thing . . . quite apart from anything Claremont had offered at that point."

Indeed, in a very real sense, GLIE is simply the part of CLUB that survived, albeit altered in form and purpose. Many of the CLUB founders became active in GLIE. And, GLIE continues in the same tradition as CLUB—with its roots in the church and dedication to the community of the South Bronx. As Sister Lorraine explains: "We really are [confined to the Bronx Community]. . . . We might help another group get started, you know. But I don't think the Board would go along. . . . Anything within the community . . . fine, but outside the community . . . no."

Since its founding in 1972, GLIE has expanded its board membership considerably beyond the core group [e.g., Waldron, Goytia] from CLUB. Membership now includes the chairperson of the local community planning board, a nurse and active member of the Baptist Church, a probation officer, a university professor, a bank employee . . . all people with an active involvement in the local community and/or professional interest in youth problems.

However, the selection of board members became considerably more "worldly" as Sister Lorraine describes: "The Volunteer Urban Consulting Group . . . had a book called *Candidates for Directors* . . . published yearly . . . of graduates of Harvard who are interested in becoming members of boards of directors. So we went through that book and picked [three men] . . . called them up and out of that three, two were interested . . . [eventually one] came on board."

Until 1979, the board of directors had not been particularly influential in setting policy for GLIE compared to the single-minded style of Lorraine Reilly's leadership. But Gary Waldron saw this changing: ". . . We have gone through some redefinitions of board roles and board memberships and needs of the board. We are getting a lot closer to goals and measurement than we ever were before. We have gathered some very, very interested members to the board. I think these two things alone are going to help to make the board more effective. This is one half. The other half is that as that board becomes more effective, it is going to contend with her [Sister Lorraine] more. . . . There is going to be more contention . . . and she is . . . just not going to be allowed to do some things that she would do in her own pioneering way. Probably it will create some boxes [constraints], some parameters of her actions. . . . It may make her uncomfortable because of the style that she had enjoyed for a long time. . . ."

Fund-raising is one illustrative area, where Sister Lorraine has essentially been a one-woman show. Waldron continues: ". . . She has done it in the past. You know, she would get wind of a proposal and she would go out there and . . . get our proposal approved. . . . She did virtually all of that. I got some IBM funds, and a lady from Morgan Guarantee [got] a few thousand dollars, but the big funding sources were primarily driven by Lorraine. . . . She is kind of a magic lady. . . . She would come in and be able to sell them stuff. And they would agree with it, and would fund it for her."

General organization and management have also revolved around the personality of Sister Lorraine. As noted above, GLIE is decentralized to suit her own "fast-moving" style and disdain for administration. And GLIE's decentralized style of administration extends into its philosophy of growth, where Waldron notes: ". . . She believes that there ought to be a series of . . . small programs that grow on their own, eventually spin-off and become independent things."

CHRONOLOGY OF EVENTS

1965—The Claremont League begins informally (without a name) as a community project by Our Lady of Victory Church and Parish. CLUB begins to work with gang youth in the Webster-Butler housing projects.

1967—CLUB receives a $5,000 grant for an advocacy program on behalf of families in difficulty from Catholic Charities.

1968—CLUB is incorporated. By this time it has two storefront operations. One provides tutoring and job counseling services for youth. The other provides day care and recreation programs, and general advocacy activity.

1968–1972—CLUB does considerable work with youth and gangs, including provision of shelter in the abandoned buildings over the storefronts. Funds are received from Greater New York Fund as well as Catholic Charities over this period.

1972—CLUB applies to the city and state to develop a group home for adolescent youth, but the state refuses to grant CLUB status as a child caring agency. The city's Director of Special Services for Children, Barbara Blum, suggests that the proposed program affiliate with an existing child care agency. As a Dominican Sister, Lorraine Reilly approaches St. Dominic's Children's Home (in Blauvelt, New York) for the purpose of obtaining sponsorship.

GLIE opens as a single group home for girls, separate from CLUB, under auspices of St. Dominic's, which operates as receiver and administrator of funds. The arrangement calls for GLIE to work towards autonomy within three years.

1973—CLUB dissolves.

1972–1975—GLIE develops two additional group homes for adolescents, making a total of three short-term (90 day) residences—one for boys and two for girls.

July, 1975—GLIE incorporates as an independent, nonprofit child care agency, and formally separates from St. Dominic's.

July, 1976—GLIE is one of three New York City programs to receive federal funds under the Runaway Youth Act (Juvenile Justice Act of 1974). It establishes a 24-hour emergency placement unit (8-bed crash pad) intended for lengths of stay up to two weeks.

December, 1976—GLIE contracts with the New York State Department of Mental Hygiene to provide urban group home care for twelve multiply handicapped and retarded youth from the Willowbrook State Hospital (or similar institutions). Such children were being moved from Willowbrook under state decree. Implementation of that decree was administered by Barbara Blum, appointed as Assistant Commissioner of Mental Hygiene for that purpose.

January, 1977—An innovative long-range program of independent, apartment living is developed for older (16–17 year old) adolescents.

1977—GLIE receives a grant from the Greater New York Fund to establish the groundwork for a program for autistic children. The agency also requests permission of the New York City Board of Education to develop an alternative high school for truant youth.

CONTEXT

GLIE has grown up at the intersection of several social crosscurrents. Its roots in the Claremont League recall the poverty program era of the mid-sixties, when community organizing and advocacy on behalf of deprived minorities in the cities were in full bloom across the nation. So, too, CLUB was a manifestation of a new activism of the clergy in bringing about desired social change at home and abroad (e.g., Vietnam). Certainly CLUB was a response to the deterioration of the city, especially the social pathology associated with the large, impersonal, low income housing projects that were built in the fifties and sixties to house the inflow of blacks and Hispanics and to replace older deteriorated housing.

In the world of urban decay, the South Bronx had become the symbol. National recognition was underlined in 1977 when President Carter personally visited the area and promised a program to rebuild from the devastation. But the deterioration had become obvious and widespread long before that—as early as the late fifties. By the mid-sixties the South Bronx was already in terrible shape, with rapid abandonment of buildings by landlords, soaring rates of crime, frequent fires, and so on. The education system was another victim, and the impacts of deterioration were felt particularly hard by youth.

Some of these youth became "urban nomads," a particular variety of "runaway" who remained in his community but spent little time with whatever family he might have. Rather, he or she hung out with others in a gang and sought whatever shelter was available. This is the type of youth that was attracted to CLUB, and was ultimately served by GLIE. Thus, another social crosscurrent surrounding GLIE was the phenomenon of runaway youth.

In a photo essay for *U.S. Catholic* magazine in 1977, Sister Lorraine implies that youthful runaways are akin to discoverers and explorers, and are part of a long-standing history of transients in Western civilization. Be that as it may, it is clear that the runaway phenomenon came to national prominence in the late 1960s with the flower children of Haight-Ashbury in San Francisco.

In the early seventies the flow of young runaways into the sex industry, particularly on the "Minnesota strip" in the Times Square area of New

York City, came to light. Through organization and lobbying by people like Rev. Bruce Ritter and Lorraine Reilly, the federal Runaway Youth Act was enacted in 1974, providing funds for information exchange and program development. In New York State, runaway legislation was passed in 1978 to fund sanctuary and other types of programs for runaway youth. From its beginning GLIE has serviced the runaway youth of the South Bronx, especially those that improvised shelter in the burnt-out and abandoned buildings. In 1976 it received one of the earliest allocations of federal runaway funds to establish its emergency shelter "crash pad," the only existing 24-hour emergency service in the Bronx.

Finally, GLIE has been entwined in the changes taking place in the governmental social services systems at large. For example, GLIE joined the child care system at a time when it was becoming clear that the population of children requiring foster care was changing radically in age composition from younger to older children, and from relatively "normal" to behaviorally difficult youngsters. GLIE proposed to serve this new breed of foster child. Indeed, GLIE's emergence coincides fairly closely with the establishment of a separate reimbursement rate for group homes by New York City's Office of Special Services for Children. Despite the reluctance of the State Board of Social Welfare to authorize GLIE as an independent agency in 1972 (see Choices, Constraints below), it was undoubtedly these social imperatives that brought forth support and encouragement for GLIE by the City, especially by Barbara Blum, then Assistant Commissioner in charge of Special Services for Children.

Another crosscurrent, later in GLIE's history, was the deinstitutionalization movement as it applied to mental hospitals in New York State. Of particular interest, a court decree in 1976 ordered the State to dismantle its Willowbrook institution for the retarded and multiply handicapped, and to place its residents into community-based programs. The job of implementing this decree was given to Barbara Blum, and it was GLIE that responded within its own mandate, with a program to service (largely Bronx-originated) Willowbrook children, in a group home setting.

Sister Lorraine is quick to contend that if those involved in GLIE had not responded to the various social needs emerging in the South Bronx others would have. This hypothesis may be questionable, but the social context certainly inspired and strongly shaped the founding and development of GLIE.

CHOICES

The founding of GLIE involved several stages of decision-making. The first stage was based on the realization that current CLUB activities on behalf of local youth were not adequate or sustainable indefinitely, and that more substantial services and support were necessary. Sister Lorraine explains the need to undertake residential services: "We tried [counseling and referral to other agencies] . . . but [in] the end . . . we found ourselves putting [up] more and more . . . kids [in the abandoned buildings]. . . . Their [problems were] family dysfunction and their needs [were] to get out. . . . [Often it was the] healthiest kid [in a family] who wanted out, even if it was for only a short period of time. . . . Sometimes [when] you really did intensive therapy, it was better to separate the youngster from the problem, so he could look back and see the problem . . . then he could go back in, and do very well. But when we found ourselves setting up so many kids a month in an old abandoned building . . . it seemed ridiculous."

One obvious alternative was referral to existing agencies and institutions, all of which were some distance from the South Bronx—usually in upstate New York. But this proved not to be viable: "Kids whom you finally convinced to go . . . [wouldn't stay there]. You'd take them up there and tell them; 'Look at the beautiful trees. Ah, it's great!' [But] by the time you'd get back to New York, they were sitting here on the steps. They hitch-hiked back. They couldn't deal with it."

In any case, referral to other agencies did not, for the most part, represent a viable solution: "We thought of . . . not developing [our own program and] sending the kids into the other recognized child care agencies. But these were . . . older adolescents. The child care agencies didn't want anybody over 14 in 1976. Now they'll take them up to 16, but then they didn't want to hear about them. So we . . . had no place to go with our kids. . . ."

The first inclination of Sister Lorraine, and others involved in GLIE, was to seek private funding, which would preserve flexibility: "Originally . . . in '70, we put in a proposal to the National Campaign of Bishops. . . . They were going to fund us . . . because it was a good idea. This was minority kids, gang kids, the whole list. Then they sent it back to the Archdiocese of New York and said, you fund half of it and we'll fund the other half. [But] it was the Archbishop [of New York] . . . who said, 'No, we are not going to fund that program because there's a [government] system in child welfare that they can get into. . . .'" The lack of church support was certainly a factor in turning to government sources, especially in 1972 when church resources for the Claremont League itself were precarious.

Having resolved to seek governmental support, there was another basic choice for GLIE promoters to make. The issues of stigma and labeling of children were of paramount importance: "We didn't want to go into juvenile justice money. Kids have to have a name on them. . . . They would be branded. . . . We didn't want to go after drug money because a lot of the kids had brothers who were already into drug rehab programs and it also meant that they had a stigma attached to them. . . . So, we felt that the city, whose foster care system . . . should have been providing some kind of prevention programming for kids living in the ghetto . . . [was the appropriate choice]."

The intent to seek support through the public foster care system strongly influenced a number of subsequent organizational choices. For one thing the effort would have to be organized on a nonprofit basis. This was no problem since CLUB was already an incorporated nonprofit organization. However, passing thought was given to the possibility of direct public provision through city government. Sister Lorraine recalls, ". . . The City has a program for hard-to-place youngsters . . . [but] . . . it's been closed since. It was known to be a horrendous place . . . all kinds of atrocities were going on there. They had two settings, one for boys and one for girls. . . . Two short-term facilities . . . and they were really in bad shape. . . . There was no reason to think that the City was going to put on a better show. . . . [But] I don't know that that might not be a [good] thing. You see, one of the underlying goals of GLIE is to employ community people and to make sure that that is stable employment. That's very important to us. So I'm not so sure that would have been a bad idea, if the city government was a little more avant garde and progressive. It could really pull off an awful lot of good programs."

The fact that CLUB was nonprofit was not qualification enough for status as a child care organization eligible to receive public (per diem) funding for residential child care services. The founders would be forced to choose between CLUB and the GLIE program, and between an independent GLIE and one affiliated with an existing authorized agency.

The initial application did envision CLUB as the organizational auspices, but the broad mandate and informality of CLUB became an issue: ". . . As a child care agency we couldn't do the kinds of advocacy work [that CLUB did] . . . and we [couldn't] set up an umbrella agency in that way. . . ." Indeed, CLUB would have had to be radically changed in terms of mission and structure to conform with Board of Social Welfare licensing requirements. Even with the willingness of CLUB to do so, however: "The State of New York would not recognize us as the Claremont League for Urban Betterment and refused to amend the charter. . . ."

According to Sister Lorraine, the basic problem was the South Bronx itself: "At the time, there were . . . no group homes in the South Bronx, not one . . . because the City and State officials felt that this was a deteriorating neighborhood. Nothing could be done here. . . . Listen, let me tell you we had one commissioner who wouldn't even walk down the street.

"We were talking about . . . opening up in a very deteriorated community . . . *for* that community's stability. We were trying to tell them that you would stabilize the South Bronx [this way, but] . . . they could not see. . . ."

Gary Waldron sees the issues in a somewhat different perspective: "As a separate group home, it was indeed an experiment. . . . There were two issues as I understand it: [First] the credibility of community agencies in general. . . . There was a lot of scandal and a whole lot of reverends and the like ripping off monies. . . . Secondly, the novelty of the program. There was not universal agreement that that type of a program [urban group homes] would be acceptable. . . . Most of the eggs were stored in the other basket . . . kids went somewhere else in an institution setting outside of New York City."

Fortunately, the founders of GLIE had a receptive ear in the City's Director of Special Services for Children, Barbara Blum. Mrs. Blum wanted to see GLIE get off the ground, and suggested another alternative to Sister Lorraine—affiliation, at least temporarily, with an established agency. With that suggestion things began to fall into place in 1972. Sister Lorraine says she really had not previously seriously entertained the notion of using the services of another agency, must less formal affiliation. But, given the idea, Sister Lorraine pursued it effectively. As Waldron described it, ". . . Only because she was a Dominican nun dealing with a Dominican home, was [she] able to convince them to take a shot at trying it this way . . . a different approach than used in the past. . . . It was indeed an experiment. . . . St. Dominic's was an established agency. If it would support the experiment, then the City would fund [us] through St. Dominic's. . . ."

Sister Lorraine elaborates on the arrangements, ". . . If we could display to the City and the State what we were talking about . . . then we could get our own charter. . . . We would have three years to do it. . . . If within three years we did not [secure] our own charter, St. Dominic's would claim any group homes that we had opened. . . ."

Affiliation with St. Dominic's was not the preferred arrangement for the founders of GLIE. Indeed, if Sister Lorraine had it to do again, she says, ". . . We definitely would not have gone to St. Dominic's. We would have fought for our charter. . . . That was a mistake." Nonetheless, the arrangement did allow the GLIE program to get started. Gary Waldron questions whether it would have been possible otherwise. But Sister Lorraine is proud to point out that independence was achieved within two and a half years.

The arrangement with St. Dominic's was, from the start, intended as temporary. And the operation of this arrangement strongly reaffirmed this initial preference. Sister Lorraine bristled under the wing of St. Dominic's, and the feelings of officials of the parent agency were probably mutual. A large part of the problem was money since St. Dominic's claimed a good fraction of GLIE's reimbursement for overhead expenses. In addition, St. Dominic's tended to impose its policies on staffing and other program parameters.

On the other side of the argument, an official of the State Board of Social Welfare indicated that St. Dominic's might actually have been losing money, because of loose bookkeeping and reporting by GLIE, i.e., that reimbursement was not being made for all children actually in care. Gary Waldron, who was GLIE's Treasurer at the time, gives a more balanced appraisal. ". . . The [problem was] over an allocation [of funds] which was very fair in St. Dominic's eyes. . . . It turned out to be 50 percent of her [Sister Lorraine's] reimbursement that St. Dominic's was keeping, in effect. . . . [Sister Lorraine] was fair in believing that she was not getting the right end of that deal. However, on the other side of the coin . . . [they] were providing some accounting services and support services. It was an accounting and billing process. They were going through the direct billing from the City. . . . I'm sure they were sharing a part of the cost of their whole office staff." In any case, ultimate separation from St. Dominic's was never in question, as far as the two principals were concerned.

In terms of programmatic content, GLIE's apartment-like group homes were pretty much an outgrowth of the impromptu activity begun under CLUB. But design parameters were influenced by child care regulations. According to Sister Lorraine, ". . . We were . . . obliged to listen to what the bureaucrats wanted. . . . For instance, for us to open a group home, we never thought of boys separate from girls, or six year olds not in the same apartments as their mothers . . . or single parents and a boyfriend not living in the same apartment. . . . Whereas immediately all those host of rules came in, so all the types of apartment development we had gotten [into] with young people in abandoned buildings . . . was now thrown out. . . ."

Later programmatic decisions of GLIE were shaped by a combination of unanticipated opportunities and an underlying desire to escape the narrowness of the conventional child welfare system. The program of group care for the multiply handicapped was a response to solicitation under the Willowbrook decree. A new program for autistic children follows a similar scenario: "The Bronx Chapter for the Autistic came to our open house [for] the two units for handicapped kids. . . . We hadn't thought of . . . ever doing anything like [a program for the autistic] but we said we would help. . . . The board said, 'Look into it, Lorraine. Do a little research . . . and tell us what you think. . . .' My research [showed that] a large number of autistic children in the Bronx were out of state. Wasn't that a good enough reason to develop a program, if their families were asking that they be close [by]? . . . [So we went to] look for a grant. . . ."

Another example is the runaway program. "Once we got the temporary houses [group homes] going, we realized we could only take in those children that the Bureau of Child Welfare decided we could take in, which still left out a lot of gang members . . . a lot of really nomadic, homeless youth . . . which were words the City didn't even know. So we went after [funds under] the National Runaway Youth Act . . . in '74 when it first came out. We did it again in '75 and we got the grant in '76, [and] . . . opened the Crash Pad. . . . [Now we could say], 'City, we don't need your bread. No, we'll show you, who you should be caring for.' . . . We'd take in a kid and we'd call up and say, 'Listen, this kid has bruises all over him; it's an abuse case, and you have to accept the case.' . . . We had the federal grant to help us. . . ."

In sum, the choices made in establishing GLIE and developing its program have been pragmatically designed to ensure success. A preference for autonomy was temporarily subdued to achieve operational status. Constraints were accepted to secure resources, but additional resources were sought to loosen the constraints. In no case were the restrictions crippling, and/or indeed permanently oppressive. And while the choices have produced a variety of programs, there is an underlying consistency in terms of semi-autonomous organizational units each servicing a real need for youth in the South Bronx.

RISKS AND CONSTRAINTS

Sister Lorraine's basic style of enterprising is bold and tilted toward risk. It is an orientation that was apparent from the beginnings of her GLIE-related activity: "My own religious community thought that it was crazy, and I knew I was at risk. . . . Becoming politically involved for me was very risky. I really didn't know anything about politics . . . [although] I think I've enjoyed . . . becoming involved politically and feeling that's really where the change has to happen. . . . If you don't get to that, than whatever you're stirring up will definitely die."

The risk-taking behavior of Sister Lorraine has been precipitated largely on her perception that that is how you get things done in a world of pernicious bureaucratic constraints and subterfuge. With respect to the establishment of GLIE, the conservatism of government officials was manifested in skepticism about the viability of any enterprise in the South Bronx. Another barrier that Sister Lorraine cites is the existence of some eighty other child care agencies in the City, and hence the official reluctance to approve "yet another one." But at the core of Sister Lorraine's perception, and the barriers she and the others who founded GLIE faced, is the system of Catch-22 regulations in which the developers of a new child care agency in New York seem to be caught: ". . . Once we decided to go [for child care status], then we had to go by all their regulations in forming a board and bylaws and what not. As a matter of fact, we had the bylaws sent back to us . . . three times because in the charter . . . we put . . . things like 'advocating for community youth.' They didn't understand that. You don't have that in a child care charter [so] we deleted all that kind of stuff. . . .

"[Then] . . . we took building commissioners to thirty-three apartment dwellings here . . . before they would allow us to open up one single group home. They said [there] was a major violation to every apartment . . . [but] when I asked them to write down those violations on behalf of [a] number of families living in the building, they refused. No, they were only there because of child care, looking [at] the group home!

"I think we have one house still in operation that the State Board [of Social Welfare] has not licensed. You just can't wait for them . . . and their regulations as to square feet between beds, and square feet in rooms, and number of full bathrooms and number of half bathrooms. You know, if they would tell you actually that we don't want you here because [our] worker is afraid to stay on the street . . . then I would live with that. . . . Okay, we'll put a bodyguard next to your working people. That's a fine way to keep you from achieving what is in need!

"It's horrendous! Some of these laws are ridiculous. [For example, to open] . . . these two units [for multiply handicapped children], their funding source would be different. They would be called ICFMRs . . . Intermediate Child Care Facility for the Mentally Retarded. Now the regulations for an ICFMR are all institutional regulations. We have these youngsters living in two apartments on 149th Street. There's no way I can make that apartment building meet the code for an institution. And at any rate, none of those kids lived in an institution that met those regulations, anyway. You know [it's as if] . . . it's wrong for the community to be doing it and yet the State and City never do it. So it's Catch-22. You have to work through it. You know, you have to either ignore them and keep on going, or try to work through as much of it as possible."

OUTCOMES

GLIE is a success story, having rooted itself in a devastated urban area, and grown from a single group home and budget of $75,000 to a multifaceted, million dollar program over six years. The program has diversified from its original focus on gang-oriented youth, growing somewhat by happenstance in a decentralized mode into new dimensions of services. But the themes are still fundamentally troubled youth and the community of the South Bronx.

ANALYSIS

The social chemistry which results in the birth of a new agency is a multifaceted and complex phenomenon—usually a combination of conscious intent and fortuitous circumstance. In the case of GLIE, there were some fortunate occurrences, most particularly a timely suggestion that GLIE could begin operations by affiliation with an established agency.

This idea, although accepted with reluctance, accelerated (if not simply made feasible) the birth of GLIE. However, it had little influence on its eventual form.

The environment in which GLIE developed, on the other hand, was inauspicious. Certainly there was a host of legitimate social problems to address in the South Bronx, and there were new opportunities emerging for support of child care services to older, runaway, and handicapped youth. But there was a great distance to be bridged between the opportunities and the reality of services.

Primarily, therefore, the emergence and early growth of GLIE is attributable to the bold and risk-taking, yet pragmatic behavior of its primary entrepreneur, Sister Lorraine Reilly. Her willingness to force the issues and test and challenge the bureaucratic constraints, sometimes overstepping the bounds of technical legality, was instrumental in overcoming the odds against successful enterprise in the devastated environment of the South Bronx. This risk orientation is a product of the distinctly and intentionally independent and unencumbered style that Lorraine Reilly personified.

Much of GLIE's organizational form also reflects Lorraine Reilly's style. Program units are small and decentralized because this allowed Lorraine freedom of action, and keeps each unit close to the grassroots, where Lorraine thinks they belong. A variety of programs have emerged because GLIE has been attuned from the beginning to expressions of need from the Bronx community, but also because some sources of funds (e.g., federal runaway funds) offer the prospect of loosening the bind of current funding agents (e.g., the local child welfare system) and permitting more discretion.

Finally, the GLIE experience reflects the tensions that inevitably arise when an enterprise founded in advocacy enters the regulated, bureaucratic environment of social service delivery. For GLIE the trade-offs between the advocacy and service delivery missions were apparent from the beginning, as GLIE was forced to separate from CLUB and drop its explicit advocacy orientation. Subsequently, the leaders of GLIE had to swallow hard many times, accepting constraints such as oversight by St. Dominic's and compliance with rules and regulations on services and facilities that inhibited a quick response to perceived service needs in the community. In essence, GLIE had to learn how to become part of the service producing establishment without losing the energy that had sprung from its idealistic roots.

Group Child Care Consultant Services (GCCCS)

PRÉCIS

GCCCS is a consulting service affiliated with the University of North Carolina (UNC) School of Social Work that provides management assistance, program consultation, and staff training to residential child care agencies primarily in the Southeastern region of the U.S. While never formally incorporated, GCCCS operated essentially as an autonomous nonprofit organization from 1956 to 1972, when it was formally absorbed by the university. Since 1956 demand for the services of GCCCS has grown rapidly, but the organization itself has experienced continual financial and managerial problems.

THE ENTREPRENEURS

There are a number of individuals who were instrumental in establishing and nurturing GCCCS—known as the Group Child Care Project until 1968. These include Dr. E.F. Gettys, Isaac Greer, and Weston Reed of the Southeastern Child Care Association (SECCA) who originally broached the idea of a consulting group based at UNC that would visit child care agencies on-site to provide staff training; these men did much of the organizational spade work (recruiting client agencies, obtaining financial commitments, etc.) for GCCCS and became directors on the board of the project. Marshall Pickens and later Bob Mayer of the Duke Endowment were instrumental in bringing financial support to the project and inspiring some key programmatic initiatives. Early staff members such as Alton M. Broten also helped shape the enterprise. But the common denominator throughout the history of GCCCS[1] is Dr. Alan Keith-Lucas, the administrator from the beginning in 1956 until 1968, and a participating consultant to the organization thereafter.

Dr. Keith-Lucas, who since became Alumni Distinguished Professor Emeritus, was a full-time faculty member of the University of North Carolina School of Social Work from 1950 to 1975, serving as Acting Dean

---

[1]Called Group Child Care Project until 1968. GCCCS is used for convenience throughout the chapter, however.

of the school in three different years over the period 1950–1975. Thus, administration of GCCCS was never his full-time occupation. Nevertheless, Dr. Keith-Lucas, known as Keith to his friends, has been GCCCS's shepherd throughout, formally until 1968, and in spirit thereafter. It was he who provided the thread of continuity, credibility, and elan that enabled the organization to get started and to hold together over time. Indeed, GCCCS was developed with Keith as the focal point. The original organizers from SECCA wanted Keith, who then directed the successful Chapel Hill Workshops, an annual conference at UNC for child care agency staff and professionals, to serve as their consultant for on-site training. As Keith's other commitments did not permit this, the idea of a full-time consultant working under Keith's supervision was formulated, and eventually arranged by SECCA and UNC.

It is possible to describe Keith as a "reluctant entrepreneur," in the sense that he had no inherent interest in amassing or controlling enterprises or even accomplishing social reform, but was anxious to respond, out of personal, professional, and religious conviction, when he felt he could be of service. In Keith's words, ". . . We didn't start with a dream here . . . except with the dream of being helpful. . . . We didn't start out to reform children's homes or to produce a certain kind of child. We started as a response to [the agencies] desire for training." Keith's style and motivations appear to explain much about the history of GCCCS— particularly its constant work overload, the high regard in which the services have been held, the underfinancing, and the reluctance to incorporate separately from the university or to take initiative towards putting the organization on a firm economic base.

THE ORGANIZATION

Since its founding in 1956, GCCCS has gone through three distinct phases of organizational structure: from an autonomous project operating through the UNC extension service; to a more formally structured, but still unincorporated, nonprofit organization; to a service formally absorbed within the UNC School of Social Work.

The roots of GCCCS lay in the Chapel Hill Workshops and the Southeastern Child Care Association. The Chapel Hill Workshops, begun in 1945 and run by Keith from 1951 to 1973, were also organized as an extension service of UNC and provided an annual forum for child care workers and professionals. They are, in Keith's words, ". . . one of the few truly national or even international activities of the University, and the nearest thing the United States has to a national conference on the group care of children."[2] Nonetheless, the Workshops, organized largely

---

[2]Alan Keith-Lucas, unpublished draft.

on the initiative of the child care agencies originally, failed to adequately address the training needs of participating child care agency staff. According to Keith, "Despite the popularity of the Workshops . . . both the children's homes and the School recognized their inadequacy to reach even the beginning needs of staff. . . . In 1953, however, a group of administrators of [SECCA] . . . came up with a new idea . . . a traveling consultant . . . employed under Dr. Keith-Lucas's supervision, to be based in the School of Social Work. . . ."

SECCA is essentially a trade association and vehicle for collective action of the administrators of residential child care agencies, largely denominational (Baptist, Methodist, Presbyterian, Church of Christ, etc.) in heritage, in the southeastern part of the U.S. With Keith as the focal point, the members of SECCA developed the resources and constituted most of the governing board of the original project. UNC, a state university whose principal facility is in Chapel Hill, was a willing partner, through its extension service which was intended to be sensitive to political demands for service throughout the State. The Duke Endowment, under Marshall Pickens (and later through its child care service director Bob Mayer) was an early financial supporter of the project. This fund, set up (by Mr. Duke) for charitable causes in the Carolinas, has historically been active in child care and support of the Workshops.

In its initial form, the project, begun in 1956, consisted at the staff level of a single consultant under the supervision of Dr. Keith-Lucas, who served as (part-time) administrator. The governing board consisted two-thirds of representatives appointed by SECCA and one-third appointed by the UNC Chancellor. (Significantly, Keith comments, ". . . Perhaps to show our independence of the school, it was the Chancellor who appointed, not the Dean of Social Work.") The project was financed by twenty-two member agencies who pledged to pay for five days each of consultation time ($300 per year), plus the donation by UNC of space, utilities, secretarial help, and part of Keith's time (although he received no reduction in his other university duties). In addition, a three-year starting grant of $5,000 per year was received from the Duke Endowment. The project remained essentially in this form until 1968, when, because of workload, financing, and leadership problems, the staff and board organized a two-day retreat, at Quail Roost Conference Center where major reorganization decisions were made. The board was broadened to include 25% at-large representation, 25% representation of member agencies, with SECCA itself and UNC equally sharing the remaining 50% of the seats. A decision was made to employ a full-time director (to succeed Keith). Finances were restructured by establishing fees for member agencies over and above consultation charges. Limits on staff consultation loads were set and staff salaries were made more competitive. The budget was tripled, from $39,000 to $109,000, with an expectation that a full-time director would be able to finance part of the increase by outside fund-raising. A decision was made to change the name to GCCCS and call it a national organization, but to maintain the focus on group child care rather than more general child welfare issues. These decisions taken, GCCCS appointed a full-time director in 1969; Keith stayed on as a consultant and "father figure."

GCCCS remained in this form until 1972, continuing to grow but experiencing internal staff difficulties, and facing in 1971 a questioning by the university of staff salaries and issues of control. In 1972, GCCCS came under control of a new Dean of the School of Social Work and the GCCCS governing board was relegated to an advisory status. Internally, however, the project continued to operate in much the same manner, with minimal support of the UNC.

From the beginning, the relationship of GCCCS to the University of North Carolina had an ambivalent quality. Logistically, the project utilized the university's administrative machinery, yet has always been separate and apart. According to Keith, "It had a [separate] budget and that budget was carried for a long time in the Extension Division of the University, then was transferred to a special grant fund. . . . But it was a very casual relationship with the university. . . . University professors don't participate directly in this, except that . . . [the] staff are officially lecturers in the University. We can . . . buy our car through the university. . . . We do our expense accounts through the university. . . . As far as a staff consultant is concerned, he is "technically . . . paid by the university, I mean he got his check in the same mail . . . and became part of the retirement system and that kind of thing. But actually, the money came from a special fund set up in the Extension Division."

The University essentially viewed GCCCS as an extension service over which it had jurisdiction, in ". . . the long tradition in this state [to] provide the services to the people. . . ." This accounts for the concern on campus in 1971 when ". . . the governing board approved a salary raise above the university as a whole. And the university began to challenge this [saying] 'Hey, what right have you to do this?' This was just as we were changing deans . . . and the new dean, when he came, said 'This is part of the School of Social Work . . . I want it established as part of the School of Social Work." Despite these intermittent expressions of proprietorship by the university, GCCCS was mostly ignored, even neglected (certainly in terms of resources), by the university for most of its history.

Internal operations posed another source of problems for GCCCS. In keeping with Keith's style, the project ran in collegial fashion. This was fine as long as the organization was small and Keith was around to provide guidance as the respected elder. (Several of the staff consultants have come from the ranks of Keith's former students.) But as the organization grew, and as Keith's attention was diverted to other matters, tensions rose. The conference at Quail Roost in 1968 recognized the difficulties and attempted to right them, but the problem of leadership was not easily solved, either by appointments from within or outside. Keith reviews the post-1968 situation: ". . . We had an awful lot of staff difficulty, particularly with [the first staff director]. . . . It was a mistake to appoint him. We should have gotten somebody from outside. . . . But then with the second [outside] director . . . staff meetings became impossible. . . . They were too democratic. . . . They'd spend the whole entire time discussing whether a meeting should start at 6 or at 7, and this kind of thing. They were intolerable. At the same time there was great resentment when the executive made a decision. It was a kind of damned if you do, and damned if you don't. . . . The executive had not enough status. As a matter of fact, the staff recognized that he was inferior . . . rather than superior to them.

"It's a difficult organization, very difficult organization to administer because you've got four or five people who are tops in their field. . . . It's very difficult to take a peer out and put him over [them]. . . . Now I could fulfill that role because I was the original teacher. Do you see that? Somebody else would find it almost incredibly difficult. . . . So [the first director] was eased out . . . and we brought a man in from outside who was a complete failure. And after [that] . . . Mr. Sanford [the current director, a staff consultant for eleven years and originally one of Keith's students] was appointed."

Financially, GCCCS was continually problematic. Part of the problem stemmed from the uncertainties of the relationship with the university, and from the inherently discontinuous (albeit substantial) nature of support from sources such as the Duke Endowment. But the problem was more fundamental than this, stemming in part from the basic nonprofit rationale under which GCCCS operated. Keith explains: "The problem, financially, has been that it costs a great deal more to put a consultant on the road than we can charge in fees. . . . You see, we're in [a] situation [where] every new agency we take on, we lose money. [We don't raise consulting fees] . . . simply because that would put out of business a good number of the poorer agencies who need consultation the most. . . . In order to get a first class consultant, you probably have to pay up to $30,000 [per year] and that is so far above what the agencies are paying their people that they see the costs of consultation [as exorbitant]. We charge $200 a day and it costs $400. . . . A private guy would charge considerably more . . . $300 to $500 a day. . . . So we have to make [it] up either from grant money or Duke money. And we've always been in [a tough] financial situation, [but] . . . we've always survived; we've survived 23 years now."

Clearly the financial problems were related to self-imposed constraints on program purpose, e.g., the desire to serve (less prosperous) child care agencies in the region and indeed to confine attention to residential child care per se. In later years this began to change, under pressure of a new dean. Keith observes: ". . . It's still fundamentally a group of child care people [but] what the dean has done is undo one thing that we said in '68 . . . [that] we will specialize [solely] in group child care, rather than . . . run a competition [with] the Child Welfare League of America. . . . I think he sees [GCCCS] as a model that he can use in other ways and he doesn't have our commitment to group child care as a motivating force."

CHRONOLOGY OF EVENTS

1945—The Chapel Hill Workshops begin at the University of North Carolina, as a joint venture of the Southeastern Child Care Association, the School of Social Work, and nominally the Child Welfare League of America. The Workshops initially service executives of child care agencies and focus on the training of child care personnel (houseparents).

1946—Planners of the Workshops decide to offer sessions to child care workers and houseparents as well as executives.

1949—Alan Keith-Lucas, the supervisor of Children's Services for the State of Louisiana, participates in the Workshops for the first time.

1950—Alan Keith-Lucas joins the UNC School of Social Work facility and becomes director of the Workshops. He takes charge of the 1951 sessions, and continues to do so until 1973.

1951—The Workshops are popular but fall short of demand for staff training. The children's homes (SECCA) and UNC School of Social Work begin to explore more intensive means of providing staff training. The possibility of a six-week course at UNC is broached, but potential funders fail to respond.

1953—The Workshops change format to utilize advisor/consultants, rather than lecturers, for sessions. Workshops are organized around specific topics, with session participants producing their own reports. The Workshops begin to publish these reports and disseminate them as training materials.

1953—A group of administrators in SECCA propose the idea of a travelling consultant based at UNC under supervision of Keith-Lucas to provide on-site staff training.

1954—The consultant project is approved by SECCA and by UNC. UNC agrees to provide space, utilities, secretarial help, and (unofficially) part of Keith-Lucas's time. Twenty-two agencies agree to pay for five days of consultation each ($300 per year). A governing board is elected, and Keith-Lucas becomes administrator.

June, 1956—Appointment of the first staff consultant is made, and the project begins to function.

1956—The Duke Endowment pledges $5,000 per year for a three-year trial period, at the solicitation of Dr. Greer and of Weston Reed, Chairman of the GCCCS Board.

1959—Duke support begins to phase out, with intent that the project become self-supporting by 1962. Fees to member agencies (now numbering 29) are raised, and all but one agency decides to retain membership.

1960—Workload for the consultant staff has risen substantially, and Keith-Lucas is forced to undertake directly a share of the consulting load with member agencies.

1961—The original staff consultant leaves for a new job and is replaced. (Staff still consists of just one full-time consultant plus Keith-Lucas.)

1962—The Chapel Hill Workshops are formally merged with GCCCS.

1962–1963—GCCCS ventures into federal funding with a short-lived research grant.

1964—The project adds a second consultant. UNC is unable to continue its secretarial and overhead support, leaving the project totally on its own funding. GCCCS is required to move off campus, as space on campus is needed for other uses.

1965–1968—This is a period of major growth in the number of agencies served, and a struggle for staff to stay abreast. Some expedient measures are taken, including the recruitment of 15 executives and social workers from member agencies to serve as temporary consultants to smaller and less sophisticated member agencies. Project staff are also permitted to "moonlight," to supplement low salaries, by providing private consultation over and above the stipulated 110 days per year. Also, from May, 1965 to Summer, 1966, Keith-Lucas serves as Acting Dean of Social Work, followed by a semester on leave in the Fall of 1966, creating a serious leadership vacuum at GCCCS.

1966—The Duke Endowment offers GCCCS $10,000 per year to develop an extensive Certificate Training Program for child care agency personnel. GCCCS staff conduct a feasibility study and the program opens in 1968 with classes for child care worker supervisors.

1968—Problems of staff overburden, leadership, and finances inspire a two-day retreat at Quail Roost at which GCCCS staff and board members make some major reorganizational decisions. (See Choices).

1968—The new Dean of Social Welfare (Dean Anderson) temporarily assists GCCCS in its financial problems by putting GCCCS consultants on state salaries for part of the year. One of the staff consultants is appointed Acting Director, replacing Keith-Lucas.

1968–1969—Two more consultants are added to the GCCCS staff.

1969—The acting director is confirmed as full-time director. Staff problems ensue as the new director is unable to command necessary staff cooperation.

1969–1972—Demand for GCCCS service (77 member agencies by

1972) grows, but internal problems and financial difficulties continue to mount also.

1971—The GCCCS Board proposes an increment to staff salaries greater than the university-wide increment, raising significant administrative problems. As Keith-Lucas points out, ". . . The university questioned the dean's lack of control over such matters."

1972—A new dean (Dean Teicher) is appointed to the School of Social Work. He insists that GCCCS give up its semi-autonomous status and come formally under his control. The board of GCCCS accedes to this demand. Bylaws are revised and the board assumes an advisory capacity. The dean now formally controls GCCCS policies and personnel.

1974—The first full-time executive resigns under pressure from staff, but continues as a staff member. A new one is appointed from the outside. He also encounters rough going. Research specialists are added to the staff.

1975—The agency continues to run a deficit, imposing new burdens on its staff who are required to teach summer courses without additional compensation to allow UNC to cover expenses. GCCCS moves back on campus, again receiving housing and utilities from UNC.

Fall, 1977—GCCCS appoints its third director since 1968, this time an insider, Cliff Sanford, a staff consultant originally appointed in 1966. The agency begins to attract federal grants for training programs and curriculum development and to broaden its scope to include projects on child abuse and neglect.

CONTEXT

As already noted, GCCCS has its roots in the Chapel Hill Workshops and in the southern, church-affiliated child care agencies which were largely responsible for initiating those workshops. As far back as 1938, these agencies solicited UNC and later succeeded in getting Duke University to provide training courses for child care personnel. The Duke extension courses ran from 1939 to 1941 but were terminated in 1942 due to war-related travel restrictions. However, the initiative was picked up again by the Superintendent of the Baptist Orphanages of North Carolina (I.G. Greer), resulting in the first workshop in Chapel Hill in 1945.

The Workshops are significant to the development of GCCCS in several respects. First, they are the product of the same kind of inspired leadership by a few southern child care executives, that led ultimately to the establishment of GCCCS. As Keith observes, these leaders were not responding to a particular problem or crisis but ". . . they were the people with the dream, in a sense. . . . Their dream at that point [1953] was only a better trained staff. But then when we moved into the field . . . of training the staff, I think we began to raise problems with them. . . . And they [would] say, 'Well, help us with it!' "

Although the setting is the South of the early to middle 1950s, it is not hard to understand the initiative of forward thinking executives, for improving agencies' staff personnel. These men were in touch with the social work field which was beginning to professionalize and rethink its old-line institutional practices. And, while the social fall-out of urbanization may not have been as serious a concern in the South as it was in the North and West, this was a time of social change, with the Supreme Court decision (Brown) on school desegregation, and other civil rights activity. The churches, of course, would become an important element in this struggle, and this would inevitably affect the thinking of church-affiliated child care people.

Once the Chapel Hill Workshops were organized, they became a breeding ground for progressive thinking and questioning of current practices. Executives and agency staff mingled with academics, and hashed out their ideas in small sessions. Renowned child welfare experts were brought in as speakers and consultants from all over the country, controversial subjects were discussed, and social mores began to be challenged. Thus, the workshops nurtured an atmosphere in which demand for more knowledge, reform, and improvement of practice on the part of child care agencies would grow. And as Keith notes, the solicitation for GCCCS ". . . simply came as the agencies began to realize that we had advice to give them."

Still, Keith also makes clear that the culture of the South has much to do with the manner in which the training and advisory service evolved. For example, GCCCS developed only after a bond of trust and mutual respect had been built up. Keith writes: ". . . They were somewhat wary at that time of social workers but trusted me because of the Workshops which I had conducted for three years."[3] This bond of trust permitted GCCCS ultimately to bring about significant changes in some very conservative agencies. An important key to this process was the religious factor. Keith explains: "It may seem a very paradoxical thing to say, but in one sense those agencies which have changed in accordance with the [current] fashion are the ones that are capable of the least change. They become doctrinaire. Whereas the old established agency, even though it's very conservative on some points, is not committed to any doctrinaire position and is ready to change . . . if it once sees the advantage of changing. . . . [One] very conservative agency [was] able to change, partly because it had [religious] ideals and it [was] struggling towards these [but] it had no very clear professional knowledge of how to get [there]. . . ."

In sum, the southern, religious culture, combined with the progressive

---

[3]Personal correspondence.

yet sensitive elements enmeshed in the Chapel Hill Workshops, created an environment in which the child care agencies could change in their own manner. This environment nurtured the demand for, and helped shape the nature of, the consulting services of GCCCS.

CHOICES

GCCCS developed, since 1954, in an evolutionary rather than abrupt manner. The project was born of the Workshops, grew and modified its services in an adaptive way, and adjusted to the shocks of changes within the UNC. Still, there were some important conscious decisions along the way. At three different points in time (1954, 1968, and 1972), for example, decisions were made to maintain affiliation with the University of North Carolina, rather than to incorporate separately. The decision to be structured, and to remain nonprofit rather than profit-making was similarly affirmed. In 1968, conscious decisions to formalize the organization structure, and broaden its mandate under full-time leadership, were taken. And the consultative rather than standard-setting modality of GCCCS, and broadening of its original outlook from staff training to general child care agency problem solving, was endorsed.

As observed earlier, the relationship of GCCCS to the university was an uncertain one. But the forces binding these organizations were strong enough to withhold any strains. In the beginning (1954), the university setting was mutually attractive to the SECCA sponsors and to Keith. The university provided convenient administrative and logistical support through its Extension Division (handling pay checks, providing space and utilities, etc.) so that GCCCS would impose a minimal administrative burden on Keith, given his other responsibilities and activities in the School of Social Work. At the same time, the affiliation with UNC was comforting to the sponsors. Rather than simply hire a private consultant, which they were leery of (as Keith was not himself interested in taking on a private contract), they could secure Keith's supervision and the fallback of the university's commitment. As Keith saw it: "It was a way of making sure that I supervised it, I think. . . . [Also] it had something to do with the prestige and value to these people, of UNC." (It also came at a price that a wide range of SECCA members could afford.)

But as GCCCS grew, over the years from 1954 to 1968, the university did not always treat it kindly. When the conference at Quail Roost was called in 1968, affiliation with the university was again on the agenda. As Keith recalls: ". . . The alternative was raised of an independent organization and offering me the directorship. . . . [But in the first place] . . . I wouldn't accept the job. . . . I think [also] it was the same feeling that there was a great advantage in being part of the university. [For Keith and the staff consultants] there was a more attractive job within the university because of retirement [benefits] and because there is a certain status in belonging to the faculty of UNC. I mean it is, in the South, a very prestigious university."

The real test came in 1972, however. By this time, GCCCS was more formally organized, essentially independent of the university for decision-making purposes and headed by a full-time director. But, sparked by the controversy over pay scales, the new Dean of Social Work, with backing of UNC (because GCCCS had become, according to Keith, ". . . a sort of maverick agency [which] didn't fit entirely within the university structure"), forced a decision. GCCCS would either submit to the dean's control, or be banished from the university. The board of GCCCS chose to submit, and to relegate itself to advisory rather than trustee status, for the same apparent reasons that it had always favored university affiliation. Independence was not so important as the comfort and assurance associated with continued affiliation.

Although never officially incorporated, GCCCS was consciously developed on a nonprofit basis. The tie to the university clearly required this. Originally (in 1954), the SECCA sponsors probably would have accepted a private contract with Alan Keith-Lucas as an individual (proprietary) consultant, for it was his services they were after, and he would, in any case, come with the university label. Even in 1968 or 1972, an independent, private corporation headed full-time by Keith might have been accepted by staff and board. But in no case did Keith want to assume this level of responsibility, to the exclusion of his professorial and administrative duties at the school, nor did the notion of a profit-making unit have any special appeal to him, or his staff colleagues. To the contrary, such status would have precluded philanthropic subsidization of fees to permit assistance to less well-to-do child care agencies. Thus it was no surprise that in 1968 (and thereafter), when an independent status was considered: ". . . There was never any suggestion that it would be profit-making."

The 1968 decisions at Quail Roost to formalize the project, including the appointment of a full-time director, restructuring of finances, and adopting the new name GCCCS, represented the accumulation of pressures emanating from growth. Keith recalls the circumstances leading to Quail Roost: ". . . If you look at the statistics, I think you will find that the big growth years [are] '65 and '66. . . . Suddenly from being a nice little activity that I could handle with my left hand, it suddenly became a major operation. . . . We were much more scrambled to get the job done. We were beginning to live under crisis, a crisis business. [And] we didn't have enough money to pay . . . the consultant fees. There was a critical mass and we had reached it. . . . And [there] was [a] feeling that [we] needed to build a [stable] structure. . . ."

GCCCS began as a consultative service on staff training for residential child care agencies in the Southeast. As the agency grew, it diversified its services and clientele, but remained essentially loyal to its origins. Nonetheless, its programmatic commitments have been challenged, stretched, and reaffirmed at various points. Between 1954 and 1968, the project essentially adapted to the problem-solving needs of its clientele, and to the expanded membership—diversifying the kinds of advisory services it offered, as required. Keith recalls: ". . . There was never a conscious decision. . . . It was something simply that developed. . . . I mean it was as if one day we looked at it and said, 'Gee, we're not [solely] staff training any longer are we? We're doing something quite different.' That partly arose from the philosophy that we developed . . . that we would help an agency with anything that it wanted to do that we felt was reasonably sound . . . a philosophy of consultation really, rather than being a standard setting agency [like the Child Welfare League] or having something [preconceived] we were trying to get agencies to do. . . . Therefore, consultation became [a] very, very varied thing, and still is. . . ."

In 1968, at Quail Roost, the diversified and expanded program was both consciously affirmed and elaborated. The decisions here attempted to shore up GCCCS to allow it to continue its basic mission. The decision to "go national," for example, would provide a wider basis of support (given the redesign of the fee structure to include membership dues). Similarly, the decision to diversify into research could be viewed as a means to attract future grant support, but also to allow GCCCS to continue more effectively in the mode of adaptive consultation. Thus, in the years following Quail Roost (1968–1972) the program was still overwhelmingly consultative, and focused on the southeastern agencies, although there were structural, administrative, and financial changes designed to cope with current difficulties. One thing that the formalization (and growth) of GCCCS might have changed, however, is what Keith calls the "spirit" of the enterprise. Talking about one of the early consultants, Keith recalls the pre-1968 days: "I would say to him at the beginning of the year, 'Sam I haven't the vaguest idea whether I've got enough money to pay your salary.' And he would say I have faith in what we're doing . . . I'll stick. [This] spirit . . . disappeared . . . a little bit . . . with the reorganization. . . . With the gathering of more consultants, it became more an agency rather than a cause, and something of the spirit went out of it . . . something of the tremendous enthusiasm that the early consultants had [was lost]."

By 1972, the inevitable transition from the early missionary zeal to a more stable and pragmatic foundation had occurred. Coupled with the continued internal problems of leadership and concern over financial stability, this loss of inspiration may have contributed to the rather passive submission of GCCCS to the School of Social Work, and to a degree of erosion in the original purpose.

RISKS AND CONSTRAINTS

As enterprises go, GCCCS cannot be considered a terribly risky one for Alan Keith-Lucas. After all, his position in the university was secure throughout and his writings assured him a place of respectability in the social work profession. Keith himself admits there would have been no tragic consequences had the project failed, particularly in its early days: "It wouldn't have made any difference. I mean, I would have been sorry because it was something I wanted to do. And you don't like to start something and see it collapse. . . . I think we would have had the same sort of feeling [as] if you put on an institute during the summer and nobody came to it . . . that kind of thing."

Still, there were more subtle risks. Despite his seemingly cavalier attitude about possible failure, there were times when Keith wore himself to a frazzle to help meet the workload, as demand for GCCCS services began to grow. There was a clear personal health danger associated with overwork, as Keith coupled GCCCS to his other duties. Furthermore, there were certain characteristics of the GCCCS enterprise that risked disfavor with the social work profession at large. The sole focus on group care, for example, was definitely at odds with the growing national emphasis on deinstitutionalization, and orientation to other approaches such as foster family care, adoption, and preventive maintenance of families. Similarly, Keith's explicitly religious orientation raised some eyebrows in the profession. Keith, however, was aware of these risks, and dismissed them with his general self-characterization as a maverick: " . . . It's not entirely popular in the profession to work with group care, and it is not entirely popular within the profession to work with religious agencies. And one of the things you have to do on this job is to really be able to talk religion. . . . But then I had already made myself unpopular with the larger profession. I mean, I was already a controversial figure . . . particularly after an article I wrote in '53 that really set the profession by its ears. . . ."[4]

Keith was able to cope with these professional risks rather easily. He cites ". . . the complete support of the dean." He was based in a southern university where the religious context and group care orientation were more comfortable. Furthermore, his record of publications and professional participation was impressive and hard to discredit. A man of lesser stature might have been more intimidated.

All along, constraints on the GCCCS enterprise were numerous. Given the nonprofit rationale, i.e., the desire to keep fees within bounds of agency capabilities, and the limited financial resources of the university, financing depended on philanthropic sources. Yet there was never much

---

[4]Alan Keith-Lucas. The political theory implicit in social casework theory.

slack in staff or leadership time to engage in fund-raising. Indeed, following the start-up period, such funding came largely on the initiative of the Duke Endowment itself, substantially in connection with the Certificate Training Program.

Financing limitations are one manifestation of the larger problem of the leadership resource constraints that continually plagued GCCCS. From the beginning Keith was explicitly part-time. As the organization grew, and as external demands on Keith also increased, the supervision of staff, policy-making, fund-raising, — essentially the capability to grab the bull by the horns — was foregone. These problems were recognized at Quail Roost in 1968, but leadership scarcity continued to be a problem. A respected elder like Keith was needed, but hard to find. Finances were involved here, too. According to Keith: "I don't think we ever had the finances to get the only kind of person who could have [handled it]. I mean if we had been able to get Gula or Treischman or Berman [it might have worked] . . . but they are people in the $35,000–$40,000 figures and at that time [1968] we were talking about $15,000 to $20,000, you see."

Another limitation on acceptable candidates for the directorship in 1968 was cultural. As Keith puts it: "I was afraid of a child welfare expert coming in who would not understand the agencies we were working with, who wouldn't have the religious base or the cultural base of the South . . . and who would try to turn all the agencies into treatment centers, which is not the role that most of the agencies either want or really should develop."

Contributing also to the post-1968 leadership lacuna was uncertainty over what a director was supposed to do. As Keith recalls: "Sometimes I think all you really need is a business manager. On the other hand, there is a great deal of feeling among some of the staff that they want someone who can give them new ideas, who can approve them, who can tell them they're doing a good job, who can somehow be a leader. And then there is the third possibility . . . someone who simply would be a money raiser. . . . None of our . . . executives managed [to] raise money."

Finally, GCCCS operated (by choice) within the confines of the university. As we have observed, this setting also imposed its limits. The events of 1971–1972 demonstrated that if GCCCS wanted the comfort and convenience of university affiliation, it would also have to curb its autonomy. Prior to 1972 this was subtle and unwritten. After 1972, it became explicit, and took its toll in terms of ability of the organization to pursue its own administrative policies or its historically favored mission. GCCCS would have to attend more seriously to the university rules and to the more catholic interests of the school.

OUTCOMES

Despite its sometimes turbulent history, GCCCS managed to grow throughout. Even in 1968 Keith obsesrves: "[It was] wrong . . . to think of it as an impending crisis. . . . It was a flourishing organization. The question was, 'how should it be managed?'" Indeed, beginning with some 22 agencies and one staff consultant in 1956, it grew to some 66 member agencies and three full-time consultants by 1966, to 86 member agencies in 1978.

Clearly there was satisfaction with GCCCS's services, and its reputation grew. Indeed, despite any explicit motive in this direction, GCCCS served as a model for efforts elsewhere. Keith notes, for instance, that ". . . the Texas agencies talked for two or three years about setting up a similar [organization]. . . . They even wanted to get one of us to go to Texas for a year and start the agency. . . ."

Nonetheless, through the sixties and seventies, GCCCS never succeeded in solving its own financial problems. Keith writes, "Since [1968] the agency has been in financial trouble. . . . In 1975 the agency ran a deficit of $50,000." There was a possible silver lining in this chronic cloud, however. For the first time (in 1978) there was the promise of stable leadership, under a director, newly appointed but long associated with GCCCS and respected for it. The new basis of affiliation with the university also brought some reason for optimism. By diversifying its outlook, GCCCS now had more options for solving its problems of organizational maintenance, without wholly sacrificing the essence of its original mission.

ANALYSIS

In a very real sense, the experience of GCCCS was the product of the ambivalent yet dedicated entrepreneurship of Dr. Alan Keith-Lucas. Driven by a religious and professional desire to be of service, he nurtured a program that was obviously responsive and appreciated by his clients. Yet this dedication to purpose came at a price to organizational maintenance. The nonprofit orientation, essential to the assistance of less prosperous agencies, and the headlong response to requests for help, created a financial bind, while the preoccupation with group child care displaced exploration of other areas that might have eased the budget squeeze.

Of equal consequence, the basic loyalty and affinity of Keith and his staff to the university, and the lack of any strong material or power-seeking motive, precluded any effort to have GCCCS escape the restraints of the university, by separately incorporating, or to resolve the problems of leadership scarcity, by having Keith assume full-time responsibility. Lacking Keith's full attention and unable to find a proper substitute, GCCCS was in no position to establish a stable operating environment.

It is interesting that GCCCS would have such severe leadership problems following Keith's withdrawal. Selecting leadership from among a group of professional peers seemed not to work. Peers were poor supervisors of peers. Effective leadership seemed to depend on a father figure like Keith, or someone else with sufficient charisma. Either that, or the role of leadership in such an organization of professional consultants as GCCCS required redefinition. Perhaps as Keith seemed to imply, a more specialized business manager or fund-raiser would do, leaving GCCCS to be governed like a law firm with senior and junior partners.

Still, the nurturing of GCCCS and the early definition of its mission required the dedication and sensitivity of a Keith-Lucas. With that foundation, growth was evolutionary rather than planned. A relatively small and informal agency responding to its environment grew inevitably larger and more formal. As a result, long-run survival seemed to mandate a more flexible service agenda and more conscious attention to organizational maintenance.

POSTSCRIPT

In April of 1969, Dr. Alan Keith-Lucas was involved in a serious automobile accident, in which his wife and sister-in-law were killed. I met Keith's wife Jill only once, but her warmth and hospitality impressed me.

Jill was not merely an emotional support for Keith, but more of a partner in his work. Keith recalls, for example, that "for fifteen years she put on parties, at our house, for as many as 200 people at a time, largely because she realized that child care workers attending the Workshops vastly appreciated being asked to someone's home rather than be entertained at a formal party in some community building."

Bob Mayer expressed it best when he wrote: "One had only to visit their home or be with them to realize Keith and Jill exemplified the qualities of caring and sharing he spoke about so often." This case is dedicated to Jill Keith-Lucas.

—D.Y.

NEW ORGANIZATIONS PARENTED BY EXISTING AGENCIES

Child Welfare Information Services, Inc. (CWIS)

PRÉCIS

CWIS is a management information service established to provide computerized reports about client populations, to New York City and some 80 voluntary agencies in New York City's foster care system. CWIS was founded in 1972 as a nonprofit corporation, jointly governed by representatives of the City, State, and voluntary agencies. It was nurtured in embryonic form by the Council of Voluntary Child Care Agencies (COVCCA) under the leadership of Joseph Gavrin, and developed cooperatively with officials of New York City.

THE ENTREPRENEURS

A number of key individuals were instrumental in the development of CWIS. Initially, officials of COVCCA including Ted Burbank and Morton Deich helped explore and formulate the idea. Later, a partnership between COVCCA and City staff, especially Barbara Blum, carried the idea to fruition. The first executive director of CWIS, Robert Gundersen, shepherded the organization through its early years. But the person most responsible for devising the idea, translating it into a concrete proposal, organizing the effort, and seeing it through, was Joseph B. Gavrin. The effort to establish CWIS began late in 1968, some six months after Gavrin was hired as executive director of COVCCA, an organization which represents the voluntary child care agencies in their relationships with the City and State.

Joe Gavrin described himself professionally as a "community organizer" who operates in a style of "indirect leadership." That is, he tended to work behind the scenes, as a catalyst to recruit and mobilize others into developing self-sustaining organizational activities. Although not an academic, Gavrin was a serious student and comfortable in the world of ideas. He counted some of his teachers among the strongest influences in his life, crediting them with orienting him ". . . more towards a career of service rather than money as an objective . . ." in developing a "skeptical rationalism and the necessity for clear thinking," and learning the principles of "indirect leadership." The rational, intellectual dimension was a

basis for action throughout Gavrin's career. His "major intellectual satisfactions come out of phrasing a new idea or concept which resolves a difference or provides a new rallying point. [He puts his] trust in intellectual, rather than political or numerical clout: out-think the other person
. . . have the facts and the concepts clear . . . and take advantage of an
opportunity to thrust them forward."

Gavrin's apparent motives in the CWIS venture were highly consistent
with his orientation to rationality. Commenting that the beginnings of
CWIS preceded some of the crises and calls for "accountability" that hit
the New York City child care system in the early 1970s Gavrin notes: "A
number of us within the system knew that [the system] needed to be ra-
tionalized . . . and that we often did not know what the consequences of
our actions were. We really didn't know who was in care . . . and so on
. . . and that since this [computer] technology was available we should
use it. . . . If you could have computerized information to control who
was going to sit on an airplane . . . you should be able to have computerized information for something much more important . . . namely, child
care."

As a newly appointed director of COVCCA, representing close to 80
diverse voluntary child care agencies, and aware of existing efforts in city
government to develop a computerized child care data system, it is certainly easy to understand why Joe Gavrin in 1968 would have a special
interest in improving his own information base concerning the activities
of the agencies he represented. But there was more to it than this. He inherently preferred a more rational way of doing things, and furthermore
was inured with a civil libertarian view of government: "I was concerned
about . . . civil liberties and . . . [the notion] that knowledge and information are power. I did not want to have all that power in government. . . .
This is just a point of view that I've had for a long, long time and goes
back to certain Jeffersonian antecedents in my thinking. . . . In addition
. . . we were in the early Nixon days and we'd had many examples [with
Nixon and Johnson] and what happened with Vietnam . . . where government manipulated information for its own purposes, and I wanted to be
able to guard against that."

While Joe Gavrin and COVCCA were the major elements in the founding of CWIS, the cooperation and partnership with the local public sector
was absolutely essential. In this regard, the contribution of Barbara
Blum, the key public sector proponent of CWIS, was particularly crucial.

Barbara B. Blum has been widely described as one of the finest public
servants in the mental health and social services areas of New York City
and State government. As a staff member in the Lindsay years, she was
part of the team effort of that administration to bring rational planning
and analysis to city government. In 1970 she headed a task force of the
Mayor's Policy Planning Council, to review New York City's child wel-

fare system. From there, she rose in meteoric fashion, first as a staff director of the City's newly created Interagency Council on Child Welfare and shortly thereafter as Assistant Commissioner of Social Services in charge of the City's child welfare services. In 1974 she was appointed as Assistant Commissioner of the New York State Board of Social Welfare, with responsibility for child welfare services of the metropolitan region. In 1977 the governor appointed Mrs. Blum as the State's Commissioner of Social Services.

For the CWIS venture, and Joe Gavrin, there could not have been a better public sector ally than Barbara Blum. As an analyst, she was sympathetic to the goals of information and planning, and as a rationalist with no particular axe to grind, she understood the virtues of a jointly sponsored effort between the public and voluntary sectors. The combined efforts of "believers" in rational planning, such as Gavrin and Blum, enabled the anchoring of CWIS in a sea of narrowly defined interests and skepticism. This sea was never a calm one, and once CWIS was officially launched, the navigation depended largely on Bob Gundersen, the executive director. Gundersen was an "in-house" candidate for the directorship, having been hired by Gavrin as a staff member to work on the CWIS project under COVCCA. Familiarity with the goals of social work and the needs of administrators were Gundersen's strengths. By his own reckoning: "My primary concern is not with data processing or information systems per se, but with the management of human delivery systems." He would hire a competent technical staff to master the nuances of data collection and programming. In view of the problems involved in managing a corporation like CWIS, jointly controlled by the public and voluntary sectors, Gundersen's identification with social work and his leaning toward the administrative rather than technical aspects of the enterprise may have been advantageous, though problems lay ahead in both spheres. Looking back from 1978, Gavrin viewed Gundersen's stewardship as a success. If he had a serious fault, Gavrin noted, it was that he was too much the optimist, down-playing problems and latent hostilities and not acting on them soon enough.

THE ORGANIZATION

CWIS is an offspring of the Council of Voluntary Child Care Agencies. The Council was established early in 1968 as a representative of the voluntary agencies that provided child care services under contract to New York City. COVCCA was to serve as the agent for the agencies, in their contract negotiations with the City, as well as to speak for the agencies, and serve as a forum for discussion on a variety of child care issues.

COVCCA is essentially a membership organization whose budget is supported by dues of the member organizations. COVCCA's board of directors consists largely of officials of the member agencies, but includes a number of at-large members and is not weighted towards the larger dues-paying members.

COVCCA is a small operation in terms of staff. Even in 1978, after having become statewide, its staff numbered under a dozen with only five professionals, and a budget of $323,000. At the time CWIS was embryonic, the staff of that project represented a major proportion of the whole COVCCA operation.

CHRONOLOGY OF EVENTS

1965—New York City begins development of a child welfare management information system, with the CONSAD Corporation.

January, 1968—COVCCA is incorporated.

April, 1968—Gavrin is engaged as executive director of COVCCA.

November, 1968—Gavrin discusses the CWIS idea with Ted Burbank, COVCCA board member and head of its Committee on Meeting Community Needs for Foster Care Services.

January or February, 1969—Idea for CWIS is presented to COVCCA's Committee on Meeting Community Needs.

Spring, 1969—COVCCA board authorizes Gavrin to move ahead with the CWIS idea.

Fall, 1969—Gavrin and Burbank go to Philadelphia and Cambridge to talk to people at the Wharton School and at Harvard.

April-May, 1970—A Wharton team presents its ideas for a system to the COVCCA member agencies. The agencies and COVCCA Board reject the proposal as too elaborate.

Late Spring, 1970—COVCCA obtains a small grant from the Edwin Gould Foundation to continue exploration.

Summer, 1970—System Dynamics Corporation is engaged by COVCCA as a consultant to write a new proposal.

August, 1970—Mayor Lindsay asks his Policy Planning Council to examine the child welfare system and develop recommendations. Barbara Blum is assigned to head the task force.

October, 1970—The System Dynamics report is approved by the COVCCA board. COVCCA then seeks HRA Commissioner Goldberg's endorsement, but this fails.

Late Fall, 1970—Goldberg is replaced by Jule Sugarman as HRA Commissioner. Sugarman (and Barbara Blum) are receptive to the CWIS proposal.

Late 1970—Mayor Lindsay organizes New York City's Interagency Council on Child Welfare which begins to work cooperatively with

COVCCA and New York City's Office of Special Services for Children, on the CWIS idea (Ericksen, 1974). Barbara Blum is appointed as director of the council, and a Management Information System Committee is designated whose goal is "the establishment of a comprehensive data bank that could be utilized to identify need and plan appropriately from a system-wide information base."

April, 1971—A formal proposal is submitted by COVCCA to the Rockefeller Brothers Fund, requesting $180,000 over three years to develop the CWIS program.

June, 1971—The Rockefeller Brothers Fund approves funding for the project.

Summer, 1971–Spring, 1972—An interagency advisory committee to the CWIS project, representing New York City, COVCCA, and various voluntary sector organizations, is set up as the predecessor to CWIS's board of directors. Project staff is hired by COVCCA (with committee advisement) and system development and organizational work is begun. Discussions and meetings are also held by COVCCA to familiarize its member agencies about CWIS.

May, 1972—CWIS is separately incorporated as a nonprofit organization, and the board of directors is appointed (Barbara Blum as President)

January, 1973 Robert Gundersen is hired by COVCCA, for the CWIS project.

March, 1973—Gundersen is appointed as executive director of CWIS.

July, 1973—CWIS physically moves out of COVCCA headquarters and into its own offices.

CONTEXT

Symbolically at the very least, CWIS is a product of both the high expectations and the subsequent disappointments associated with government in the 1960s. It also reflects the changing relationships of voluntary organizations to government, and the growing clouds of crisis in the child welfare services of New York in the early 1970s.

First at the federal level and later at the state and local levels, rationalization of public budget-making and service delivery became the themes of the sixties. Beginning with program planning and budgeting in the Defense Department, the notions of setting goals and measuring them, and allocating resources by cost-effectiveness criteria began taking hold. The year 1965 may have been the high point when President Johnson asked all federal departments to follow a program budgeting format.

At the local level, the Lindsay administration in New York City was pioneering in the application of analysis and rational planning to municipal services. Dozens of bright young planners were employed, the New

York City Rand Institute was established as an experimental think tank for the City, superagencies designed to coordinate related service functions were created, and analytical projects flourished in various departmental offices.

The early efforts of the Department of Social Services to develop a comprehensive computerized child welfare management information system was part of the overall trend. The CONSAD corporation was engaged in the mid-sixties to develop a prototype system, although that system never succeeded in getting off the ground. Several of the voluntary child care agencies in the City's system were also beginning to experiment with computer information management, including a group of nine agencies under the Catholic Charities of Brooklyn federation.

As a member of the advisory committee to the CONSAD project, Joe Gavrin was obviously in a good position to discern potential threats to the voluntary agencies, of a government-dominated information system. But Gavrin, too, was in spirit part of the rationality cult and to develop CWIS was consistent both with his official responsibilities to his constituency and with his own personal beliefs. Furthermore, as a member of the CONSAD committee, he was able to learn from the mistakes of that effort.

Overall, changing technology proved to be both a boon and a bane for the CWIS venture. Obviously, the advent of large, fast computers enabled the CWIS enterprise to occur in the first place. As Gavrin noted, computers in the late 1960s were being used in a myriad of functions from airline reservations to social science research, and it became clear that the child welfare field would ultimately exploit their benefits.

As CWIS got underway, however, the pace of technological change seemed to accelerate. Microminiaturization made computers even faster, with greater storage capacities that were more economical, and this made widespread use of small business computers practical. CWIS, however, was designed as a centralized, batch-processing, limited-capacity system with a slow turnaround time. As it became operational it started to obsolesce. "Real-time" input and output from multiple, remote terminals were becoming feasible, as did larger scale multifunction government computer systems, as well as small-scale business computers for individual child care agencies. By the late 1970s the changes in technology contributed to a major rethinking of CWIS's program and its role in the child care system.

The late sixties and early seventies are associated in most minds with the failures and disappointments of government planning. The Vietnam debacle reached its climax, and government generally was being called to account for its actions. Accountability became the watchword. What were citizens receiving in return for their billions of tax dollars? While the growing skepticism over planning did not bode well for a proposed system like CWIS, the call for accountability boosted the public sector's support of this project. For accountability took on a special meaning in New York City's child welfare system. Most children in the City's foster care system (some 85%) were in the care of voluntary agencies, and the budgets of these agencies, like those in other social service areas, had changed from basic dependence on philanthropy (in the 1950s and earlier) to close to total dependence on government sources. New York City's foster care budget had reached the neighborhood of $200 million per year and most of this went to the voluntary agencies. The City now had a strong vested interest in learning how public funds were being spent by the agencies.

Joe Gavrin correctly points out that the origins of CWIS predate the very serious crises in the New York City child welfare system of the early 1970s: Beginning in late 1969 and continuing into the mid-1970s, that system received a series of major blows, starting with a scandal emanating from overcrowding in the public children's shelter, and continuing through a class action suit charging discrimination in placements, new laws requiring court review of individual placements, and ultimately the City's fiscal crisis which imposed severe limitations on child welfare budget allocations. Had the CWIS system not been under development, something like it would have been called for, perhaps of a much more hastily conceived design.

CHOICES

A number of deliberate choices were made in the design and implementation of CWIS, in terms of programmatic content, corporate structure, and financing. Some of these choices, especially the programmatic and organizational ones, were crucial to the success of the venture.

Programmatically, it was important to have clearly in mind the function which CWIS was to serve. The basic choice was between a "data-based" system and a "case management" system. The differences here concern both the level of detail of information and the intended uses and users. A case management system would be oriented to the caseworker and would be capable of reporting case records in all their detail. Prior to the CWIS venture, a system of this nature was undertaken within at least one individual voluntary agency, without success. One of the problems, Gavrin indicated, was that it could not accommodate the diverse needs of practitioners. (With the advent of larger and faster computers, however, case management systems continued under active development.)

The data-based approach is aimed at administrators and system managers. It is much less intensive in the number of data items (per client or case) it collects and processes, focusing basically on "critical indicators" of a client's status or progress (e.g., how long has he or she been in care, etc.). Such a system attempts to produce meaningful aggregate statistics, comparisons, and other reports in order to signal (and help correct) problems at various levels of (agency and systemwide) organization.

In some minds, it was desirable for a new system to do both case management and data-based monitoring and analysis. In other minds the two functions were incompatible. For Joe Gavrin, CWIS was intended as a data-based system: ". . . Some place along the line I . . . made the decision that we were not going to go after a so-called case management system but after a data-based system. The difference [was] that we were not going to try to work out . . . a system which would enable each agency to manage its own internal operations because there were . . . too many variations among the agencies. . . . It was going to be much too elaborate. What we wanted to do was to generate information that would be helpful to the child welfare system as a whole. And that turned out to be a much more crucial decision than I realized at the time, because later on many people felt that one of the reasons . . . CWIS succeeded, whereas other groups did not succeed, was that a data-based system . . . wasn't overly ambitious to begin with."

The mandate for a data-based system evolved more clearly out of initial explorations for the CWIS project. One of Gavrin's first initiatives (in Fall of 1969) was to approach the Wharton School in Philadelphia with a request to develop a proposal for COVCCA. In the Spring of 1970, the Wharton people presented plans for a very detailed (multipurpose) management information system. The elaborate nature of the proposal led to its rejection by the COVCCA Board. According to Gavrin, ". . . The Wharton project . . . would have been . . . a two or three year thing before we reached any kind of conclusion, and that was one of the reasons . . . it got chopped down. It seemed too ambitious and the fruits too far removed. So we learned something about how to deal with the issues. . . . In the last analysis . . . we were better off by being more modest. . . . Inadvertently, Ted Burbank and I and that [COVCCA] committee had become overly ambitious too soon." In 1978 Bob Gundersen, Executive Director of CWIS, noted in an interview that "CWIS is basically set up to provide an accountability mechanism, a planning mechanism, and a possible base for research and evaluation" (CWIS, 1978). But this centralized orientation continued to be a concern. For one thing, the basic data for any system would have to come from the individual agencies and caseworkers, and these parties would have to perceive some benefit from the exercise in order to cooperate. An aggregate-oriented system whose utility was completely centralized would not do. A letter from COVCCA to the Rockefeller Brothers Fund in April of 1971 soft-pedaled this dilemma: "We believe that by the end of the three years [requested funding period] it will have been possible to develop an adequate central system to meet the needs of both the voluntary and public agencies and, at the same time, enable individual agencies to decide on sub-systems tailored to their own needs but also compatible with the larger effort."

As it became operational, CWIS developed a formatting of periodic computer reports, at three levels of aggregation: total system, groups of agencies (by religious affiliation or federation membership), and individual agencies. CWIS began to demonstrate its potential at both the agency and system levels. According to Gavrin, ". . . The initial reports were designed to give the agencies basic information. . . . [For example] . . . the child register so that they would have the list of all youngsters . . . so that they could know what the plans for the children were . . . how many children had adoption plans, how many were returned to their own families, how many were discharged to their own responsibility."

Despite its data-based design, CWIS also began to spin-off information at the case level as well, e.g., issuing "ticklers" and providing other data for filling out government-mandated reports.

The corporate status and structure of CWIS required careful deliberation, and had much to do with the venture's ultimate fate. Three interrelated organizational parameters were of key interest—the status of CWIS as an independent corporation, its nonprofit status, and the specific composition of CWIS's board of directors.

Spinning CWIS off from COVCCA was consistent with Joe Gavrin's personal preferences ("[I] didn't want a big, cumbersome program . . . to administer."), but it was also essential for the venture's success. Just as a fully governmental management information system was objectionable to the voluntary agencies, so would the public sector have withheld support from a system which operated under the organization which represented the voluntary sector. An independent organizational structure, responsive to both government and the voluntary sector, beholden to neither but accountable to both, was required. As ultimately incorporated, CWIS became a separate nonprofit corporation, whose 24 member governing board is composed of eight representatives of various New York City public agencies, eight representatives of voluntary child care agencies, four representatives of New York State agencies, and four from other private nonprofit agencies with interests in child welfare.

Joe Gavrin explains the need for independence and balanced governance of CWIS: ". . . I saw it conceptually that just the way government shouldn't run it for fear that it could be manipulated, I felt that the voluntary agencies shouldn't run it. . . . It needed to be governed by a balanced group. . . . The governance issue was important from the beginning."

While in concept CWIS was always intended to become independent, the "emancipation" came much sooner than initially expected. Gavrin explains how the failure of the Wharton proposal pushed this matter to the forefront: ". . . Until we had that experience with Wharton, we didn't really think of it as a separate corporation. . . . The Wharton project would have been as a contract with COVCCA . . . and Wharton would have developed a detailed system. [When] that got slapped down . . . we . . . developed the idea of doing it ourselves and then spinning it off. . . . I always had in mind that eventually it would be a separate corporation, but we saw that further down the line, so that the timetable for incorporating CWIS was accelerated."

The experience with the Wharton proposal not only speeded up thinking about the auspices for CWIS, but it affected the organization of the developmental groundwork. In particular, the Wharton episode interrupted the momentum of the CWIS initiative, so it became important that demonstrable progress be made quickly, to revive the project. In this connection, Gavrin and his colleagues at COVCCA began to see how they might be able to do things more effectively and economically, in-house: "[Originally] we thought about a longer leadtime. . . . Wharton would develop a plan over two or three years [and] give us a price tag for it, there would be some decision as to whether [to] go ahead or not go ahead, and . . . only then would you begin to wrestle with the question of . . . [under] whose auspices would the system be run. When that was shot down . . . we . . . went to Systems Dynamics as a consultant . . . to keep the momentum going. . . . It was important to get moving. So rather than have a contract with anybody to do it, which . . . would also involve . . . a [large] administrative overhead rake-off, . . . it seemed to us that we could do it much less expensively if COVCCA got a grant and hired people on our staff. . . . So then it became an internal project rather than a contracted-out project."

Immediately following the failure of the Wharton proposal, COVCCA obtained a small grant from the Edwin Gould Foundation with which to retain System Dynamics Corporation to write a new proposal. Within six months a proposal was written and endorsed by the COVCCA Board and within a year a grant from the Rockefeller Brothers Fund was received to begin development work. Over the next year COVCCA hired a small staff which began to design the system.

It seemed quite natural that CWIS, having developed in embryo under the wing of COVCCA with its own project staff, would retain its nonprofit status and utilize its own staff rather than contract out, once it became independent of COVCCA. But given the substantial data processing industry in the business sector, this scenario was not inevitable. Indeed Gavrin indicates that private vendors had to be consciously resisted, and that developing CWIS as a nonprofit, with its own in-house operations, was a way of accomplishing this: ". . . One of the problems we ran into in the beginning, and one of the reasons for having a new voluntary corporation was that we were, in effect, inundated by various potential vendors . . . who wanted to get in on the act. . . . At various points it became very difficult in terms of dealing with personal relationships, fending off all these different vendors, some of whom were related to different people [I knew]. . . . In my thinking, one of the ways to fend them off, and not be involved in trying to choose among vendors, was to have our own operating entity."

And that operating entity would have to be nonprofit. Gavrin explains that "If we had set up a new profit-making corporation, then we would have no advantage over any other profit-making corporation. The advantage of CWIS, the way . . . it could effectively [eliminate] all these other vendors . . . was the fact that it was *not* for profit."

Given the decision to incorporate CWIS as a (jointly governed) nonprofit, it was still possible, of course, to contract work out to private vendors. Even this option was scrupulously avoided, however. Private vendors had developed working relationships with various organizations in the voluntary and public child welfare sectors, and putting work out to bid would engender the same kinds of conflict of interest pressures as noted above. Furthermore, and perhaps more fundamentally, CWIS has been an innovative and evolutionary development, requiring constant discussions and revisions along the way. As Gundersen notes: ". . . There are a series of secondary goals [for CWIS] that have come about because of what we have experienced as we have developed this system over some five years now . . ." Gundersen counts the development of a common data base for governmental-reporting requirements by child care agencies, the training of child care agency personnel to properly supply system data, and the application of CWIS to fiscal administration of the child care system, as unforeseen functions that emerged over time. In this type of adaptive developmental environment, the specification and administration of work tasks by contract becomes unmanageable. An operational, in-house staff, amenable to continuous revision of mandates and in close touch with the users, is required.

Some of the same issues that determined the choice of organizational structure influenced the financial strategies selected to develop CWIS and subsequently fund its ongoing operations. The decision to develop CWIS under COVCCA, and subsequently to organize it as an independent nonprofit, made the voluntary sector a logical source. For example, Gavrin never seriously looked to the large profit-making corporations for money because ". . . the corporations who might be interested would be those who would be in the business, and then you'd be beholden to Burrough's or Xerox or IBM or whatever. . . ."

Obtaining a direct grant from government entailed similar problems. Gavrin notes: "I was adamant against going to government for money because, again, if we went to government they could control. One of my major motivations was that this shouldn't be controlled by government—city, state, or federal. I wanted to be able to develop it on a voluntary basis and then present it to others." Gavrin also notes that obtaining foundation money (from Rockefeller Brothers Fund) was accomplished very quickly, and at a time when keeping the momentum for CWIS was very important. In his view, this fast response ". . . would never have happened with government."

But why was external development funding necessary at all, when CWIS was to perform a service to the City and voluntary agencies? Apparently these potential clients needed convincing. The agencies needed to see results they could use and the City needed to be persuaded to give up its developmental effort with CONSAD. Gavrin recalls: ". . . We knew we had to get a grant in the beginning because until it [CWIS] showed some results, there was no way that we could get either the City or probably the agencies to fund it."

Ultimately, of course, the City pitched in staff time to the development effort, and arrangements were worked out for ongoing support of CWIS. According to Gavrin, "There had been some thought, not really serious thought, I would say . . . in the beginning . . . [to get CWIS] . . . completely funded by foundations so it wouldn't cost either the City or the agencies anything. That was never realistic. . . . It had to be funded on a fee-for-service basis. [It was] just a question of . . . whether the fee was going to be paid by the agencies or paid as part of a [direct] contract with the City."

Ultimately, some adaptation was necessary on this point. As Gavrin describes it: ". . . The financing of CWIS has changed. . . . In the beginning it was on the basis of the agencies paying so much for each day of care . . . with that being a reimbursable expense (by the City). After a [while (1975)] . . . it seemed better, and certainly the City preferred it, that . . . there be a direct contract between the City and CWIS . . . and that's what we did."

It is interesting that after less than two years of operation that Gavrin and his constituents would feel comfortable with direct financing of CWIS by government. But the child care agencies themselves were very heavily dependent on government money anyway, the direct contract was simple, and apparently the balanced governance of CWIS had taken hold and seemed to be working effectively. In view of later developments, however, this change may have been more significant than was realized at the time. [See discussion below.]

RISKS AND CONSTRAINTS

The CWIS initiative came very soon after COVCCA was established and Joe Gavrin hired as executive director. As such, the project, if it failed, could seriously impair the ability of COVCCA and Gavrin to become effective. Gavrin expands on this point: ". . . [CWIS] became a major programmatic effort of COVCCA and the prestige of the organization was put behind it. If it failed, it could be a body blow to COVCCA. . . . As a matter of fact, this crisis . . . in 1970 when the Wharton School put forth a proposal which was voted down, did create almost that kind of situation. Some people were [asking] 'Was COVCCA viable?' and 'Where was it going?' and so on. . . . There were lots of risks involved in terms of the success of the organization, and if it failed then I might very well be blamed for it and could lose my job . . . and there were professional risks. And I had to keep fending off people who were worried about confidentiality [of child care records] and worried about this, that, and the other thing."

If there were risks involved in failure, there were even more numerous sources of resistance to the successful establishment of CWIS. Early on in the venture various sources of opposition could be identified. The private vendors were perhaps the most apparent. As early as the Wharton proposal, according to Gavrin, "the [other] vendors . . . ganged up and helped knock it down." These vendors were ". . . connected into the [various child care] agencies" and either coveted the CWIS project or were fearful that CWIS would supplant their own agency-client businesses.

Another source of initial resistance was New York City itself. As noted earlier, the City had already invested in system development by the CONSAD corporation and was reluctant to give up on this. According to Gavrin, "The fact that CONSAD technically was out there was both a help and a hindrance. It was a help in the sense that we could hopefully develop a better track record because they had failed. It was a hindrance because the public department [of Social Services] had this investment, literally a financial as well as a conceptual investment in the success of CONSAD and it took them a while to recognize the fact it never would fly. . . ."

Indeed, Gavrin and COVCCA were rebuffed by Social Services Commissioner Goldberg in mid-1970, and the City's cooperation on the CWIS project had to wait for a new Human Resources Administrator, Jule Sugarman. Sugarman and Barbara Blum eventually sold Mayor Lindsay on the venture.

According to Joe Gavrin, ". . . The cost was not a major deterrent because it didn't seem that expensive and even now it isn't that expensive. . . . Now [1978] the total budget of CWIS is under $2 million. . . . That's a drop in the bucket when you talk . . . about what is being spent . . . in the state on child care. . . ."

With the development of CWIS well underway, under the wing of COVCCA in early 1972, the process of incorporation for CWIS proved to be the next high hurdle. Some of the problems were related to simple administrative bungling, and others due to substantive issues of confidentiality, conflict of interest, and bureaucratic "turf." Since CWIS was classified as a social service program, its incorporation had to be approved by the State Board of Social Welfare (BSW), which at that time was a regulatory agency separate from the State Department of Social Services. However, the BSW was only used to dealing with child care–producing agencies. When CWIS came along, notes Gavrin, "they didn't know what to make of it. . . . There was no precedent for it."

Substantive issues and power struggles did arise in this process of incorporation, however. According to Gavrin, the BSW was ". . . concerned that there not be a violation of Section 372 of the Social Services Law which has to do with confidentiality [of child care records]. . . . So we had to phrase things in such a way in the Certificate of Incorporation that we would not be violating that. . . . And then when we came to develop the board [of directors] we ran into certain conflicts of interest issues, and we had to have understandings about that, too. . . . [For example] if a public official on the Board of CWIS has to make a choice then that choice would be made in terms of his official [public] responsibility and that would not be construed as a violation of his or her duties as a trustee. So various kinds of compromises had to be made."

Perhaps the most serious threat to CWIS's incorporation was a late-breaking imperialistic design of the State Department of Social Services whose commissioner, according to Gavrin, ". . . felt that [CWIS] should be run by the State. We had to go through the whole rigamarole again. . . . I think [the Commissioner's] motivations were essentially that of a high-level . . . bureaucrat. In the last analysis most of the money is going to be State money because the State will be reimbursing the City. [So] why should the State have to get permission from some third thing, namely a separate voluntary corporation, in order to get the information which [it] thinks [it] needs? I think there was [also] a certain amount of organizational jealousy . . . [in the sense of] why didn't they think of this [themselves]."

Finally implementation of CWIS, following incorporation, involved some serious institutional problems. Social service caseworkers, on whom primary data collection depended, were uncomfortable and antagonistic to the notions of coded and computerized reporting about children. Gavrin notes that he was "appalled by the degree to which CWIS has to be involved in [in-service] training. . . ." in order to properly integrate the caseworkers into the reporting system.

OUTCOMES

Despite early struggles to gain acceptance and to establish working relationships (including a smooth and reliable data reporting system) with its client child care agencies, CWIS managed to survive and grow in its first five years, under guidance of its first executive director, Robert Gundersen. Its budget more than tripled, from approximately $400,000 in fiscal year 1974 to $1.4 million in fiscal year 1978. Staff increased from 13 to 50 in that period.

Growth was accompanied by adaptation and response to new opportunities. For example, CWIS developed ". . . a common data base to meet all the various reporting needs that the agency and the public body itself are subject to. . . ." [CWIS, 1978].

Indeed, having begun fairly simply as a system oriented to planning, accountability, and research, CWIS became more of a multipurpose management tool, producing over 200 different types of reports tailored to various managerial levels including caseworkers, supervisors, and executives. These reports range in orientation from "ticklers," i.e., reminders to workers or managers that certain actions (reports) are now due, or microfiche reproductions of computer files of individual children, to aggregated statistical profiles of children serviced by a given agency or group of agencies, and specially prepared research reports. Rather than maintain a rigid distinction between what constitutes planning information and case management information, CWIS management adopted a flexible stance (Annual Reports, 1976 and 1977): "From the beginning, CWIS has been . . . and will continue to be . . . responsive to the people who are actually doing the work. Therefore, suggested modifications . . . to CWIS reports . . . are all given consideration. . . . Literally hundreds of changes to the CWIS system have occurred this way."

Gavrin's original insistence on a simple, data-based design served well to launch CWIS successfully. As the organization established itself and became more sophisticated, however, the distinction seemed more obscure. While still basically a planning-oriented system, CWIS moved significantly to assist with case management as well. Nonetheless, Gavrin maintained that CWIS remained essentially true to its original intent: The ticklers and assistance with case-level reporting have, in his view, essentially been spin-offs of the main thrust of planning-oriented activity.

With the advent of New York City's fiscal crisis in 1975, CWIS was perceived as a valuable resource. According to Gundersen, "CWIS was started to deal with programmatic concepts and programmatic concerns but rapidly we found that there were significant savings that could be effected for both the City and for the voluntary agencies through the use of information contained in the data base. The programmatic improvements that are made as a result of CWIS reports obviously have fiscal ramifications; if a child is adopted sooner, that means the public is saving money. Those things are important. We've found other ways as well; through streamlining billing and some rather sophisticated financial arrangements, we've been able to save close to $10.00 for every dollar that CWIS costs."

Whether Gundersen's claimed cost/benefit ratio is accurate or not,

CWIS did receive some substantial endorsements. In 1976, New York State created with the Department of Social Services the Child Care Review Service to carry out statewide the same kinds of management information functions that CWIS had undertaken for the City. Logically, CWIS was selected as the contractor to implement such a system. Also in 1976, CWIS was one of 20 human service systems, and the only child welfare system, selected as a model for inclusion in U.S. H.E.W.'s data bank of systems to be shared with local governments throughout the country.

Given the foregoing recognition that CWIS has received, there is no little irony in the fact that by 1979, major changes were in store for CWIS. As Gundersen notes, CWIS now seemed better appreciated outside New York than within. In particular, the New York City and State governments decided to take over the data collection and processing functions of CWIS, and to restructure them for integration within a more comprehensive framework of computerized management information for human services. While CWIS would not be "cut off without a penny," the functions of CWIS and the nature of its contract with government would change drastically. A review by CWIS is fairly candid about reasons for the change [Prospectus, 1978]: "Recently . . . both the New York State DSS and New York City's SSC have indicated that they would like to take over much of the data collection, reporting, and distribution functions currently performed by CWIS, to alleviate what they perceive as current problems with regard to CWIS:

(1) CWIS is limited by the constraints of its hardware and funding, to a batch-entry, paper-form system, with rather long turnaround time.
(2) Government at both the City and State levels feel [sic] the need to integrate the child welfare information with other systems they have (or intend to have) on their own computers with a goal of less duplication of information, greater operational efficiency, and control of their data bases, as well as more effective data entry mechanisms."

To Joe Gavrin, this shift in government policy towards CWIS hinted at how successful CWIS had been. Government had now become so enamored with computers that it has invested enormously in its own computer capacity. Such investment was spurred by New York's fiscal crisis in which the substitution of capital for (clerical) labor has been looked to as a source of savings. In any case, having made such an investment in capacity, the state apparently felt impelled to use it. Gavrin wryly called this "Parkinson's Law of Computers."

Whatever the reasons, technological or otherwise, the abrupt shift in state and city government policy was traumatic to Bob Gundersen, although it quickly became viewed by CWIS officials as an opportunity as much as a setback. In particular, a prospectus for "ÇWIS II" was written, which emphasized management consulting and moved CWIS away somewhat from direct data processing as well as exclusive service to New York City and State. Four specific missions were delineated for CWIS II [Prospectus, 1978]:

— analysis — of significant trends/problems in the delivery of child welfare services . . . on a system and agency/district level, using modern interpretive techniques.
— training of child care administrators in the understanding and use of information and its translation into action.
— management support, including especially development of a data processing system geared primarily for the needs of agencies, to run on their own mini-computers.
— a "monitoring" function over government's development and operation of child welfare [information] systems [data bases].

Early in 1979, the City and State tentatively agreed to the first three of these new missions.

ANALYSIS

If Joe Gavrin and his colleagues at COVCCA had not taken the initiative that led to CWIS, a computer management information system for the New York City child care system would probably have developed ultimately, but not in the same form or as quickly. The unique characteristics of CWIS are its nonprofit, jointly governed corporate structure and its system-wide management orientation. In CWIS's absence, government would probably have imposed its own system, or a patchwork of private vendor systems might have evolved out of fragmented efforts of various groups of voluntary child care organizations.

CWIS was shaped heavily by Joe Gavrin's own set of beliefs — that the child care system needed to be managed rationally and that information was subject to abuse and should be controlled jointly by affected parties. The latter precept happened to coincide with the best interests of COVCCA and its constituent agencies, in the sense that a model like CWIS would preempt a solely government controlled system of the type then under development by the City (i.e., CONSAD).

The organizational form of CWIS also coincided with Gavrin's innate working style preferences. Another entrepreneur might have struggled to keep CWIS under the wing of its parent organization (COVCCA), or to assume control of the new unit, as part of an exercise in empire building. This was not Gavrin's style or preference.

Had Joe Gavrin attempted to maintain internal control of CWIS as a COVCCA program, the project probably would have failed. It might also have failed if Gavrin had not been so sensitive to conflicts of interest or had groomed himself for the directorship of CWIS.

The CWIS initiative planted itself on fertile (although not troublefree) ground in several respects. Similar-thinking, rationalist officials like Barbara Blum bubbled through the public sector at the same time, and were receptive. In addition, the public sector was struggling with its own faltering information system efforts, at a time when the accountability imperatives for government were beginning to grow. Third, CWIS was proposed in a form that sympathetic people in government could accept —jointly governed, self-contained, independent of other organizations, and relatively free of the morass of potential conflict of interest problems associated with the interaction of voluntary, proprietary, and political activity. Fourth, the programmatic concept of CWIS was purposely made simple, adaptive, and pragmatic. Operational status could be achieved in relatively short order, after which the system could presumably evolve according to user needs.

Overall, CWIS was formulated on a basic rationale of nonprofit organization; namely that such corporations can be established as independent units to resolve potential conflicts of interest and purpose, in a manner that is still responsive to those divergent interests. Unfortunately, the joint governance structure proved to be unstable in this case. The City representatives on the CWIS governing board were more powerful, and clearer about what they wanted from CWIS than their voluntary sector counterparts. And the transition to a direct service contract, from the original fee for service routed through the voluntary agencies, drew the purse-string controls of government tighter.

While changing technology helps explain the need for CWIS to reorient itself, it also appears true that government control hindered the ability of CWIS to adapt to new conditions. CWIS could not garner the resources to preempt the more comprehensive "real-time" management information systems that government had in mind, as the new technology began to allow it. Nor could CWIS, with its growing centralized government orientation turn its attention to the emerging minicomputer market as a more flexible mode of response for the individual voluntary child care agencies. In effect, CWIS was hemmed in by its relationship to government, and its initial investments, and could not muster the entrepreneurial initiative to break free, until it was pushed.

The takeover of data collection, processing, and distribution by government represents a failure of one of the initial objectives of CWIS, especially if data-base monitoring of the new government system is not accepted as one of CWIS's new functions. Perhaps this usurpation was inevitable in view of the continual pressure from government from the very beginning, especially by the State, for more control. Joe Gavrin was ahead of the pack in establishing CWIS, and he succeeded in preempting government's ultimate control. It worked for five years but time eventually caught up to it.

REFERENCES

Annual reports: fiscal years 1976 and 1977. New York: CWIS, Inc.
A prospectus for CWIS II, New York: CWIS, Inc., 1978.
CWIS: What it is, what it does. New York: CWIS, Inc., 1978.
Ericksen, K. *New York City's Interagency Council on Child Welfare: An evaluation*. New York: New York Community Trust, March 1974.

POSTSCRIPT

On October 2, 1979, Joe Gavrin died on his way to work. The circumstances of his death testified to his dedication. In his last letter to me he wrote about reading the draft of this case: "After a busy, busy week I read it on the train going home. It was great fun to read and gave a lift to the coming weekend. [I] truly enjoyed seeing the history set forth."

I am glad he had this pleasure as a small token of exchange for the guidance he gave me on this and other projects. I dedicate this case to him.

D.Y.

Harlem-Dowling Children's Service

PRÉCIS

The Harlem-Dowling Children's Service is a nonprofit agency that provides foster care, adoption, and related services to the Harlem community of upper Manhattan. Harlem-Dowling was founded in 1968 as a satellite of the nationally known, New York-based, Spence-Chapin nonprofit adoption agency, whose intent was to build and spin-off Harlem-Dowling as an autonomous agency, indigenous to the Harlem community. From 1969 to 1979 Harlem-Dowling operated semi-autonomously under the wing of Spence-Chapin. In 1980, it achieved status as an autonomous voluntary child care agency.

THE ENTREPRENEURS

A number of individuals were instrumental in initiating and organizing the Harlem-Dowling project: Spence-Chapin board members Alice Hall Dowling and Marjorie Bienstock were active in convincing the board to undertake the project and in raising funds for the venture; first Program Director Joseph Smith was largely responsible for establishing a community base and building the organizational structure from scratch; Program Director Doris Douglas was the midwife ultimately helping to bring Harlem-Dowling out into the world on its own. The basic determination, initiative, and momentum, however, came from Jane Edwards. Harlem-Dowling was her first major project initiative as Executive Director of Spence-Chapin.

Jane Edwards is an attractive, articulate, effervescent, career woman, especially attuned to broad social issues and current professional thinking in her field of social work. She rose from the ranks of casework positions in Spence-Chapin to become a dynamic executive, recognized for her leadership in the social services.

Mrs. Edwards pictures herself as a "change agent" for social reform. She says she is specifically not a grass roots community organizer, nor simply a management executive, nor a practicing caseworker. Her approach is both activist and intellectual. She seems driven by both a sense of competitive excellence and a genuine sense of social concern. She is a conscientious reader of social work journals, saying that she generates ideas through reading, soliciting staff proposals, and talking with professional colleagues. She makes herself aware of the broad social issues and tries to respond in terms of "seeing . . . what is wrong or needed and then going about to change it." Her "audience" is more national and professional than local or intraorganizational. While much of her work at Spence-Chapin has been stimulated by specific New York City problems, the perspective, consistent with the national orientation of her organization, is considerably wider. Asked why she and Joe Smith spent so much time on the road, talking about their experience with the Harlem-Dowling program, Mrs. Edwards replies: "To show people how they could do it. It was a national problem. . . . The problem really exists in every major city in the United States, that black children are in foster care, and there are not enough adoptive homes."

If Jane Edwards was the driving force behind the Harlem-Dowling project, Joseph Smith was her right arm. Mr. Smith was recruited specifically to head the project, having previously led a respected career as a social worker and administrator. Smith's responsibility was to organize Harlem-Dowling, and a large part of this task was to have the proposed new agency gain acceptance and support by the Harlem community. Smith was ideal for this mission. He lived in Harlem and is, by nature, a conciliator and peacemaker who could bring antagonistic factions together.

With Jane Edwards as the driving force, Joe Smith as the implementor, and supportive Spence-Chapin board members, Harlem-Dowling started with reasonable odds for success, despite the inherent problems of planting a new agency from the outside in the rocky soil of the Harlem ghetto.

THE ORGANIZATION

Spence-Chapin was incorporated in 1948. It emanated from the merger in 1943 of two informally run efforts, organized around the turn of the century by Clare Spence and Alice Chapin, to place babies of unwed mothers into adoptive homes. The roots of Spence-Chapin, its adoption orientation and its governance by civic-minded, well-connected members of New York society, continue in evidence, but the agency itself has grown considerably in size and function since 1948.

In particular, Spence-Chapin has become the largest adoption agency in the U.S., and the best endowed of all private agencies whose business is primarily adoption services. Its $5 million endowment has been built up over the years by charitable gifts and bequests and from fees paid by middle class parents who have adopted children through Spence-Chapin.

By the late 1960s Spence-Chapin could no longer be thought of as primarily an adoption agency, nor an agency that supported itself primarily on privately derived revenues, nor even an agency that was predominantly white, middle class in its orientation. In 1962 the agency began a foster boarding home program for nonwhite infants, in response to a burgeoning problem of abandoned babies left in city hospitals. In terms of budget and clientele, the foster care program came to dominate Spence-Chapin. In fiscal year 1977, for example, 75 percent of the agency's operating expenses went toward foster boarding care services, while 80 percent of incoming revenues were derived from government reimbursements. Nonetheless, as far as New York City child care agencies go, Spence-Chapin could still be described as less dependent on government fees, and having a more comfortable endowment cushion to fall back on, than most. In spirit, however, it remains an adoption-focused agency whose clientele are essentially young children and mothers, and adoptive parents.

There are other distinctive features of Spence-Chapin, as well. Despite its base (headquarters) in New York City, it considers itself a national agency which places children into adoptive homes all over the country. The agency is also very much attuned to the educational aspects of the profession and considers itself a leader in training and development of methods and materials.

Perhaps the most significant feature of Spence-Chaplin, especially for Mrs. Edwards, is the activist tradition the agency had developed through some of its board members, and the previous executive director, Helen Montgomery. Mrs. Edwards recalls some of her anxiety on assuming the directorship: ". . . When I accepted the position of . . . executive director, I accepted it knowing that the Spence-Chapin board is not a do-nothing board and they don't conceive of Spence-Chapin as an agency that just rocks along, not expanding, not getting into new programs. . . . I just felt that this is a tremendous job because I know fully well that our agency wants to keep doing things. . . . The former executive . . . was one of the most outstanding executives in this country, I think. Most people don't come up to that level. . . . It's easy to take somebody's place who was mediocre but when you take somebody's place that was outstanding, in an agency that considers itself a moving, developing agency, it's a big responsibility. . . ."

Despite its forward-looking orientation, Spence-Chapin has a few attributes that were potentially troublesome for embarking on a venture like Harlem-Dowling. First, in terms of governance, it has been an essentially white, upper middle class agency. As its first black director, Mrs. Edwards had some initial qualms about the Harlem-Dowling venture as a result, although race was never a factor in her relationship to the board: ". . . We had to do something that helped minority kids . . . and I thought that would be very difficult for me. . . . I had all kinds of mixed feelings. . . . Our board . . . was largely white . . . and [here it] gets a black director and the first thing she wants to do is take all of our money and [put it] up in Harlem. I said, you know, really a white director is better for an agency in some ways, to develop a program for black children. . . . But . . . I found out . . . my board didn't look upon me in any racial way. They put all their faith in [me]. . . . They trusted me . . . and I didn't have a personal problem. . . ." Nonetheless, the image of a white agency moving into Harlem was a problem that Spence-Chapin had to consciously deal with.

Another aspect of Spence-Chapin that appeared to clash with the Harlem-Dowling venture was its mode of central control. The rationale of Harlem-Dowling demanded autonomy for this new program unit, yet Spence-Chapin's operation, consistent with Mrs. Edwards' own style was neither decentralized nor used to spinning-off programs on their own. Somehow the management of Spence-Chapin would have to learn how to loosen controls and let go.

As it has turned out, over the ten-year period in which Harlem-Dowling operated under Spence-Chapin's wing, the degree of autonomy for the former has been mixed. Intake and program development, staff training, and direct services were run independently by the Harlem-Dowling staff. However, all personnel decisions, budget decisions, approvals for fundraising, and the like, have gone through Spence-Chapin. Overall, the staff of Harlem-Dowling felt that it operated with considerable independence, while the Harlem-Dowling Advisory Council, set up to eventually assume the functions of a board of directors, felt impotent and impatient.

CHRONOLOGY OF EVENTS

1960—New York City begins to experience a serious problem with increasing numbers of healthy minority children remaining in hospitals, for whom adoptive and foster care placements cannot be found.

1962—Spence-Chapin begins a five-year foster care demonstration program intended to provide long-term care for healthy black children left in hospital wards, through foster care, work with natural parents, and adoptive placements. Jane Edwards is named to head this program.

October, 1967—Mrs. Edwards is appointed executive director of Spence-Chapin, on the death of the previous director, Helen Montgomery.

1967-1968—Spence-Chapin is one of several agencies studied by Andrew Billingsly, for his PhD dissertation entitled, *Children of the Storm*. Decisions are due regarding the future of Spence-Chapin's long-term foster care demonstration project.

November, 1968—Mrs. Edwards proposes the Harlem-Dowling project to the Spence-Chapin Board of Directors. Board President Alice

Hall Dowling is especially receptive and promises to work on behalf of the project.

December, 1968—The Spence-Chapin Board of Directors approves the Harlem-Dowling proposal and begins to organize the project, including solicitation of local leadership in Harlem.

May, 1969—The first meeting of prospective members of the Harlem-Dowling Advisory Council (intended ultimately to become a board of directors) is held at Spence-Chapin offices. A core group is selected for the Advisory Council.

June, 1969—The Advisory Council meets to select an agency name and to develop by-laws.

October, 1969—Harlem-Dowling moves into office space in Harlem.

November 17, 1969—A press conference is held to announce the program's opening, and intake begins.

1969-1979—The Harlem-Dowling program develops and expands.

1977—Joseph Smith, nearing retirement age, joins the central staff of Spence-Chapin. William Ballard is appointed Acting Director and later permanent Director of Harlem-Dowling.

October, 1978—Doris Douglas replaces Ballard as Director of Harlem-Dowling.

1978—Harlem-Dowling staff actively prepare a charter and other papers required for incorporation as an independent child care agency.

Spring, 1979—Harlem-Dowling submits its application to New York City and State to become an independent voluntary child care agency.

April, 1980—Harlem-Dowling officially becomes an independent child care agency.

CONTEXT

Despite Spence-Chapin's national orientation, specific circumstances in New York City heavily influenced its decisions with respect to the development of the Harlem-Dowling program. Two sets of events in particular—the developing crisis in New York City's foster care system in the 1960s, and the fiscal crisis of the mid-1970s—were especially important. Beyond these municipal circumstances, the Harlem-Dowling venture was also shaped by attitudes in the local Harlem community, as well as current professional thinking vis-à-vis service to black children.

Spence-Chapin was basically an adoption agency and, except for a small preadoptive program, did not seriously undertake to provide long-term foster care until 1962. The stimulus for that undertaking was a crisis in New York City's hospitals caused by an accumulation of nonwhite abandoned babies. Spence-Chapin's *Annual Report* of 1977 recalls: "In 1962, at then Mayor Wagner's request, we started a demonstration program to take infants out of the city hospitals and shelters that served as their homes. These babies for one reason or another had been abandoned by their parents. The cost to the City of keeping them was unaffordably high—over $100 a day in hospitals and $40 a day in shelters. In addition, the babies suffered from severe maternal deprivation, a truly devastating affliction."

Jane Edwards elaborates: ". . . New York is largely a sectarian city in relation to child welfare services. The children [in hospitals] were Protestant. The Catholic and Jewish agencies took their children out of the hospitals. The Protestant children weren't taken care of because the Protestant agencies didn't want to expand their programs. They felt they couldn't afford it. . . . [Also] most of them thought that this was a city problem [and] the City ought to do something about it. Well, the City wasn't prepared to do anything at that time. . . ."

Spence-Chapin's response to the hospital crisis of the early 1960s was to set up a five-year foster care demonstration project. Mrs. Edwards explains the rationale: ". . . The hospital commissioner called to ask the agencies to take those babies . . . [but] various executives . . . said: 'Well, first of all there are no foster homes; we just can't find any foster homes for these [black] kids. Number two, if you could find the foster homes, you can't get the staff.' And so we were trying to show that we could not only get the homes, but we could train staff. [Furthermore, we would demonstrate that we] would eventually lead into permanency . . . a great many children . . . because we would find parents [who] would take them. . . ."

The foster care demonstration program contributed to relieving the hospital baby crisis and it led to Spence-Chapin's permanent involvement with provision of foster care.

But despite this program, which served some 1,700 children by the end of the demonstration period (1968), hundreds of healthy babies were still in hospital wards. It had become apparent that the root of the hospital children problem—children being born of unwed mothers in nonwhite, low income areas of the city, was hardly being addressed. In his 1970 speech to the Child Welfare League regional conference, Joseph Smith noted: "Illegitimacy rates in deprived areas were skyrocketing, with the highest percentage in central Harlem. During the first ten months of 1968, there were 1,400 more out-of-wedlock births than during the same 1967 period."

Mrs. Edwards elaborates: "We learned . . . around 1968 . . . that despite the fact that we had served so many black and Hispanic unwed mothers that there were still many, many thousands of unwed mothers in New York City living in Bedford-Stuyvesant and living in Harlem who were not coming out of their communities. . . . There were a few government projects in those areas—maternal and infant care projects. . . . The federal government was paying for these projects to help . . . unwed mother[s] to take their babies home, get the proper medical care, etc. . . . [But] . . . there was [no] alternative. Many of these girls cannot keep their babies . . . many of them are in school. . . ."

The problem of providing a foster care alternative, or as Mrs. Edwards puts it, providing "another way of planning for their children, placing them in adoptive homes [or] placing them in foster care temporarily" was one of access. Teenage girls would simply not respond to agencies outside their own communities. This realization coincided in time with research undertaken by Andrew Billingsly on the plight of homeless black children. Mrs. Edwards recalls, "I had just . . . been interviewed by Andrew Billingsly . . . who was then [investigating] . . . child caring agencies to see how many agencies were really placing . . . black children into adoption. He subsequently published his study in a book called *Children of the Storm*. . . . [In] his book he mentions Spence-Chapin [and that] 10 percent of its adoptive placements were black [and] that this was not enough. . . . And that what agencies needed to do was to really have a separate program . . . a full blown program to place black children in adoption . . . [i.e.] to establish black agencies [which] . . . devoted all of their time to . . . [black] children. . . ."

Billingsly's thesis had a profound effect on Mrs. Edwards. " . . . I would say the strongest influence on my decision to bring this [Harlem-Dowling proposal] to the board's attention was Andrew Billingsly's support. I was really quite stunned . . . to have him view us simply along with all the rest of the agencies as doing [just] a little something for black children when I thought that we had done a tremendous job—far more than any other agency, far more than the City of New York. . . . The . . . City told us . . . that we took 5 to 8 times more children into care, when children had no place to go. We took them from shelters. . . . We had a tremendous staff . . . a lot of minority people. And we just thought that if there is a black unwed mother somewhere in New York, she must be coming through Spence-Chapin.' And then we found out from Billingsly . . . that there were still blacks . . . not being served . . . [and that he viewed ours as still a token effort]."

In Philadelphia there was a small black agency under the Women's Christian Alliance, which was a precedent for Harlem-Dowling. Billingsly argued that, despite its smallness compared to Spence-Chapin's efforts, it was following the philosophically correct approach by having its roots and attention exclusively in the black community. This was the course on which Spence-Chapin was to embark.

The Harlem-Dowling venture was begun in 1968, a time of social activism in the country and especially in black communities. It was an especially hostile atmosphere in which to try to establish from the outside a social agency in Harlem. Developing grass roots support was Joseph

Smith's first priority. Mr. Smith describes the environment in which this effort took place: "At this time we were right in the height of the very militant [period]. The Black Panthers were very active. Two blocks from where the office was set up, the Welfare Rights Mothers [were located]. . . . I remember after we got started . . . [some] Black Panthers . . . met two of our young workers on the street [and] . . . told them that two of their members were incarcerated in the Women's House of Detention and they were pregnant, and they wondered if Harlem-Dowling would service these [women]. . . . [We told them] that we were there to give service to anyone in the community who needed it and we were not concerned about . . . their religious or political affiliation . . . The young ladies never came, but it was all sort of testing out to see what [we] would do."

One of the concerns of black activists at the time was community resentment over social agencies moving into Harlem. Joseph Smith recalls: "They were very suspicious about agencies coming into Harlem. [Other] agencies came in . . . brought their own staff from downtown and . . . imposed their own policies and programs . . . [with] money from the government. . . . They didn't hire anybody from [the] area. . . . They got the benefit of whatever . . . they could from the area and then left. . . ."

Harlem-Dowling did eventually succeed in achieving community confidence and support. Partly this was due to the plan, right from the beginning, to make it an autonomous agency indigenous to Harlem. The plan was for autonomy in about five years. However, the New York City fiscal crisis of 1974–1975 intervened to help postpone autonomy another five years. The crisis hit hard at the child care agencies which contracted with the City to provide foster care services. Mrs. Edwards recalls, "The City froze all [reimbursement] rates, salaries as well as rates for the boarding care of children. . . ."

With rates frozen, Spence-Chapin began running a large deficit on its foster care operations, especially its Harlem-Dowling division, which Mrs. Edwards estimates was losing $250,000 per year. Spence-Chapin had to make this up out of private funds. The fiscal crisis also precluded obtaining a separate, higher reimbursement rate for Harlem-Dowling that would enable it to survive on its own.

CHOICES

Major decisions pertaining to the Harlem-Dowling venture were made at three distinct periods in time. In the 1967–1968 period, basic decisions were made to undertake the venture and to shape it in its particular form. For example, it was decided that Harlem-Dowling would become an autonomous agency in five years. In the 1974–1975 period, the determination was made to postpone autonomy past the five-year target. In 1978, it was decided that the time for autonomy had finally come. The initial decisions (1967–1968) on Harlem-Dowling were based on professional goals and principles, and spurred by internal events at Spence-Chapin. The decisions of 1974 and 1978 were shaped largely by the changing fiscal environment and internal progress of the emerging Harlem-Dowling program.

Two converging events made 1967–1978 a time of basic policy decision-making at Spence-Chapin. First, the executive director, Helen Montgomery, died and Jane Edwards was appointed as the new director. Second, the internally imposed five-year tenure of the agency's foster care demonstration program was expiring. Major policy options were due to be considered.

For Jane Edwards, it was imperative that she begin to clarify her position on the agency's future with due haste: "I knew I had to do something. . . . The board members were [saying] to me . . . 'as soon as you get settled, as soon as you find out where you're going, let's talk about a new program . . . and wasn't it family service or something we were thinking of? . . .' And I just kept saying 'yes.' And then I did some soul-searching and decided in good conscience [that] I could not go into family service because family service was already being done. What we had to do was something that helped the minority kids; this was a big problem in New York. . . ."

The five-year point in Spence-Chapin's foster care program coincided conveniently with Mrs. Edwards ascendency to the directorship (and also with Billingsly's study). In any case, decisions were due on the foster care program. Joe Smith writes: "In 1968, after six years of expansion, the Spence-Chapin Adoption Service began slowing the acceptance of unwed mothers whose children would go into foster care because the agency was outgrowing its facilities. It was necessary to consider expanding physical facilities again or think of another way to serve this clientele."

The foster care program was, on its face, successful in the sense of expanding to serve a substantial clientele population. But by 1967 it was beginning to overwhelm Spence-Chapin and cramp its heretofore flexible, adoption-oriented, nationally focused style. And there was concern over a mismatch between the white middle class image of Spence-Chapin, as it may have restricted its effectiveness with nonwhites. Mrs. Edwards reflects: ". . . In relation to [our] finishing up our five-year project in 1967, [we were] realizing that we really were expected to [continue to] accept children [but] we really were not the best agency, I don't think, to relate to the problems of the City."

Furthermore, some of the original demonstration objectives were not being achieved. Mrs. Edwards explains: ". . . It was a demonstration project where other agencies would follow suit. But other agencies were not following suit, in taking in and serving those people. . . ."

Nor could Spence-Chapin make a significant dent in the problem of service to minority children by itself: ". . . We had gone as far as we could. We had served . . . by that time, thousands of children . . . 1,200 children in care at the time, black children. And the City was literally asking us to continue. [But] we didn't feel that we really could manage such a continuing adding of children to foster care. They were being added faster than we could get them returned home or placed in adoption."

Spence-Chapin could not very well suddenly drop its foster care operation. But it could consciously decide to limit its growth and to move to a new approach. The Billingsly thesis, while disconcerting in its judgement that Spence-Chapin wasn't doing enough, was appealing in providing a way out, consistent with Spence-Chapin's predilections to preserve its professional flexibility, to innovate, and avoid being overwhelmed by its foster care division, while continuing to serve its clientele in good conscience. As Mrs. Edwards puts it: "We felt that we could get more black adoptive homes if we established an agency in the black community. . . . They would come to an agency they felt identified with . . . [which] was concerned about the community. . . . The main thing we would do was to set up a board of people who live in that community so that they could manage their own destiny and . . . their own program, and relate to the community in a way that was appropriate for . . . that community, rather than by the way we [at Spence-Chapin] would relate to *our* . . . national and international . . . community."

Once taken, the decision to establish the Harlem-Dowling project required a number of strategic choices. Should the agency be fully autonomous, and when? How should the venture be financed? How should it be organized programmatically and as a corporate entity? Some of these choices were explicitly considered; others emerged naturally from circumstances.

Spence-Chapin had never before developed programs just to spin them off as independent units. It has been a consolidated, centrally administered and controlled organization. So, too, it is Mrs. Edward's general preference to keep programs directly under her watchful eye. Nevertheless, the ultimate autonomy of Harlem-Dowling was never really an issue —just the timing. Basically, the concept of Harlem-Dowling, as a professional innovation in response to the particular social problem, required an indigenous, autonomous agency in the black community. Mrs. Edwards summarized the argument: "We started the Harlem [program] for two different reasons. One was [that] we felt that not enough agencies were spending . . . enough time on adoption of black children. And two, the black clientele were not leaving their communities. . . . [Harlem-Dowling] was sort of a community-based agency. We didn't take our agency up to Harlem and say, 'Here we are to help you.' We said, 'Here is an agency that you can develop on your own, to be your own. To run it the way you want to run it, in relation to the community needs and lifestyle.'"

The financing of the Harlem-Dowling venture followed pretty much from its roots in the voluntary sector. Start-up money was sought in the form of grants from a variety of sources. Mrs. Edwards says that ". . . All possibilities were considered and reached out for—government grants, . . . foundation grants . . . [etc.]. . . ." The vigor and social position of some of Spence-Chapin's board members were especially important in securing funds. Mrs. Edwards recalls that Mrs. Dowling and Mrs. Bienstock were notable in their initiatives. For example: "Mrs. Bienstock . . . had many friends who were heads of foundations . . . so she was able to get us a great deal for Harlem-Dowling. We also got money from the New York Foundation and from United Fund. . . ."

Unlike the parent agency, however, Harlem-Dowling would have to be almost exclusively dependent on government money for foster care services. It would not be in a position to generate revenues or build up an endowment cushion from fees charged to adoptive middle-class parents, as Spence-Chapin had done over the last three or four decades. Both Spence-Chapin's private sources and Harlem-Dowling's heavy dependence on government were to play an important role in the timing of Harlem-Dowling's emancipation.

The initial five-year plan for Harlem-Dowling's autonomy was simply a target, not a binding decision. Five years was felt to be a short enough period to demonstrate that Spence-Chapin was serious about letting go, but long enough to allow Harlem-Dowling to become established with a viable program and organizational structure. As the project got underway, however, various trade-offs developed, as seen from downtown (Spence-Chapin) and uptown (Harlem-Dowling).

Seen from uptown, the approaching autonomy was fraught with both promise and uncertainty. Doris Douglas, director of Harlem-Dowling, explains the staff view: ". . . People have always felt two ways about [it]. They have felt very much proud of, and comfortable with, and wanting to be a part of Spence-Chapin; and they have also felt very much wanting to be 'their own boss' and [have] their own programs. . . . Some of us [including Mrs. Douglas] were originally from Spence . . . [but] we want [also] to expand and relate . . . to this [Harlem] community. . . .

". . . [Overall] we had some comfort from being with Spence-Chapin and I think that we may have moved more slowly until there was really . . . some emphasis [to separate]."

Some of Harlem-Dowling's Advisory Board, which remained relatively impotent during the agency's period in utero, pushed for early autonomy, but overall it seems ironic that Harlem-Dowling was cautious over the issue of autonomy. More and more, the push was to come from the parent agency, Spence-Chapin.

Essentially, the "downtown" perspective involved several different strands. No one wanted to see the venture fail for want of support. For one thing, Harlem-Dowling had, in a sense, become a professional showpiece for Spence-Chapin. Furthermore, some board members began to feel, after a while, that Harlem-Dowling had become an integral part of Spence-Chapin's operations and should not be hurried away. But others began to see Harlem-Dowling as an increasing drain on Spence-Chapin's treasury and advocated separation as soon as Harlem-Dowling could survive on its own.

The issue of autonomy first came to a head in 1974, six years after the beginning of the Harlem-Dowling project. In terms of the original intent at least, it was time to seriously consider separation. But as Mrs. Douglas explains: ". . . At that point we still needed some of the services of Spence-Chapin. We did not have all of our professional services [fully] developed. . . . I don't know if we were quite ready . . . in 1974. . . . We were still building professionally, so that the original date of 1974 . . . might have been a bit unrealistic. I think maybe that it takes longer than that to set up a program . . . [of] this scope . . . [i.e.,] a full-service child welfare agency. . . . As it approached 1974, I don't know that we all felt the push, that this was the time. . . . Then came the whole financial crisis. . . ."

Indeed, an even more cogent factor mitigating against autonomy in 1974 was New York City's fiscal crisis. In order to survive, Harlem-Dowling would need a substantially higher rate of per diem reimbursement than Spence-Chapin was then receiving. But the City was not about to grant such a rate, and discouraged autonomy for that reason. Indeed, it preferred to have Spence-Chapin, with its relatively comfortable cushion of private funds, absorb whatever losses the Harlem-Dowling program generated, at least until such time as the fiscal crisis eased. Mrs. Edwards elaborates on this, downplaying the readiness issue and emphasizing the fiscal problems: "[Harlem-Dowling was] supposed to become autonomous within five years, and they were fully ready to become autonomous at the end of that fifth year, but the City of New York was in a financial crisis at the time and they were concerned about losing the agency. . . . Agencies were folding in New York because they didn't have funds. . . . [So] despite the fact that Harlem-Dowling wanted to be autonomous, they were [also] afraid of . . . closing up. . . . [And] since Spence-Chapin does have quite an endowment fund [postponement of autonomy seemed wise]. . . .

"The City froze all rates . . . for the boarding care of children and [Spence-Chapin was] frozen at a very, very low rate . . . far less than our costs so that Harlem-Dowling had almost a $250,000 [annual] deficit. And [the Harlem-Dowling people] knew that they couldn't raise that much money . . . so Spence-Chapin . . . had to pull·them out of this deficit [during the] financial problem period in New York City. . . ."

Still, looking back on the 1974 period, Mrs. Edwards reflects that perhaps Spence-Chapin was too cautious and conservative: "I think that at the end of [the] five years designated time we should have gone through the procedure to see if . . . it could become autonomous at the scheduled time. . . . Despite the crisis I should have encouraged the agency to seek autonomy. And if denied a charter at that time, I would have felt better if they had tried, instead of discouraging it."

From Spence-Chapin's viewpoint this is easy to understand. Harlem-Dowling, as well as Spence-Chapin's own foster care program, became more and more of a financial drain under the frozen rate structure. Efforts were made to negotiate a higher overall rate for Spence-Chapin, and/or to establish a separate, higher rate for Harlem-Dowling, but none were successful. By 1978, despite the City's continuing fiscal problems, the pressures were sufficient for Spence-Chapin to vigorously encourage emancipation. By this time also, the City's fiscal condition would permit the granting of a realistic new rate to Harlem-Dowling, despite the essentially continuing overall freeze. Finally, the staff of Harlem-Dowling was now itself ready, and indeed also feeling the economic pinch. According to Mrs. Douglas, ". . . The [Spence-Chapin] board voted and . . . felt it wisest for us to become chartered. And they gave reasons for this. . . . One [was] we could not continue forever to operate at a deficit . . . caused by not having sufficient reimbursements. . . . We could cut staff, we could cut all kinds of things . . . but that would not help us face [the real issue]. . . . We could not postpone it any longer [even] if we wanted to because the agency was just getting a bigger and bigger deficit. So that our population, our foster care population, fell off . . . because for every child that we had, we had an increased deficit."

Mrs. Douglas explains that by 1978 autonomy really became the only way out of the financial bind: ". . . It seemed like this would be a good time to fulfill the commitment . . . [because] we could apply for funding. This was a good time to become autonomous . . . There was some chance because the [current] freeze does not [prevent the City from] setting new rates. The freeze affects existing rates [only]. . . ."

Despite the financial imperatives of the parent agency, Mrs. Douglas says that Harlem-Dowling was encouraged rather than pushed into seeking autonomy: ". . . Encouraged to become autonomous—[yes]; pushed as to setting a date or time—no, no. But . . . I am sure that if we went in and said, 'Gee, why, we have changed our minds and we are not going to be autonomous anymore. That was a nice little idea, but we looked into it and it is a bit more complicated than we thought, and we would just as soon [not].' Well, [we wouldn't get away with that]."

RISKS AND CONSTRAINTS

While the Harlem-Dowling venture was a professionally exciting outcome of the policy deliberations at Spence-Chapin in 1967–1968, it was also a gamble in a number of respects. For Mrs. Edwards, the venture would affect her credibility as a newly sworn executive director: "[If it failed] it would have been embarrassing amongst my colleagues . . . because most of my fellow executive directors were discouraging. They said, 'It's the wrong way to go. . . . You needed integration. You're setting up a black program in Harlem, and it's not going to work.' Some of them called up and said, 'You're a damn fool, you're not going to be able to get anybody to go up there to work. They're going to be afraid, and they ought to be afraid.' I'm ashamed to say that some of my black colleagues also said I was crazy. . . . So it would have been embarrassing [if it] failed. . . ."

In contrast to some of her professional colleagues, the board members of Spence-Chapin apparently gave Mrs. Edwards solid support: "I don't think the board would have [been embarrassed]. Very unusual people. They don't get embarrassed about anything." Thus Mrs. Edwards' job was not immediately at risk. Still, there was some concern, even among board members, about the safety of a Harlem-based project. According to Mrs. Edwards, ". . . Some of the board members were not entirely in favor of us setting anything up in Harlem. Harlem is a dangerous place for staff to go. . . ."

Perhaps of greater concern to the board, the Harlem-Dowling venture represented a potential albatross—a burden that would restrict the agency's freedom of action. While, to the contrary, the project was intended to ultimately relieve the growing weight of Spence-Chapin's own foster care operation, it might succeed in simply changing its form. As Mrs. Douglas explains: ". . . Spence has been able to pick up and go with needs that have just gone unmet for years. . . . It is kind of a fallacy that Spence-Chapin needs that foster care program to exist. Without that foster care program, they could really do some exciting things in mental health [for example]."

While some of the initial fears about Harlem-Dowling were overcome, risks surrounding the emancipation decision as seen from uptown, still loomed large. Mrs. Douglas reflects: ". . . There are people who wonder what is going to happen. . . . If people felt that somehow we were going to go down the drain, they would [say] . . . that is terrible. . . . Who is going to be left here, and who is really going to want to work in Harlem? . . . How could we have let this happen? . . . This is the community that always suffers. . . .

"[Concerning the staff], our working conditions [with Spence-Chapin] are not by any means lavish. . . . But we do have a pension plan. . . . We don't know whether the new agency will be able to afford one. And I think that people are really concerned about it. They [also] wonder if we are going to be as large as we have been. And whether there will need to be staff cutbacks. I think that is all part of a major change. . . . People . . . wonder what is going to happen to them."

At the beginning (1967–1978), the most serious institutional barrier to establishing Harlem-Dowling was gaining the acceptance of the Harlem community. As noted earlier, there was both local militancy, and suspicion of being "ripped off" by agencies from the outside. Mrs. Edwards recalls, "[Joe Smith] and I went to Harlem to every conceivable organization we could find to . . . tell them what we had in mind and ask their approval. We went to welfare people . . . ministries . . . Harlem Neighborhood Houses . . . hospitals . . . the Urban League. . . . They came down here to talk to us . . . and they were very suspicious. . . . They wanted to know how the money was going to be controlled, who were the staff going to be, who were the people on the Advisory Council. . . . They said they would reserve . . . further comments until they could see how it was developing. Then they welcomed it after they saw [we meant] business, [that] we were going to have a board up there . . . [of] people in Harlem.

". . . We didn't want to be picketed. We didn't want them to prevent us from coming into Harlem, which they could have done. If they had caused too much of a problem, I think our board would have said no. Some organizations had been run out of town, and then they just forgot about it. . . . They said, 'Well, . . . we came here to do good [but], if they don't want us, let them do it themselves.' . . . So we didn't want to run into any [of that] difficulty if possible."

Having eventually overcome the entry problem into Harlem, what remained was to build the program internally and to negotiate the labyrinth for seeking charter approval from the City and State, for independent child care agency status. The former was done under the nurturing wing of the parent agency.

The chartering process itself was thwarted in 1974 by the City's position not to authorize any new agencies nor grant necessary new per diem rates. When the serious autonomy initiative got underway in 1978, the direct staff work was principally left in the hands of the Harlem-Dowling staff. As Mrs. Edwards explains, the charter itself had to be written in a simple and direct fashion: ". . . The name of the game is to first think about what you want to do in relation to services, and secondly to make your charter as simple as possible. . . . If they add things into the charter that they're [just] thinking of doing, it would involve having [to deal with] too many bureaucracies. . . . For example, [they're] . . . working through the State Department of Social Services for this charter. If they

add in to the wording of their purposes 'day care' then they've got to go
to some other governing body. . . . Although they would like to have . . .
day care in Harlem . . . they dare not put it down at this point. . . ."

Other aspects of the chartering process also represented constraints.
The new agency must be nonprofit, and it must demonstrate financial viability. The latter of course was contingent on being able to get the City to
agree to pay a substantially increased per diem reimbursement rate.

OUTCOMES

Over the 1969–1979 period, the Harlem-Dowling program grew into a
$1.4 million program, approximately a sixth of the total Spence-Chapin
budget. In terms of clientele it represented an even larger proportion. According to Mrs. Edwards, "It has been one-fourth the size of Spence-
Chapin for the past five years . . . but it's the size they intended it to be.
They did not want it to become a tremendous foster care program. They
thought that their maximum number of children in foster care should be
somewhat around 300 and that they should continue to keep those numbers low and concentrate on working with natural parents and getting the
children back home [or] . . . placed in adoption. . . . They have increased
the number of children they've placed in adoption regularly each year and
they have also returned a large number of children back to their natural
parents."

Harlem-Dowling thus became a fully functioning foster care program.
By the summer of 1979, it had completed its application for a charter as
an independent child care agency. The application was approved less than
a year later by the State Department of Social Services.

The most important implication of emancipation is that Harlem-Dowling must survive financially, on its own. Programmatically, Harlem-
Dowling essentially operated independently already. In other ways, however, a close relationship with the parent agency, Spence-Chapin, would
continue. As Mrs. Douglas envisioned it: ". . . I would feel that I could
pick up the phone and call them. I would also feel that . . . if we have
children who need a service . . . right away, and we are calling other
agencies, [that] we [would] tend to call Spence first. . . . They tend to call
us first [and] I imagine that will continue. When they have training [semi-
nars] we are invited. When we have things, they are invited. . . . I would
expect that to . . . continue."

ANALYSIS

In a number of ways, Harlem-Dowling seems an unlikely venture for
an agency like Spence-Chapin. Historically, the parent agency derived
from white, upper middle class society and has mainly served middle

class adoptive parents. To the contrary, Harlem-Dowling is rooted in the black community, serving low income black mothers and children. Spence-Chapin conceives itself as an adoption agency, nationally focused, and integrally involved in professional training and social work education. Harlem-Dowling is a locally based service program with primary emphasis on its foster care division. Finally, Spence-Chapin is a centrally controlled and consolidated agency, whose director likes to maintain a close eye on operations. To the contrary, Harlem-Dowling has operated semi-autonomously from the start, with the intent of being spun-off.

The apparent anomaly of Harlem-Dowling is explainable by the combination of motives and circumstances that brought it into being. Despite its national viewpoint, Spence-Chapin was already involved in foster care and related services to minority children and unwed mothers, as a response to local problems and pressures in New York City. And in certain respects, this involvement was not proving to be satisfactory to the parent agency. Overall, Spence-Chapin was not receiving much professional credit for its efforts. Its foster care demonstration program was not succeeding, for example, in inducing other agencies to make similar strides. To the contrary, Spence-Chapin was lumped together with other agencies by Billingsly's study which viewed current efforts as tokenism. Finally, the foster care program easily had the potential to overwhelm Spence-Chapin in terms of size, and to fundamentally limit and restrict the agency's flexibility and penchant for innovative, education-oriented, professional activity.

The Harlem-Dowling venture was a novel response to the concerns generated by Spence-Chapin's foster care program. It was a concept that simultaneously would attract professional recognition but would allow Spence-Chapin to preserve its own identity without simply abandoning responsibility. But the concept did not simply fall into place. It was put into motion as a result of the determination of Jane Edwards. The Harlem-Dowling idea appealed to Jane Edwards personally, in a number of respects. As a black woman, she was not about to abandon agency efforts on behalf of minority children. As a fierce competitor, she was sensitive to criticisms of the limited impact of the foster care program, which she had administered, and was not about to accept this judgement passively. As a professional, attuned to current thinking in her field, and with an eye to this wider audience, she was fascinated by Billingsly's thesis and its potential for an innovative project. The Harlem-Dowling venture provided an exciting new thrust with which Jane Edwards could begin her tenure as executive director of Spence-Chapin.

In many ways, the form of the Harlem-Dowling program has been heavily influenced by its parent agency. Its internal structure resembles that of Spence-Chapin. And it is nonprofit, not only because this conforms to requirements of the local child welfare governmental per diem reimbursement system in which it is designed to operate, but just as fundamentally because this is the way Spence-Chapin knew how to (and preferred to) do things. Start-up money for the venture, for example, was raised through philanthropy by influential Spence-Chapin board members. And guidance could be offered by Spence-Chapin staff on internal organization, setting up a board, conformity to regulations, and requirements for chartering.

The issue of autonomy pulled two ways for Spence-Chapin, at least initially. Spinning-off an autonomous unit ran against the organizational grain, but it also promised to relieve the strain of a threateningly large foster care operation. More fundamentally, however, the promise of autonomy was essential for success of the project. Without autonomy, the Harlem community would view the venture as a (perhaps predatory) intrusion from the outside, and would not support it.

Ironically, once initial community skepticism was overcome, and the Harlem-Dowling program began to operate, the impetus for autonomy came more strongly from the parent agency than the offspring. A comfortable relationship with Spence-Chapin, combined with a hostile fiscal environment, dampened the Harlem-Dowling staff's enthusiasm for immediate independence. The fiscal environment worked in reverse for Spence-Chapin. The losses associated with Harlem-Dowling as a result of the City's refusal to grant a (separate) increased reimbursement rate, became more and more serious, even for this relatively well-endowed agency. By 1977–1978, Spence-Chapin still took pride and wished to see its offspring succeed, but given the somewhat improved fiscal environment, it was time for it to move out of the house.

The Lower East Side Family Union (LESFU)

PRÉCIS

The Lower East Side Family Union (LESFU) was established in 1972 as a purposeful innovation in the delivery of social services to children and families. Organized as a nonprofit corporation, LESFU was modelled on the concepts of neighborhood-based service delivery, community governance, and preventive services to families in order to reduce the need for foster care of children. In its short history, LESFU has been the subject of a remarkable level of attention, both in the literature and among influential people in government, the voluntary sector, and the social work profession. The present case study recounts the circumstances and motivations surrounding the birth and early development of LESFU.

THE ENTREPRENEURS

The early history of LESFU is dominated by one man, Bertram Beck, then Executive Director of the Henry Street Settlement on the Lower East Side of Manhattan, and now General Director of the Community Service Society. A strong supporting role was played by Trude Lash, then Executive Director of the Citizens' Committee for Children of New York, and later staff scientist for the Foundation for Child Development. As the effort was mobilized, directors of other settlement houses on the Lower East Side, officials of the City, and project staff employed by Beck and Lash were instrumental in LESFU's development.

Bert Beck is a dynamic and charismatic character on the New York social welfare scene who knows how to garner resources. As Harold Weissman puts it in his recent book about LESFU: "In a field where money is always a source of anxiety and charisma is scarcer than money, he had both."

Beck is a man of restless inventiveness who would not be happy with a large and prestigious but routine organization: "I am very interested in . . . excitement. If I were just running a program that was doing good day after day, and there weren't a lot of new things happening . . . new ideas, new people, success, failures . . . it wouldn't turn me on. . . . At Henry Street my attention was always with the new programs. . . ."

THE ORGANIZATIONS

The establishment of LESFU was essentially a small group effort, initiated by Bert Beck in 1971, and developed over the next three years by Beck, Trude Lash, and Mary Goldson, a social work professor hired by Beck and Lash in 1972 as project planner. While the initial effort did not involve, in any major way, the staff or internal decision-making of existing organizations, several organizations contributed to the development of LESFU.

The role of one organization, the Citizen's Committee for Children, of which Lash was staff director, and Beck, a member of the Committee's board of directors, is somewhat cloudy. Much is made, in Harold Weissman's account of LESFU, and in the public relations literature of LESFU, of the Committee's 1971 report *A Dream Deferred*, as an antecedent of the LESFU initiative. That report reviewed the difficult, often tragic, history of foster care in New York City, and called for a new type of service system which would focus on families and the prevention of need for foster care of children. However, while the LESFU model is consistent with the Committee's recommendations, there seems to have been no direct connection between the report and Beck's initiative, nor did the Committee, a large and distinguished panel of prominent New Yorkers interested in children, play any substantive role in getting LESFU under way. According to Beck, ". . . I was chairman of the group that did *A Dream Deferred,* but my leadership was nominal. The report was very good. . . . I was familiar with the general thrust of the report. . . . That was [the] Citizen's Committee for Children . . . party line. . . . So I was very familiar with what the issue was, but there wasn't really a one-to-one relationship between *A Dream Deferred* and the founding of Lower East Side Family Union. I felt there should be a local family service, and I'm sure I was influenced in that thinking because of what I had been exposed to at the Citizen's Committee. So that was a connection. . . ."

Once Beck had begun his LESFU initiative he apparently tried to get the Citizen's Committee to back him, but "[they] didn't ever get that involved the way I wanted them to be. . . ." Perhaps one reason for this was the fact that the Committee had already experienced one failure with a program concept like LESFU. Several years earlier, Dr. Lash recalls: "I felt that . . . the Citizen's Committee for Children should try to start a neighborhood organization of this sort, and I went to a foundation and got $25,000, and sent somebody into East Harlem . . . to find out whom we can interest in developing a neighborhood-helping system. . . . After a while we realized we couldn't do that . . . coming in from the outside . . . and I returned the money."

As far as the Citizen's Committee's contributions to LESFU are concerned, however, one thing is clear. The report, *A Dream Deferred*, did serve as useful ammunition for Beck and Lash in their efforts to raise funds for LESFU over the planning period of 1972 to 1974.

A more important group in the establishment of LESFU was a committee of five directors of settlement houses on the Lower East Side, of which Beck was chairman. In 1971 the group, consisting of the executives of Henry Street Settlement (Beck), University Settlement, Hamilton Madison House, Grand Street Settlement, and Educational Alliance, had been meeting regularly to discuss problems in their area of the city. It was to this group that Beck first floated his ideas for LESFU. But, as Beck recalls, he took almost all of the initiative and ". . . the other men sanctioned it but didn't do much about it." One good reason for this lack of response back in 1971–1972 was that LESFU was assumed to be simply another of Beck's own programs within Henry Street. Nonetheless, the committee of settlement house directors ultimately became an integral part of LESFU. From the beginning, Beck realized that he needed the support of his colleagues, or at least needed to avoid their opposition, if he was to be able to sell LESFU to government and private foundations—especially, as the LESFU concept required an integration of services on the Lower East Side. That is, LESFU was based on a general practitioner model of service to families in which LESFU staff would engage specialty services, as needed, from existing social agencies in the area, *including* those organizations headed by the other directors.

By 1972 the directors committee had become a legitimizing base for LESFU, serving as an advisory board to the project, and the kernel for what ultimately became LESFU's board of directors. (In 1972 membership was expanded to include the directors of three additional Lower East Side agencies—Gouvernor Hospital, Church of All Nations, and Mobilization for Youth. However, efforts to bring community residents at large onto the board, following LESFU incorporation in 1974, met with little success.) While members of the committee began to play a more active role by 1973–1974, e.g., the director of University Settlement arranged to have the LESFU papers of incorporation prepared, the influence of the directors was more subtle than this. The fact was that the other directors were suspicious of Beck, and initially viewed LESFU as an exercise in empire building at Henry Street, involving possible incursions into their own areas of "turf"—through comprehensive integration of services to families on the Lower East Side. Talking about the motives of his fellow settlement house directors, Beck observes, "Some of them are more concerned than others . . . about services [to] the people. Then there's [concern over] turf, prestige. . . . I think with the settlement directors . . . a lot of the [LESFU activity] . . . was going on in their turf. [And they were]

. . . making sure that they were in on what's happening." As discussed later, this territorial concern was a factor in having LESFU spun-off as an independent corporate entity, separate from Henry Street.

Given this background, perhaps the most important organization involved in the establishment of LESFU was Henry Street Settlement because it gave Beck his base of operations. Henry Street is perhaps the best known of the settlement houses which developed on the Lower East Side of Manhattan around the turn of the century, to service the general social and recreational needs of European immigrants. Since that time Henry Street has continued to serve the changing groups of low income minorities that have lived in that area of the city to the present day.

Prior to Bert Beck's tenure as director beginning in 1967, Henry Street had been under the direction of Helen Hall for some 34 years. As Beck recalls, "She was . . . a very well known social reformer [of] the early settlement type," so that the agency was inured in a tradition of innovation. However, in contrast to Beck's style of building, the previous director "spun things off all the time."

When Beck joined Henry Street he found a rather informal organization with a relatively modest annual budget of $800,000. He maintained that informality but shielded himself from day-to-day operations in order to explore various new programmatic enterprises, which ultimately increased the budget eightfold. By 1971, Beck's reputation was well established at Henry Street: "The board admired me . . . [and] I was kind of in that swing of thinking up things . . . getting them financed, and making them happen." It was in this context that LESFU was born.

CHRONOLOGY OF EVENTS

Early 1971—As director of Henry Street, and as chairman of the committee of Lower East Side settlement house directors, Bert Beck floats a proposal for the LESFU concept. He then (in April) writes a letter to Jule Sugarman, administrator of New York City's Human Resources Administration, which is positively received and helps Beck to begin fundraising.

May, 1972—The Lower East Side Family and Children's Services is established as a project within Henry Street Settlement, with the settlement house directors committee serving as an advisory board. Trude Lash is engaged as a volunteer adviser and Mary Goldson is hired as project planner.

Later in 1972—The advisory board is expanded to include representatives of three additional Lower East Side Agencies—Gouvernor Hospital, Church of All Nations, and Mobilization for Youth.

August, 1972—The name of the project is changed to LESFU, reflecting development of the concept to include a dual emphasis on advocacy activity by a "union" of community residents, as well as a service-delivery program.

May, 1972–May, 1974—This is a planning period during which Beck, Lash, and Goldson work as a team to make LESFU operational. Goldson is entrusted with developing programmatic concepts, community support, and helping to prepare proposals for funding. Beck and Lash concentrate on funding. Beck raises over $200,000 from a consortium of private foundations. A major planning grant is obtained from the Foundation for Child Development in the Spring of 1973. Relationships and support are also discussed with the City, including the integration of City social service workers into the LESFU program.

May, 1974—LESFU hires its first "team leader" and a secretary. (Teams, which are geographically defined and ethnically distinct cadres of workers, constitute the heart of the LESFU delivery system. Each team includes a leader with an MS degree in social work, five social work associates, three homemakers, three housekeepers, and a clerk-typist.)

June, 1974—LESFU is incorporated as an independent, tax-exempt nonprofit corporation. In July LESFU is approved as a licensed child care agency by the New York State Board of Social Welfare.

Late in 1974—Bert Beck and Trude Lash are active in Hugh Carey's gubernatorial campaign. Carey is elected in November.

Early 1975—Beck and Lash head the Governor's task force on social services (and are widely assumed to have the governor's ear).

May, 1975—The State Department of Social Services awards LESFU $500,000 over two years from Title IV-B, preventive program funds.

June, 1975—The first contracts between LESFU and direct service agencies on the Lower East Side are signed.

March, 1976—Three fully staffed teams, including one composed of workers "on loan" from the City, become operational.

CONTEXT

While the Citizen's Committee for Children played a minor role in the establishment of LESFU, its report *A Dream Deferred* painted a detailed picture of why such an agency was desirable. The report recalled the long and disappointing history of foster care in the city, culminating in the early 1970s with overcrowding in the public children's shelters, increasing difficulties of placing older, behaviorally difficult minority group children into the City's system of voluntary agencies, and concerns over inappropriate and prolonged care and rising costs associated with children in care. The gist of the report was that a whole new system was needed —one that would minimize the need for care by ministering to families to prevent or ameliorate the crises that led to external placement of their children. Foster care was to become a last resort rather than the current primary mode of service delivery.

The organization of foster care in 1970 reflected, as Weissman recounts, a long history of development in the social services. Around the turn of the century charitable agencies were unspecialized, and organized around local geographic catchment areas. Over the years, such agencies became larger and more specialized, the social workers also became more specialized and highly trained, and large-scale government funding programs later developed along narrow functional lines. By the mid-1960s the problems of functional fragmentation were already apparent, and interest was renewed in the old idea of geographically defined, general service–delivery systems. The federal War on Poverty emphasized "model cities" and neighborhood service agencies. The City began to organize superagencies such as the Human Resources Administration that would integrate various social service functions under a single umbrella, and there was also movement toward geographic decentralization of city government.

Perhaps paradoxically, the Citizen's Committee saw an opportunity in 1971 to accomplish integration of services through the Department of Social Services directive to reorganize its own programs by separating income maintenance and service delivery functions. The Committee's report notes: "The opportunity . . . to unify the previously fragmented social services . . . those reserved for welfare recipients, and those for many 'others,' into the most efficient and effective system which can be designed, within the limits of resources and statutory requirements." (This perceived opportunity is cited by Weissman as an entry point through which Beck would float his proposal.)

There were other salient issues also that would help establish a receptive environment for initiatives like LESFU in the early 1970s. Deinstitutionalization and community-based care had become bywords not only in the context of foster care but in other areas such as mental hygiene and criminal justice. So, too, "holding government accountable" for its services was part of the popular jargon. LESFU would build on the latter, by establishing the model of the general practitioner–client advocate who would demand specific services from provider agencies and hold them to it. More generally, LESFU intended to establish a union of local residents that would keep rein on the agency and ensure its responsiveness to the community.

Given the notions of services integration, geographically (and ethnically) defined service patterns, and innovation on which LESFU is built, the environment of the Lower East Side of New York could not have been more suitable. That portion of real estate has long been associated with services to minority groups in ethnically distinct neighborhoods. Furthermore, the area was historically rich with social agencies of various types, whose services could be coordinated. Finally, the idea of generalized catchment areas was consistent with the traditions of the old settlement houses which continued to operate in the area. Thus, both the time and the place seemed right for a development like LESFU.

CHOICES

LESFU was based on several interrelated ideas in contemporary social welfare thinking, crystallized by Bert Beck in 1971 into a proposal for a new social service delivery system on the Lower East Side. Beck's original proposal was still an abstraction which would serve as a touchstone for future planning, but left considerable room for interpretation. The essence of Beck's proposal was, according to Weissman [1978], ". . . a community-based child welfare agency. . . . The basic elements of the model included teams of professionals and neighborhood residents, the concept of a general practitioner in social welfare, and the need to ensure service integration. . . . The agency would develop into a general social service agency acting as an entry point to a variety of specialized services with the general practitioner accountable for integration of services and follow through. The possibility of the agency subcontracting with other agencies for certain services and acting as an intermediary between the public and private sector was specifically indicated. Early intervention and community involvement at all phases of decision-making were signaled."

While the concepts articulated by Beck were not precisely defined, they influenced subsequent strategic choices in important ways. In particular, the original concepts were precise enough to constrain the organizational form of LESFU, yet ambiguous enough in programmatic content to permit a wide-ranging search for funding support. The ambiguity also left considerable responsibility to program planners for subsequent clarification and design and in some areas left the door open to conflicts over interpretation of program intent.

Perhaps the most significant organizational decision, and the most painful one for Beck, was whether to make LESFU an autonomous corporate unit, independent of Henry Street. Beck's inherent preference, consistent with his general style of entrepreneurship, was to keep it at Henry Street. But the pragmatic considerations of implementation, and the logic of the LESFU model, led to completely relinquishing this idea by 1973. As Beck recalls, ". . . The most difficult thing about LESFU was [that] I really did have to, and I was able [to] . . . I'm happy to say, give it up. . . . To give up the leadership of it, and really allow other people to take it over. . . ."

One factor in this decision was Beck's fellow settlement directors; especially at the point in 1973 when LESFU was in a position to receive substantial funding from the Foundation for Child Development: ". . . At the time the Union was still . . . lodged within Henry Street and the people were beginning to talk about the Union and Henry Street as identical. But I knew that if I brought large-scale resources . . . [into] Henry Street, the other settlement house directors would object. . . . You know if you're familiar with grants . . . about the indirect costs and the ways you could use [them] . . . to support an organization. . . . I would have liked to have kept it at Henry Street, but it was the feelings of the other settlement directors, who . . . were, perhaps with good reasons, somewhat suspicious of me. . . . But, if you're interested in the organization [LESFU] you will do what is necessary to sustain it. What was necessary was to make it independent."

The problem for Beck was that his fellow directors were needed as a legitimizing base for LESFU. After all, the concept of LESFU required local integration of services and could not work without the cooperation of other area agencies. In addition, the LESFU concept rested on the idea of autonomous, community-based control. Indeed, Dr. Lash ". . . assumed that it would become independent. . . . You can't prove something is able to live, and is a genuine community organization, when it is really a protected workshop, so to speak."

Thus, early in the development of LESFU, Beck realized the logic of autonomy and was able to overcome whatever personal inclinations he had to the contrary. This left him in a somewhat difficult position, however. Without his leadership, LESFU would almost certainly fall through, yet how could he continue to devote his energies and resources to LESFU at the expense of his responsibilities to Henry Street? One option might have been to leave Henry Street and take over LESFU, but Beck admits, ". . . I never thought of leaving Henry Street, because Henry Street was a much more substantial position. The Union, was to me, another . . . Henry Street program. In my head, it was quite similar to other programs I had started."

What Beck chose to do, consistent with both his desire to stay at Henry Street but also to avoid a failure of LESFU and maintain its value as a feather in his cap, was to remain active as Board President of LESFU, and to work closely with the planning team in selecting and advising leadership for the project. He continued to put in substantial time and effort, but to phase this down slowly over the years after 1973. Nonetheless, problems of LESFU leadership were considerable during this period —largely due to problems with personalities and some early confusion over division of staff responsibilities. There were some poor choices of leadership by Beck and Lash, and the other settlement directors, despite considerable time spent in the selection process. Thus, one wonders if things would have been different had Beck remained at the helm throughout.

As an offspring of Henry Street, it is not surprising that LESFU is organized as a nonprofit organization, like its parent. And of course, the nonprofit status permitted exploration of the most viable channels of funding for LESFU, both governmental and philanthropic. But LESFU is not a simple, free-standing nonprofit organization. In several respects, it resembles a cooperative. Furthermore, the LESFU model was explicitly intended as a model for *public sector* adaptation.

The cooperative aspects of LESFU are twofold, and in themselves appear to suggest the choice of the nonprofit form. First, there is the notion of services integration through the operation of general social work practitioners who would prescribe and draw upon the specialized services of other area organizations to service their clients. Thus a network of services is implied. In LESFU's case this network is knit together by its board of directors, which provides explicit representation of area service agencies who share cooperatively in LESFU's direction. In addition, the device of service contracts has been evolved within which individual agencies agree to provide specific services to particular clients, under the orchestration of the general practitioner. The participation and reinforcement of these contracts obviously requires the cooperation of leadership of the various local (nonprofit) service agencies.

The second aspect of the cooperative form has been a more explicit but less successful part of LESFU, namely the notion that a "union of families" from the community would be developed as an advocacy body that would guide LESFU service policies, and work in a social activist mode for improvements in the neighborhood. This clearly embodies a "collective action" rationale for nonprofit organization or association. The vision is described by Beck: ". . . My proposal was . . . that it would be a union of families that were interested in maintaining their children . . . and they would press us . . . to deliver services to them. . . . They would pick at us and demonstrate, and they would ask for a contract. That was where the idea of the contract came from, even though we never organized the union."

While LESFU is explicitly nonprofit, it is not altogether private. Indeed it has been intended from the start to serve as a demonstration to government as to how to reorganize its own services around the principles of the general practitioner, neighborhood-based service areas, integration of services and preventive, family-oriented care. One concrete way in which the "governmental connection" has been manifested is the integration of a service team of City employees directly into the LESFU program. The motivation for this has been as much financial (see below) as programmatic. But it has involved an interesting (although essentially academic) organizational arrangement, namely, the designation of a separate administrative board consisting of the executive director of LESFU and the director of the City's Office of Special Services for Children, to oversee the city team. However, according to Beck, ". . . That was pretty much on paper. There was an issue with the city team that came up through the [Civil Employees] union. . . . They were worried [and] needed assurance that the city team was responsible to a public official. That was given, but it never meant anything. . . . When I make my union speech I always point out that one of the significant things [about] the city team is that the [team] director is not responsible to the LESFU director, but it doesn't make a damned bit of difference . . . the director behaves as if they're responsible. [Later, the City] said [it] wanted to have someone on the board [of LESFU] which we agreed to. . . . Again, it didn't mean anything. . . . The person seldom showed up."

According to Weissman [1978], "The organization [LESFU] was basically conceived of as a quasi-governmental unit depending on public funds and providing a demonstration of how a community-controlled organization can be responsive both to its own constituency and to a city-wide governmental organization." The innocuous manner in which the City shared authority never forced the hard choice between government and private control. The programmatic rhetoric notwithstanding, and despite Beck's withdrawal of designs on LESFU as a Henry Street enterprise, it seems likely that governmental encroachment would have been resisted. At a minimum, LESFU needed the flexibility of private control to succeed as a demonstration project before it would be turned over to government.

Financing of the LESFU venture, especially in the early years, was marked by broad-gauge exploration of possibilities, and flexible adaptation of program concepts to opportunities. As Beck describes it: "I would go in all directions for funds, with the idea that if you throw up enough cards, some of them are going to land on the table. . . . It was opportunistic. . . . We wanted to start the organization and . . . we went wherever we could get the money."

This opportunistic strategy took some interesting turns, as Beck describes: ". . . After [Governor] Carey was elected . . . [Trude Lash and I] became head of the task force to plan the human services, and people attributed to us . . . power we never had. . . . There was a guy . . . in the State Department [of Social Services] at the time . . . [who] wanted to move from the State Department to [another state position]. In some way . . . he got it in his head that Trude and I were fostering his interests, which we weren't. . . . It just wasn't true, but I never disabused him of his belief, and he used his good offices . . . to get us [the state money]. . . . It was, as I say, an opportunistic approach, and this was a series of coincidences that we could use to get some money, which we did use."

From the start it was realized that public funding ultimately had to become the mainstay for LESFU's operation. Yet Beck and Lash followed a more circuitous route—first developing planning funds from private foundations and then later cultivating public sources. The strategy was both opportunistic and intentional. As a practical matter, private start-up funds could be secured more quickly (although not on a long-term basis), especially in view of Beck's considerable experience in this area. Furthermore, Beck and Lash were adroit in cultivating Lash's developing relationship with the Foundation for Child Development to secure the major planning grant in 1973. But securing funds from government was more challenging. Exploiting opportunity was certainly involved, as witnessed by the political involvement of Beck and Lash in the early years of the Carey Administration, as they secured an impressive chunk of the State's allocation of preventive demonstration service funds. (As Weissman [1978] observes: "When decisions were finally made in late 1975 on the programs the State would fund under Title IV-B for preventive programs, small, unknown LESFU—in comparison to large sectarian federations and agencies with powerful boards and contacts—was able to hold its own and received $500 thousand from the State.") Later, as the private funds and the demonstration funds became depleted, LESFU creatively used the aforementioned team of City employees, as part of the required local matching contribution to secure regular state prevention monies.

But the scramble for public funding was not totally opportunistic. Indeed, the easiest thing to do, once LESFU became incorporated as a child care agency in 1974, or even earlier through auspices of Henry Street, might have been to secure regular foster care per diem funding. This was scrupulously avoided, as it would have contradicted the very intent of the entire LESFU model. As Beck points out: ". . . [We] were in the business of trying to . . . change, in the long run, the public funding system. It's easier [for an agency] to survive now on per diem operating funds [but] that was . . . totally against the principle of [LESFU]." If LESFU was to retain its demonstration value, and be true to its original intent, the conventional source of foster care funding had to be rejected out of hand.

Weissman is careful to point out in his account that the programmatic content of LESFU was consciously kept flexible in the period when funding was sought. In some areas, this flexibility—deliberately intended to maximize funding opportunities—would lead to problems later on. For example, the concept of preventive services was kept vague. Should services apply only to families who were immediately at risk of losing their children to foster care, or should services apply more generally to all local families that needed help? Around 1975, when the State was insisting on the narrower view, the LESFU board went along in pragmatic fashion to ensure funding, but at the same time creating resistance among staff members uncomfortable with the notion of denying service to families in the wider set of potential clientele.

Just as with funding strategy, however, there were definite programmatic choices that would not be violated. Perhaps the clearest decision was that LESFU was an experimental program, whose research and demonstration value was of primary importance and not to be sacrificed. Adherence to this position required conscious effort to overcome staff resistance. As Weissman [1978] indicates, for example: "A major intent of the planning of LESFU was to document and develop the effectiveness of the new service delivery patterns . . . [but] . . . staff members gave only lip service to research; they were mainly skeptical and at times actually hostile towards it. . . . ."

But choices that involved a conflict between research and service tended to be resolved in favor of the former. Some of the pressures for this came from the State (once funding was secured in 1975) which was initially concerned with measuring "the local impact of LESFU in preventing family break-up; this caused problems because the State insisted that LESFU restrict access . . . to people living in certain . . . census tracts . . . [and by] insisting that LESFU specifically define the characteristics that would index high-risk families" [Weissman, 1978]. But even without this outside pressure, the founders of LESFU were intent on maintaining its research and demonstration value. Not only did the board, under Beck's direction, "reaffirm . . . the importance of research" in resolving such issues, but also instituted from the start . . . the documentation of a social history of the project. Here, too, the founders were resolved to prevail, despite sources of internal resistance . . . especially staff reluctance to be observed or to violate confidentiality of client relationships" [Weissman, 1978]. The explanation of this choice can again be found in the desire of LESFU founders for the project to be a showcase and a guide for system change.

RISKS AND CONSTRAINTS

The founders of LESFU took risks of both a personal and professional variety. For Bert Beck, despite his well established reputation, there was the growing fear of possible failure and damage to his reputation: ". . . The risk is you'll fall on your face . . . that you could have a disaster. The consequences of disaster wouldn't be anything terrible, but they might look terrible to me . . . that people whom I respect and want to respect me, would view me as a failure, as a person who was not sagacious or prudent or not a good leader. . . ."

Once committed to the project, the risks seemed to mount for Beck during the 1972–1974 planning period. As he recalls, ". . . In the first place, I was doing an awful lot [of other things] as I usually am, and there's the risk that [I wouldn't] give the thing the supervision or the guidance that it needed. There are a lot of details that [I was] not going to give attention to. And yet I had involved Trude [Lash] in it, you know, and a number of . . . foundations. There came a time after the planning was over [when] Trude [asked Professor] Al Kahn to evaluate it for the foundation. He gave it a terrible evaluation, which Trude showed to me. I thought Al was actually right. I explained the absence of data that Al criticized by saying we were building our base in the community. It was partly true, but this did not fully excuse our failure to amass hard data."

Another risk faced by Beck, especially once it became clear that LESFU was to become an independent unit, was that he might be faulted for neglecting his other responsibilities at Henry Street to spend time on LESFU. Or on a more personal level, LESFU might begin to cramp Beck's style, precluding him from exploring other ventures as is his custom. Indeed, it was a tightrope-walking act, with pressures on both sides of this issue. For, in addition to the personal sense of failure Beck might feel if LESFU failed, there was a kind of mixed personal and professional guilt feeling involved also. As Trude Lash explains: ". . . If this is defeated, then it's a defeat of more than LESFU, it's a defeat for a lot of things we've been saying [professionally]. . . . Maybe then it means that those of us who have given a lot of time to LESFU are . . . less critical than others, are less wise than others, are less concerned with continuity and Institutions than others. . . ."

Whether Beck and Lash allocated time "optimally" between LESFU and other responsibilities or not, it is certainly clear that they were willing to go out on a limb for the project, when this seemed to be required. Their political activities on LESFU's behalf just confirmed the pattern. Lash and Beck bet on Carey and the Democrats. A loss there conceivably might have jeopardized the chances for LESFU's survival through the instrumentalities of governmental funding.

The list of constraints and barriers to implementation of the LESFU project is not a short one, as befits a venture which attempts to substantially rearrange current, institutionalized patterns of service delivery. As a prevention-oriented program which ultimately relied on public funding, the funding opportunities were severely limited. And as a nonconventional child care agency, which contracted for foster care only when necessary, the process of licensing proved to be difficult. As a research and demonstration effort, the service-oriented preferences of hired staff had to be resisted. As a new agency on old turf, a thin line had to be walked in defining LESFU's functions—it would integrate, not duplicate, services of existing agencies; it would attempt to reform rather than replace the functions of the City's social service worker; and it would not aggrandize one existing agency (Henry Street) at the expense of others.

Perhaps the most difficult constraints were associated with the concept of LESFU as an indigenous, community-based agency. This idea contributed to the emancipation of LESFU from Henry Street. Furthermore, people from the community had to become involved in governance and decision-making at LESFU. Of all areas of resistance, this has been the most difficult. The basic problem was that the neighborhood residents never became a viable political group.

The second (and to that point only successful) director of LESFU, Ken Schuman, is quoted in Weissman's [1978] book as writing in 1977: "The Lower East Side Family Union has operated under the assumption that high-risk families can be stabilized and, once themselves stabilized, will become interested in helping their neighbors resolve problems similar to those that they experienced. As their strength and awareness increase, the stabilized families can next be involved in groups working on problems of general community concern, and finally, in the governance of LESFU itself.

"We are concluding that our original assumptions . . . may well have been unrealistic. . . . While we may be able to involve some of the families . . . most are still struggling to keep their own heads above water. . . ."

It was perhaps too much to ask of families in a chronic poverty area; or perhaps, as Weissman seems to imply, it may also have been unrealistic for LESFU staff to carry on community organizing simultaneously with the development of the new model of service provision.

OUTCOMES

LESFU's early history was a rocky one. It was a struggle of trial and error in attempting to implement in concrete form its lofty but initially vague principles—often under the handicap of uncertain staff-level leadership. (Much of the progress in program development came in the years 1975–1978, when Ken Schuman successfully provided that leadership.) Still, LESFU can point to a solid, if slower than hoped for, record of progress. The agency became operational in terms of service provision in 1976 with three service teams, and fielded a fourth team in 1978. By 1977 LESFU staff totalled 45 full-time workers and provided services to 420 families with 1,470 children (on an annual basis). The budget reached $657,000 in fiscal year 1977 of which, in contrast to the early years, two-thirds came from governmental sources. The fiscal year 1978 budget was approximately $767,000. While financing was still a struggle, LESFU seemed to have developed short-term assurances that government funds would continue, although the early foundation money was running out.

From scratch, LESFU pioneered the development of some innovative service delivery mechanisms, including the use of interagency family service contracts (between families and service agencies) to coordinate, focus, and hold accountable the services of multiple local social agencies to specific families. Through this device, the concept of the general practitioner–social worker, bringing to bear specialized services from various sources to assist his or her clientele, has taken shape in operational form. By 1977, over a dozen agencies (including those represented on LESFU's board of directors) entered into such contracts. LESFU had also developed long-term direct contracts with these agencies on the Lower East Side, in order to establish a permanent, reliable network of integrated services.

In addition to the contracts, LESFU has innovated the use of service "teams" which are assigned to particular neighborhoods within which they focus on problem families. The ethnic compositions of the teams are designed to match that of the neighborhoods. On the Lower East Side this means Chinese, Hispanic, and black teams. The teams operate as integrated units composed of social workers, homemakers, housekeepers, and a clerk-typist, designed to carry out the functions of the general practitioner as well as some direct housekeeping assistance to families in distress. LESFU also pioneered the integration of a team of City employees, into its operation. The city team operates in the same manner as the other LESFU teams. On the basis of early statistics, LESFU appeared to be having some success in reducing the use of foster care placement us an alternative for servicing the problems of families. On at least one dimension, however, the mobilization of families into an activist "union," LESFU did not succeed, although the 1977 Annual Report indicated that one of its teams had begun to undertake community organization activity in a serious way in order "to mobilize residents to organize and reverse deterioration in an area where many high risk families reside."

Given the objectives of LESFU's founders, it is particularly important to ask whether LESFU has had any significant impact on system-wide reform. In terms of publicity, LESFU has fared well, by design. It is the subject of a book by Harold Weissman, employed as a social historian from the beginning of the project; it is the focus of scholarly and popular articles by Bert Beck and others; and has been covered by the print and broadcasting media. LESFU has been the subject of presentations at a dozen national professional conferences and has been cited by U.S. H.E.W. as a model program.

The larger question, however, is whether LESFU could reasonably hope to influence the redevelopment of the current social services structure, i.e., help change it from a foster care-oriented to a preventative services model.

The 1977 Annual Report alludes to some hopeful signs, including a serious effort at data collection and evaluation capability that could help verify if LESFU is achieving its goals of preventing foster care and relieving family distress. Of more immediate interest, LESFU appears to have inspired some confidence on the part of New York City—as the City continued to maintain its cadre of LESFU team workers.

At the state level, LESFU was asked to help train a staff of public and private agencies on how to implement neighborhood-based services; this task included the writing of a manual and curriculum. And at the federal level, LESFU was selected as a model program by the Child Welfare Resource Information Exchange.

ANALYSIS

LESFU was a Bert Beck creation, one of many entrepreneurial ventures during his impressive tenure at Henry Street, where he was used to generating ideas, developing funding, and controlling the resultant programs through his administrative structure. Left to Beck's own preferences, LESFU would have remained at Henry Street. But LESFU was inherently a maverick—the concept and the circumstances in which it developed dictated autonomy from its parent organization. The concept demanded an indigenous organization rooted directly in the families of the community, and required a cooperative effort among multiple agencies. The concept could not be tested in the "protected workshop" environment of Henry Street. Nor were "competitor" agencies to Henry Street likely to engage in the cooperative effort if it were set up to directly aggrandize the fame and fortune of that agency (or its director).

Autonomy for LESFU may have had important implications for the early performance of the project. Inevitably, it meant a slow diminishing of attention by Bert Beck, its most skillful proponent. Beck remained very active in the process of selecting LESFU's senior staff and in policy decision-making. But mistakes and delays were encountered in leadership selection, and undoubtedly supervision of leadership was not as close as it might have been had Beck retained executive control. It is hard to fault Beck for his efforts, however. It simply was not within his plans to leave Henry Street for LESFU. Indeed, his level of effort on LESFU, once autonomy became clear, is remarkable, and reflects his obsession to finish things he starts. Undoubtedly, the continued involvements of Beck and Lash are also heavily explained by the demonstration value (and sheer excitement) of the LESFU experience. This was a major social innovation, in the limelight of which Lash and Beck could continue to benefit by their association no matter what the formal arrangements for control.

It must also be recognized that many of the early struggles of LESFU may have been inevitable, given the ambiguity of the concepts on which it was founded. Concept flexibility was an advantage in seeking early financial support from a wide variety of sources, but this vagueness would lead to growing pains later, as concepts had to be interpreted and made operational.

REFERENCES

A Dream Deferred, New York: Citizens Committee for Children of New York, 1971.
Lower East Side Family Union: Annual report. October, 1977.
Weissman, H. H. (1978). *Integrating services for troubled families*. San Francisco: Jossey-Bass, 1978.

Jewish Board of Family
and Children's Services (JBFCS)

PRÉCIS

In February of 1978, the Jewish Board of Guardians (JBG) and the Jewish Family Services (JFS), two large social service agencies belonging to the Federation of Jewish Philanthropies (FJP) in New York City, merged to become the Jewish Board of Family and Children's Service (JBFCS). The merger was prompted by the retirement of the executive director of JFS, but occurred against the background of a long history of attempted mergers of FJP-affiliated agencies. Arrangements for the merger were worked out jointly by the two agencies over a two-year period, overcoming various points of resistance. Through this merger, however, JBFCS became one of the largest social service and mental health agencies in the country.

THE ENTREPRENEURS

The process of merging JBG and the JFS involved the efforts of many people at the staff and board levels of the two organizations. Various committees and subcommittees were formed to explore the numerous issues and concerns associated with the merger, and to negotiate the parameters of the arrangement.

Although there is a history of "merger talk" among social service agency members of the Federation of Jewish Philanthropies, the specific chain of events leading to the JFS-JBG merger began with Sanford (Shep) Sherman, Executive Director of JFS. Mr. Sherman was contemplating retirement and identified that juncture as a unique opportunity to pursue a merger. He broached the idea with Jerome Goldsmith, Executive Director of JBG. JFS and JBG would merge and Goldsmith would become the executive of the new agency.

Shep Sherman was a career social worker and administrator, but throughout his career, he kept his hand in teaching and in practice. He was an adjunct faculty member of three schools of social work in New York City, has given courses and seminars in various other universities and agencies, has been a member of the editorial boards of two professional journals, and has written extensively on his own. Thus, despite his long administrative career, Sherman candidly admits that his heart has been in teaching and practice.

There are strong similarities but also great differences in outlook between Sanford Sherman and his JBG counterpart Jerome Goldsmith. While not a practitioner, Goldsmith is also much the scholar, having earned a doctorate in education, had several university teaching affiliations, and written numerous articles in professional journals. But unlike Sherman, who has been clearly ambivalent about his administrative role, Goldsmith thrives on his work as an executive.

As chief executive of JBG, Goldsmith followed a pattern of program building and reform, and in the process increased the agency's operating budget from some $5 million to over $12 million in a 13-year period. He views himself as "an engineer of human services" and enjoys "thinking big" and translating grand ideas into programmatic initiatives. He also enjoys the political give and take, inside and outside his agency, that is required for successful enterprising.

Jay Goldsmith says, half-humorously, that he sometimes regrets not having gone into show business, which he once had the chance to do. But his professional career has nonetheless provided him with the opportunity to occupy center stage, while at the same time allowing him to utilize his creative and political talents to dream grand designs and put them into practice.

THE ORGANIZATION

With representatives of the Federation of Jewish Philanthropies playing a background role, the process of merger required the painstaking deliberation of the two organizational marriage partners, JBG and JFS. While similar in some ways—as Jewish-oriented social service agencies—these two agencies exhibited more differences than similarities. Some of these differences represented complements which strengthened the rationale for merger. Others represented potential conflicts that required resolution to permit merger.

The strongest complements lay in the programs and services of the two agencies prior to 1976. JFS was primarily a community-based counseling agency which provided various services to Jewish families, including crisis intervention assistance, mediation service, homemaker service, legal aid, and family life education. JFS's program also included a rehabilitation service for offenders in correctional institutions and on probation, a therapeutic summer camp for children ages 7 through 11, and a Joint Passover Association which gave supplemental income allowances to Jewish families at Passover holidays. Overall, JFS defined its purpose: "To meet social and mental health needs of Jewish families and individuals . . . of the city utilizing a broad spectrum of services: guidance, counseling, psychotherapy, as well as homemaker and other material adjunctive services."

JBG, on the other hand, was a "patient-oriented" agency, attuned to the needs of emotionally disturbed children. Its services included residential facilities such as the Hawthorne Cedar Knolls School and associated group homes, Geller House (detention services), the Linden Hill School (for emotionally fragile youngsters), and the Phoenix School (for serious delinquents); plus a number of day treatment and day care programs; and specialized facilities such as the Henry Ittleson Center for Child Research and the Madelaine Borg Child Guidance Institute.

In theory, the "preventive" family therapy-oriented JFS complemented the treatment-oriented JBG rather well, providing an overall spectrum of required services for troubled families and children. The complementary quality seemed reinforced by certain common elements as well, including the emphasis on staff training and therapeutic mental health services of both agencies.

JFS cared for some 40,000 families per year, while JBG served 10,000 children. The complements and overlap in caseloads of the two agencies are nicely summarized in a 1976 memorandum: "In the large middle, JBG and JFS caseloads overlap. . . . At the extremes, caseloads may differ, but never in *opposition*. For example, at the extremes the Madelaine Borg Child Guidance Institute of the JBG will directly treat borderline psychotic children; JFS does not. JFS, on the other hand, has under treatment single adults living alone or childless married couples; JBG does not. However, in the large middle . . . there are similarities: 1) families including children with habit or conduct disorders, neurotic traits, etc., are abundantly represented in the caseloads of both JBG and JFS; 2) adolescents . . . are similarly a large concern of both agencies; 3) both agencies provide consultative mental health services to nurseries, day care and community centers, and schools; and 4) both agencies offer preventive services in the form of parent education and adolescent guidance groups.

"In the in-service training provided for their staffs . . . there is a core of teachable expertise derived from clinical experience and staff 'experts' (in the JBG, there is child development and child therapy; in the JFS, family process and family therapy). For staff training in complementary or corollary modalities (for JBG, family therapy; for JFS, child development and therapy), each agency has had to turn to 'outside experts.'"

Still, there were certain areas of potential conflict deriving from program orientations. Given JBG's more sophisticated treatment programs and residential institutions, JFS might fear being relegated to the status of an "outpatient division" of the new agency. And given JFS's particular focus on Jewish families, compared to JBG's more nonsectarian orientation, JFS might anticipate the erosion of its services to the Jewish community.

Basic differences characterized the two agencies' sizes and financial positions. A JBG prepared memorandum of early 1977 notes: "Total expenditures of JBG were $12,376,000 compared with $4,097,000 for JFS [fiscal year 1975]. In other words, JFS is about one-third the size of JBG. . . . [However] a comparison of JBG outpatient services with JFS, excluding the management and general expenses of both agencies shows that JBG's expenditures in this area were $3,693,000 vs. JFS's $3,527,000."

Jay Goldsmith provides further comparison: "JFS [had] . . . a 4 million dollar budget, primarily in outpatient services. JBG had . . . a 12 million dollar budget with a lot of residential and outpatient services. The JFS had 77 percent of its money from private philanthropy [mostly from] the Federation. . . . The JBG had about 73 percent of its money from public agencies . . . mostly public service contracts . . . [and] 18 percent from the Federation [and other philanthropic contributions]."

Of particular relevance to the merger, Goldsmith continues, "JFS had a 2 million dollar endowment and JBG had a million dollars worth of debts. That was not a good combination." Some of those affiliated with JFS would worry that its endowment would be used up bailing out JBG. (See Risks and Constraints below.)

The JFS, with its counseling orientation, brought roughly 80 social workers to the new agency, more than JBG. JFS also employed about a dozen psychologists and psychiatrists. But in this category and other staff categories such as teachers and child care workers, JBG far outnumbered JFS. Goldsmith provides an overview: "There were more caseworkers . . . from the JFS side . . . in the outpatient services. There were more [from] the residences and all other categories . . . from JBG. There were long-term, old-time, well trained clinical people in the JBG. There were more young, lesser trained . . . in the JFS, except for the top [administration]. There was a more formal structure in the . . . JBG, and a more ad hoc structure . . . in the . . . JFS. . . ."

Of particular relevance to the merger, there was no immediately obvious successor to Shep Sherman within the administrative ranks of JFS, while Goldsmith of JBG was regarded as a leading executive in the local voluntary sector. Thus the question of leadership for the new agency would not be a serious issue. However, at other levels of the organization, the staffing of positions would be troublesome. Both agencies had active boards of trustees whose officers coveted their status. And both agencies had field offices distributed throughout the city, some of which would require consolidation. The task of meshing the two structures would be a delicate one (See Risks and Constraints below). As Louis Lowenstein, first Board President of JBFCS diplomatically writes in the 1978 Annual Report: "Not only did the rationale for merging our organizations have to be explored, but we had to deal with the separate agency egos and pride in their past accomplishments. The Jewish Board of Guardians and the Jewish Family Service represent, collectively, two hundred years of service, and any effort at reshaping service delivery had to be approached with sensitivity to their histories and philosophies."

CHRONOLOGY OF EVENTS[1]

Early 1976—Shep Sherman initially explores the idea of a JFS-JBG merger with Jay Goldsmith at an informal luncheon meeting.

Spring, 1976—Sherman and Goldsmith meet at Goldsmith's initiative. Goldsmith indicates a positive response to the merger proposal and the two executives make plans for further exploration. A joint meeting of executives and board presidents of the two agencies is held. Agreement is reached to explore the possibility of merger, and the Federation of Jewish Philanthropies is alerted to this possibility.

May 20, 1976—A meeting of JBG's Professional Executive Committee is held to discuss the merger proposal. Various issues are raised by the JBG management personnel.

June, 1976—Goldsmith and Sherman circulate a memo discussing the rationale for merger with JFS, which indicates that the board presidents of the two agencies should appoint a joint committee of the boards "to begin the initial exploration of the issues raised in this memorandum and others which may be indicated as the committee proceeds. . . ."

July 14, 1976—Goldsmith asks the Executive Committee (of the Board of Trustees) of JBG to state an interest in exploring a merger with JFS. The committee authorizes a subcommittee of the board to explore the issue.

December, 1976—A joint meeting is held between staff of JBG and JFS to discuss the merger proposal. Various issues are raised in an exploratory discussion.

January 18, 1977—The subcommittee on staff of the Executive Joint Merger Committee meets to review various merger-related issues including staffing patterns, clientele, training and other items.

January 31, 1977—The subcommittee on finances of the Executive Joint Merger Committee meets to review fiscal aspects of the merger.

February 16, 1977—The merger proposal is discussed before the full JBG Board of Trustees. Previous meetings and discussions are described as "purely exploratory" and the Board is asked to indicate policy direction. Issues are discussed but no decisions are reached.

April 6, 1977—The JBG Executive Committee meets. The results of several joint JBG-JFS meetings are reported by the Executive Subcom-

---

[1]This chronology is based primarily on minutes kept by JBG.

mittee to explore merger. Enthusiasm by senior professional staff and concern by JBG trustees are also indicated.

April 27, 1977—A meeting of the JBG Executive Subcommittee on Merger is held. Goldsmith reports that he has met with the JFS Board, noting several areas of interest and reservation by that board. The subcommittee votes to recommend to the full Executive Committee that JBG go forward with *formal* negotiations for merger with JFS.

May 4, 1977—A meeting of the full JBG Executive Committee is held. The April 27 vote of the subcommittee is noted, issues are discussed, but no resolution is reached.

June 1, 1977—JBG Executive Committee meets again. Discussion of issues continues. The Executive Committee then votes to "approve the merger in principle," and to authorize the Board President to commence negotiations.

June 20, 1977—The full JBG Board of Trustees considers the recommendation of its Executive Committee and votes to "approve the merger in principle." The Board President is directed to appoint a committee to negotiate with JFS and to develop a definitive merger plan. JBG merger subcommittees are subsequently designated, at the board and staff levels, to review financial, personnel, program, and policy aspects of the merger.

July 12, 1977—A meeting of the JBG Merger Committee is held. Various structural questions including the organization and finances, board structure, and name of the new agency are discussed. The committee agrees to retain paid legal counsel to prepare a corporate charter and by-laws. On the same day, the Joint JBG-JFS Merger Committee meets for the first time. Issues of parity and structure of the new agency are discussed. A subcommittee is designated to study the issues of board and executive committee structure for the new agency. The executive directors, Goldsmith and Sherman, are asked to draft how the programs of the two agencies would be integrated, as a first step to overall consolidation.

Summer, 1977—This period is described by Goldsmith as the "summer of discontent," when proprietary feelings on both sides become ignited and the merger almost falls apart.

November 2, 1977—The JBG Executive Committee approves a plan by its merger subcommittee, for merger.

November 9, 1977—The full JBG Board of Trustees adopts the merger plan of its Executive Committee.

November, 1977—A proposal for $45,000 is submitted to the Greater New York United Fund to help defray the costs of merger.

December 7, 1977—The JBG Executive Committee meets and reports that the merger plan has been approved by both agencies, and that legal counsel has prepared the necessary documents of incorporation. Goldsmith reports having met the staffs of JBG and JFS and having discussed the merger with various City officials.

December 20, 1977—A meeting is held between representatives of JBG, JFS, and the Federation of Jewish Philanthropies to discuss the merger, especially the financial issues. On this same day, JBG and JFS senior staff meet to draft details of the board structure of the new agency.

January 4, 1978—Goldsmith reports to the JBG Executive Committee that the NYS Department of Education has approved the merger, and that approval of the State Department of Mental Hygiene and Department of Social Services and the Attorney General's Office are pending. Official declaration of the merger is described as "imminent."

January, 1978—Notices of intent to dissolve JFS into JBG, and subsequently change name to JBFCS are filed.

February 8, 1978—The merger of JBG and JFS is officially proclaimed. The process of reorganizing staff, facilities, governance, and operation is begun.

CONTEXT

Merger is not a new topic for social service agencies in the New York Jewish community. As far back as the 1930s, the Federation of Jewish Philanthropies has encouraged merger discussions among its recipient agencies. Since the 1950s particular interest in merging JBG, JFS, and the large foster care-oriented Jewish Child Care Association (JCCA) has arisen from time to time. For FJP, merger represents greater efficiency and simplicity in the funding of child-oriented social services. As Jay Goldsmith recalls the history, discussions more frequently focused on JBG and JCCA: ". . . [The merger idea] has a long history. . . .[In] 1950 . . . [for example] there was a visit from the JFS leadership to the JBG at that time to discuss cooperative efforts and mergers. . . . It has come up periodically . . . because the logic of merger had been pressing for many years. . . . The question has always been—why doesn't the Federation have [just] one Jewish children's agency that deals with all the issues of treatment and placement? . . . That was the logic, the unyielding logic that always pushed us. But . . .[there was a] fundamental lack of sympathy . . . 'sympatico,' between [JBG and JCCA] that would make it impossible for them to merge. There was a competitiveness . . . an uneasy . . . relationship between . . . the two agencies . . . [which] didn't aid the merger climate. . . . [Nonetheless], Federation, each time, even in the middle of our discussions with JFS, convened [a meeting] of JBG and JCCA to see whether that [JCCA-JBG] merger could be once again revived. . . ."

Shep Sherman recalls the debate of the 1950s: "[In] the 1950s, . . . a study was done . . . and a proposal for the merger of a number of agencies [was made]. . . . That . . . recommendation was debated and argued and [ultimately] fell apart. Then once or twice in the interim between those years and the present . . . there were starts made in this direction. . . . [Once it was proposed that] . . . the three largest agencies [JBG, JCCA, JFS] merge. . . . That fell apart in a heroic, epochal meeting in which the three boards of directors got together for a meeting chaired by a Supreme Court Judge. . . . One after another, the child care people . . . the foster care agency people . . . condemned the merger. . . . So that fell apart, and . . . [so] the thing . . . has been cooking for sometime but [has been], of course, on the back burner [of late]. . . ."

JBG, JFS, and JCCA have not been the only focus of FJP sponsored merger activity. For example, in a June 1976 memorandum, staff of JBG note: "Federation itself recognized decades ago, the value of such integration of services by creating the Westchester Jewish Community Services and the Jewish Community Services of Long Island, both of which encompass in a single agency the functions now carried out separately by the JFS and the JBG in the [city]. . . ."

In the 1970s, the rationale for consolidation and merger was strengthened in the city by the decline of the Jewish population in that locale, as well as the darkening picture of philanthropic and public funds. The aforementioned 1976 JBG memo notes: ". . . For the immediate future, the prospects are that there will be severe contraction of the real dollars available from public as well as philanthropic sources. . . . [And] the movement out of the inner city of great numbers of Jewish families continues; the number of Jewish aged will continue to rise; there is a continuing decline in the birth rate and therefore reduction in the number of 'young' families." Therefore, the call for merger by Federation reflected the need to consolidate service arrangements in view of a declining population and resource base, and an emphasis on greater efficiency.

Paralleling the economic and demographic imperatives, the trends in the social service and mental health professsions also now favored the service concepts around which the JBG-JFS merger revolved. Two interrelated points are worth noting. First, in the child care field specifically, there was a marked movement toward preventive programming, i.e., working with families to reduce the need for residential placement. A February, 1977, JBG memorandum notes, for example, that, ". . . preventive service projects aimed at 'saving families for children' . . . have been put in place in [various] children's agencies including our own. . . . These are essentially family services utilizing a variety of social services, clinical input and supporting services to help maintain children in their own homes." The implied reference here is to the 1973 New York State Preventative Services Demonstration legislation which provided funds for such programs on an experimental basis. That legislation was stimulated by a general hue and cry in the foster care field that children have been placed outside of their homes too often, and too many for long periods.

The second, more general trend in professional thinking has been towards comprehensive models of treatment services. As the June, 1976, memorandum explains: ". . . There has been an extraordinary expansion of knowledge in the field in the past several decades. The foundations for the separate identities of the JFS and JBG were laid many years ago, in a different era. . . .

"In the past two decades there have been radical changes in our intellectual approaches to social welfare and mental health work. The model of the individual patient and client treatment that had been based on *physical* medicine was considerably altered by our increased understanding of the interrelatedness and interdependence of family members, both in healthy development and in illness. Treatment has increasingly focused on the family unit and on other natural group associations. . . . The children's agency, like JBG, tries to encompass the family unit . . . in its work with children; the family agency, like JFS, increasingly includes children . . . in its work with family units. . . .

". . . Throughout the country there has been a trend in the broad mental health field toward merger of family and children's agencies. In hospitals, for example, family psychiatry has moved into departments of child psychiatry and into the training of psychiatric fellows and residents. Federal and local legislation, guided by the best of professional thinking, has increasingly favored the creation of *comprehensive* structures for delivery of service. Similarly, mental health practitioners are becoming increasingly more appreciative of the way in which individual and family disablement interlocks, and are calling for integration of practice specialties."

During the period when the JBG-JFS merger was being deliberated, the parties were aware of the current interest by the professional community. In December of 1977, Jay Goldsmith reported to his executive committee that the merger would be "watched . . . by agencies all over the country since there is a great interest now in the kind of model which we will be developing. . . ." And in January of 1978, Goldsmith reported to the same committee that, "The imminence of merger . . . has also elicited a great deal of interest in the academic community, and we have been approached by a number of universities . . . about affiliation with the JBG Educational Institute. . . ."

Thus, it is no surprise that the JBFCS Annual Report should indicate: "The decision to merge . . . is based on the conviction that the comprehensive model of service, which is being adopted by medical and social welfare organizations throughout the country, is the most effective way to deliver needed social welfare and mental health services to the community. . . ."

CHOICES

Although its deliberation transpired over a relatively short period of time (approximately two years), the merger of JBG and JFS passed through a number of distinct stages of decision-making. Initially, Shep Sherman broached the proposal. Later, board members and staff of the two agencies, after substantial study and debate, resolved to merge —based on general principles of agreement on the shape of the new agency. Finally, the particular parameters of the new agency had to be worked through, in the process of actual consolidation and redirection, by multiple staff committees under leadership direction of Jay Goldsmith.

The basic decision to merge was affected by numerous issues and concerns, almost anyone of which could potentially have sunk the proposal. (See Risks and Constraints below.) However, the merger initiative was also driven by its fundamental logic, and by a good sense of timing by Sherman, Goldsmith, and members of their respective organizations.

By early 1976, Shep Sherman was contemplating his retirement. This personal milestone required some decisions germane to the future of JFS. Clearly, alternative leadership would have to be found, but there was no immediately obvious successor in the JFS ranks. The existing deputies were either too old or ill, or otherwise unsatisfactory to the JFS board. The options were to initiate a search for new leadership, or to explore a merger. According to Goldsmith, ". . . They [JFS] really didn't have anybody in sight, and after looking around they decided there was nobody in the field that they wanted. So the idea of merger occurred to them, with an agency where it had been discussed in . . . years past and discarded. It had . . . been in people's minds from time to time, as a possibility, [so] it was decided to explore it on their part and we were approached. . . . "

According to Sherman, the search for alternative leadership was never really serious: "If the merger hadn't come off . . . we would have looked for an[other] executive. Who knows? I hadn't thought that far ahead. . . . I don't know that there would have been any other merger that would have made the same sense. . . ."

To Shep Sherman, the merger became a central theme around which he would design his retirement. It was, in his view, a "golden opportunity; . . . the reason why the other merger [attempts] really fell apart was the competitiveness of the executives as to who was going to be on top, who was going to be dispensable. . . . And I said, 'Listen, we have got a golden opportunity here. I am retiring. I want out of the administrative, executive ranks. I'll support . . . your being the executive. So there is really no need for us to compete on this thing. We are free to look at what is really desirable . . . without competitive, sibling rivalry.' And that is what made it possible. I would say that single thing . . . made it possible, because it made it possible for the executives, Goldsmith and myself, to mobilize sentiment on our boards, in favor of it. . . ."

The merger idea had a compelling quality to both executives. Goldsmith would be offered the leadership of a significantly expanded agency with a wide-open agenda, while Sherman could exit with a flourish, having made an important contribution to his field and his agency. As Sherman saw it, these two loyalties were consistent and intertwined, despite the fact that JFS's identity might be submerged by consolidation: ". . . The Jewish Family Service was my professional forum and home for over 30 years, and I have felt an attachment. [Feeling otherwise] would be like not caring what happens to your family. . . . I was deeply concerned about . . . the continuity [and] . . . the identity of the Jewish Family Service, even into the merger . . . not as an agency [per se] . . . but the tradition and the work that it is doing, and the reputation it has. . . . [The merger was a] last creative task . . . [to] approach more the concept, the holistic concept of . . . individuals and families. Children and family, family and children . . . I think being able to help the agency into a new phase of creative ferment . . . hell . . . that is exciting and rewarding, and gratifying. . . ."

Once merger talks got underway between JFS and JBG, with FJP as an interested third party, the whole gamut of merger possibilities was raised. Federation again introduced the possibility of merger between JBG and JCCA, the two child care agencies, but to no avail. (The mutual disaffection still obtained.) The possibility of a looser affiliation between JFS and JBG, short of actual merger, was also raised by JBG board members. For example, in a meeting of the JBG Executive Committee in November, 1977, it was reported that JFS was pressing JBG for a commitment to merge, and that JFS was not interested in affiliation arrangements. At least from the JFS side, the comprehensive services model and the issue of executive leadership made merger compelling, and lesser alternatives unattractive.

For JBG there were also some immediately compelling arguments for merger. One factor was JBG's strong identification with residential treatment, particularly through its large and long-established institution at Hawthorne. Such a heavy emphasis on residential care was fast becoming a liability in the view of modern mental health and social service professionals, as well as a financial burden. Addition of JFS's network of community-based services would give the new agency a more balanced image and set of resources.

For example, at a May, 1977, meeting of JBG's Executive Committee, Goldsmith indicated that ". . . merger would give us an opportunity to improve services for adolescents . . . without keeping us a prisoner of Hawthorne." And at a June, 1977, meeting of that committee, it is again noted that the merger would help free JBG "from its dependence on Hawthorne."

Another factor for JBG was JFS's strong financial position, particularly its private funding base. This was viewed as a potential source of leverage to attract more public matching funds to the agency, through the mental health system. JBG, with its mental health system accreditation, would be in a strong position to take advantage of this leverage.

A January, 1977, joint board subcommittee on staff reports in its minutes that, "The merged agency with its Federation's total grants of $4,500,000 will be in the position of drawing down, based upon the 50 percent Department of Mental Health Services (DMHS) match formula, a very substantial amount of dollars to expand mental health services for children and families. . . ."

An April, 1977, JBG memorandum also mentions the possibility of ". . . Expansion of service through utilizing the expanded pool of philanthropic dollars to match public funds." Similarly at an April 6, 1977 meeting of the JBG Executive Committee, it is noted that "the resources of the merged agency would be helpful to the City, which could use these as matching funds . . . and help draw more state dollars. . . ."

And more than simply provide additional financial leverage, the addition of JFS might provide JBG, already a major agency, with additional overall "clout" with the City and State. Such a consideration was raised by one board member in a February 1977 meeting of the JBG Board of Trustees, who noted the need for a stronger negotiating position in view of the "fiscal crunch" imposed by the City, State, and U.S. And, in a JBG memorandum of April, 1977, the possibility is noted of "increased influence over public policy as a result of the size and prestige of the merger agency."

Finally, given JBG's constant flirtation with operating deficits, the possibilities of cost savings and the addition of an endowment "cushion" that might result from a merger with JFS had to be attractive to JBG.

Consolidation of field offices and gradual shifting away from residential treatment might ease the financial problems created by the Hawthorne operation, which Goldsmith describes as a "sinkhole" for dollars.

Of course, JFS would be wary of having its endowment go down this drain (see Risks and Constraints), but JFS's financial strength was a distinct "plus" for merger, as seen by JBG.

From the viewpoint of both agencies, the attraction of merger was ultimately tied to the adaptation to a new service-delivery model. For example, Jay Goldsmith is frequently recorded as saying that ". . . if one were to initiate an agency today . . . [given] what we know about families and children . . . [we] really would not set up two separate agencies. . . . [Thus] there was an impelling logic to bring it together. . . ."

Substantial discussion centered, throughout the merger talks, on the nature of the new model. The June, 1976 JBG memorandum on exploring merger asks whether a medical model, with generalists at intake and specialists (child or family therapists, residential treatment) called in as needed, should be adopted. A February, 1977 memorandum mentions four alternative models for services integration, offered for consideration by Shep Sherman.

However, the speed with which a new model of service delivery would be implemented was uncertain. The June, 1976 memorandum also asks: "Should corporate merger be followed by an interim structure, which would provide for an integrated administrative structure but with a dual service structure (family service and child guidance) to determine whether, to what extent, and for which services full integration would be useful?"

Jay Goldsmith says he was committed to an "integration" rather than "umbrella" structure from the start, but was cautious on the timing: "I was very committed to a merging of the processes of family and child treatment. I didn't want to have a family department and a children's department, which is what most Jewish family and children's agencies have in this country. I wanted to merge the process, and we're doing it by tracking patients into service with a different kind of intake disposition conference and the utilization of criteria that select one to fifty modes of treatment at different times, depending on people's needs. . . .

"[However], the decision at the beginning was to make no changes, not to rock the boat. . . . There are certain requirements that have to take place. There are certain departments that logically ought to be questioned as to where they fit into the new service. . . . We're aware of them, but we're not moving on them right away . . . There are a lot of issues. That's one of the things the Policy and Scope Committees [of] the board and the professional staff will be doing . . . [namely] reviewing which services are still pertinent to our mission and which ought to be modified or eliminated. And we will do that."

Deference to the personnel within their respective organizations seems to have been a hallmark of strategy which Sherman and Goldsmith adopted to accomplish the merger. Having resolved to pursue the merger proposal, they were quick to involve their boards of trustees and their staffs in the deliberation process. Indeed, the executives took a back seat at first, until momentum developed. This cautious, low-key approach was in recognition of all the sensitivities involved in restructuring two large agencies. Board member and staff positions and personalities would have to be rearranged. Feelings could be hurt, and fears would arise. (See Risks and Constraints below.) A merger would have no chance unless the various personalities became an integral part of the decision process. Thus, beginning with the executive committees of the boards of trustees, and blossoming outwards to include staff, numerous committees were established to explore various issues and implications of merger, and various joint meetings were held between board members and staff members of the two agencies during the period of merger consideration. (See Chronology of Events.)

Given this cautious, participatory approach, there was, of course, the possibility that more problems would be raised than solved by the various committees. Indeed, at a May, 1977 meeting of JBG's Executive Committee (of the board) concern was expressed that it would take several years to work out all the problems. Hence two stages of consolidation were identified—legal corporate merger, followed by gradual merger of agency operations. In general, as merger discussions proceeded, the feeling grew that (legal) merger should be accomplished as soon as possible, before everything started to unravel. At the foregoing May, 1977 executive committee meeting, Goldsmith stated that he did not wish to delay any longer because "we are now at the right psychological moment." As Goldsmith recalls: "There were dozens of meetings that took place with board and staff . . . that kept coping with the issues, but one thing that came clear [was that] if you're going to do it, the longer [you wait], the more anxiety develops and the more differences begin to emerge. It began to be very clear that if we have enough confidence [that] this is the way we want to go, we'd better do it fast. Otherwise, it'll break up. . . . We'll work out the differences later. The board and the key leadership among the professional staff made that decision quickly. Otherwise [it] would have fallen apart. . . ."

Finally, as the merger of two nonprofit organizations, JBFCS would logically incorporate as a nonprofit itself. This was always assumed and never an issue. Nonetheless, the preferred mode of merger would have been to dissolve the two original nonprofits (JBS and JFS) and to incorporate a new one (JBFCS). This would have reinforced the preference (especially by those associated with JFS) that the venture be viewed as a marriage of *equals*. However, technical considerations associated with JBG's mental health accreditations required dissolution of JFS, its absorption by JGB, followed by a name change. (See Risks and Constraints below.)

RISKS AND CONSTRAINTS

While the arguments for merger eventually won the day, there was a myriad of concerns by board and staff members of both agencies, any number of which might have undermined the venture. There were, for example, certain recognized risks associated with loss of effectiveness, identity, and independence of the original agencies, and administrative overburden or financial problems for the new agency.

For those associated with JFS, which had been mostly reliant on private funds, there was the feared loss of autonomy of a new agency heavily dependent on public dollars, i.e., "that we would not [any longer] be . . . free agents," as Shep Sherman puts it. Part of the concern here involved the more sectarian program of JFS, and whether the greater proportion of public funding would mean a loss of that identity and orientation. For example, the observation was made in discussion by JBG's executive committee in June, 1977 that the City might pressure the new agency to serve more non-Jewish children. Throughout the merger deliberations the divergent orientations of JBG and JFS were recognized. For example, a June, 1976 statement on exploring merger asks: "With JFS serving a predominately Jewish caseload and JBG serving a significant proportion of black and Hispanic children, what result would the "mix" have? How could merger be directed to assure service to a larger sum total of Jewish clientele? How could the joint service not only maintain but significantly enlarge its role in the general Jewish community and in the various Orthodox Jewish communities?" The January, 1977 minutes of the joint (board) subcommittee on staff go on to state: "The issue of the JBG serving a large number of non-Jewish clients and JFS serving a predominately Jewish population was discussed. Although the implications inherent in this will need further exploration, it was pointed out that both agencies consider themselves sectarian services giving preference to Jewish applicants."

An April, 1977 JBG memo also raises the possibility that: "There might be dilution of service to the Jewish community." The concern over loss of identity with, and service to, the Jewish community, was not solely confined to the question of public funding, nor was it solely the concern of JFS. Jay Goldsmith explains that staff of the Federation were also worried: ". . . We . . . had been meeting with Federation and talking to them about this [merger] . . . letting them know of our intent. Shep and I visited [the director] . . . and he gave us his blessing and said it was a wonderful thing. . . . Meanwhile, the rumors began to creep back to us that [other FJP staff said that], 'It's not such a good idea because JBG is more nonsectarian in style and will contaminate the Jewish orientation of JFS. . . .'"

Of a more personal nature, there was fear on the JFS side, especially at the board level, that the identity of JFS personalities would be swamped by the merger. Shep Sherman notes candidly: ". . . What was unspoken is that some of [the JFS trustees] felt that they would lose identity in such a larger board. They were much bigger [fish] in a small pond than they would be in such a larger pond. . . . And [there were] . . . similar sentiments among the staff. . . . [In addition], . . . in the staff . . . the single strongest opinion was that the JBG orientation toward [institutional] practice would corrupt the JFS practice [and] they . . . would become . . . less respected and valued [and] have less status. . . ."

From the JBG side there was an even stronger concern that the merger would risk a loss of effectiveness and decline in professional reputation. In a meeting of the JBG executive committee in July, 1976, one board member expressed the fear that the merger "may require total restructuring of the services of the two agencies with the risk that you may be giving up two good things that work, for one possible [one] that won't." In April, 1977, a board member asserted that perhaps JBG should stick to psychotherapeutic treatment of children with emotional disorders and not take over a whole range of social services. In May, 1977, a board member expressed the fear that the size of the new agency and the preoccupation with merger will deleteriously affect attention to the quality of services. Perhaps the fears of a few JBG trustees were best summed up by one of them at an executive committee meeting in February, 1977. That trustee stated his opposition to merger and said he felt strongly about JBG's tradition of "quality and greatness" which he asserted was due to the fact that "we cut our cloth to a narrow pattern . . . [of] clinical treatment of the emotionally disturbed child."

An important area of risk, especially as viewed by Goldsmith and others affiliated with JBG was the prospect of an administrative morass in trying to fuse the two agencies together, and overburden in attempting to administer the new creation. Of particular concern to Goldsmith were the potential divisions at the board and staff levels. Speaking of the new trustees from JFS, Goldsmith observes, ". . . I was engaging in a relationship with a whole new set of power people . . . [some of whom] came with high levels of suspicion and even some distrust. . . . Some were supportive but generally I would say that was an area of real . . . concern, having to reestablish yourself with that group and prove your capability.

"[The merger] gave me a split board. . . . [It] carried a great division within the board *and* within the professional staff, of those committed to outpatients in community-based treatment and [those committed to] residential treatment . . . [It was a] highly unstable professional situation with a great deal of suspicion on both sides. The assumption . . . by my own [JBG-derived] staff . . . that I would betray them and their commitments to child treatment, and suspicion by the newer staff for me . . . that . . . I wasn't either acquainted or representative of their particular specialty. . . ."

Aside from the prospect of having to mediate internal divisions, there were more straightforward concerns over the potential administrative efficiency of the new, larger agency. An April, 1977 memorandum, for example, wonders if: "The increase in the number and variety of services located under the umbrella of the merged agency might pose administrative problems." While in June, 1977 a JBG trustee questions whether the larger "conglomerate" agency would become too impersonal in style. At a May, 1977 meeting of the JBG executive committee, Goldsmith notes administrative changes were already underway, consistent with the reorganization that would be necessary for merger. In particular, Goldsmith says he had already planned to be less involved in the day-to-day detail of operation but "closer to the concepts affecting the development of programs and services." Hence the merger reorganization would not be substantially different from the goal of the current reorganization of the JBG to "create a management system that will free me to deal with issues of policy."

Nonetheless, the merger represented an administrative risk if only from the viewpoint of additional workload in carrying it through. Moreover, Goldsmith was not unmindful that administrative problems of the kind potentially involved in merger, have unseated other well regarded executives: ". . . There are a few key executives in this town who have disappeared in the last few months, who had very secure positions and were very important people. That's always a possibility that . . . your job is not secure and you may not survive. And while I guess I've never really thought about that as a serious potentiality, sure, it's slipped through my mind. . . ."

One set of risks of explicit concern to both agencies was the financial base of the merged organization. While there was some thought that merging a heavily government-funded agency with one that depended primarily on philanthropy represented a beneficial "hedging of the risks" associated with the two sources, much more attention was paid to the concern that the Federation might reduce its combined allocation to JBG and JFS. After all, Federation's interest in the merger was largely in saving money, and the new agency would represent an obvious target as the largest single recipient of FJP funds. The fear of cutbacks by Federation is noted in the June, 1976 exploratory statement and later in an April, 1977 memorandum, as well as in the minutes of numerous meetings. In the minutes of the January, 1977 meeting of the JFS-JBG Merger Finance Subcommittee, it is stated: "The question of continued Federation funding was of extreme importance to the Committee since, if the two agencies were to merge, Federation's grant to the combined organizations would represent 20 percent of the total funds distributed by Federation to all agencies. The Committee expressed concern that, in this contracting climate of philanthropic giving, Federation might not be able to fund the newly merged organization even at current levels; particularly, in light of its intent to reduce the levels of grants for the next fiscal year by 1 percent and substantially thereafter."

Goldsmith reiterates the point and goes on to say, "We . . . had a . . . meeting with Federation in which the (board) presidents of JBG and JFS and . . . the professionals met with . . . leadership . . . in Federation and [we asked] . . . if we did merge, what guarantees did we have [for] Federation not to use the occasion to reduce our grant. . . . [We talked of] the concerns that . . . [we] would have . . . about being vulnerable as a large target for future cuts, with Federation's merger coming up with UJA . . . in the not too distant future. . . . And, of course, we gained a lot of reassurances . . . [and] Federation encouraged us to move ahead. . . ." Loss of Federation support turned out to be a well-founded fear, as it ultimately became difficult to hold FJP to its promises of continued funding at the old levels.

In many ways, implementing the merger was analogous to threading a needle—numerous constraints defined a narrow opening through which the venture had to be guided. Some of these constraints were simply annoying but necessary legal and logistical requirements. Others, however, represented delicate balancing of competing demands from various organizational factions.

Goldsmith acutely observes that ". . . mergers cost money. In the long run they save, [but] in the short run they cost money. . . ." To assist with the costs of merger, the JFS and JBG applied to the Greater New York (United) Fund for a $45,000 (matching) grant in November of 1977. The proposal lists $90,000 worth of short-run merger expenses including legal fees, integration of business operations, consolidation of program reporting and data processing, relocation of facilities, staff reorganization and orientation materials, and public relations materials. The actual merger process would, of course, transpire over a period of time. It is interesting, therefore, that there was some earlier discussion over how the merger costs should be paid for in terms of the treasuries of the original agencies. In July, 1977, a JBG board member (who, not surprisingly, was an opponent of merger) proposed that a holding company be set up and each agency pay separately for costs of the merger. However, this idea was rejected in favor of immediate consolidation of fiscal resources.

Legal requirements represented a tricky, but ultimately not very serious bound on the merger process. Various approvals needed to be obtained from the New York State Departments of Social Service, Mental Hygiene, and Education and the Attorney General.

A basic concern was that JBG should not lose its mental health system accreditation. Jay Goldsmith explains that JBG technically had to absorb JFS (rather than merge with it) and then change its name, in order to accomplish this assurance: "[A] real merger meant both agencies would have had to go out of existence and a new one would have come into existence. That would have meant [that] the JBG would have lost all accreditation with the Joint Commission and all of its psychiatric clinic licenses, and [would have] had to start all over. A clumsy and difficult process, so the JFS merged into the old JBG, and then the JBG . . . changed its name. . . ."

As Goldsmith goes on to observe, this technical process was not widely understood, and carried with it some trauma: "When that notice appeared in the papers, that JFS was being dissolved, all hell broke loose. Social workers who never read the financial page, read the financial page that day. . . . Nobody ever reads those notices of dissolution of corporations . . . but they saw that."

The really serious potential trauma that constrained the evolution of the merger pertained to parochial and proprietary feelings on the part of board and staff members of both organizations. The issues included use of JFS's endowment funds, job security, structuring of the new board, and the general concerns for parity in structuring the new organization.

Two intertwined issues that arose through the merger discussions were the questions of JBG's Hawthorne Cedar Knolls residential facility, and the use of JFS's endowment funds. The concern of some affiliated with JFS was that its funds would be used to finance the JBG deficits emanating from the Hawthorne "sinkhole" and other JBG residential facilities. As noted by Shep Sherman, there was the further concern by some JFS people ". . . who had had some experiences with . . . institutions that . . . Hawthorne [as] an institution that has delinquent kids . . . [had an undesirable] image in the community . . . [that] would rub off . . . on the JFS." For their part, some trustees of JBG argued that JBG should get its own house in order, and proceed with the needed renovation of the old Hawthorne physical plant, rather than divert its energies on the merger. This view is expressed by JBG board members at various meetings in 1977. But in a June, 1977 meeting of the Executive Committee, Goldsmith said that Hawthorne needs restructuring, but he didn't think it should interfere with the merger.

That dissipation of the JFS funds was a serious problem is confirmed in the January, 1977 minutes of the Joint Merger Finance Subcommittee: "Another concern appeared to be whether, by virtue of the merger, the JFS funds would or could be dissipated. Both Mr. Hirsch and Mr. Cohen [JBG trustees] indicated that once the merger had been effected, there is no way to protect the funds of either organization against the creditors of the merged organizations but that JBG's assets are substantial (although, primarily of a fixed nature) and they are not in any danger of claim by creditors in the foreseeable future although such is always a possibility."

Ultimately, the merger agreement required that JBG provide moral assurance that JFS funds would not be used simply to cover JBG debts. According to Goldsmith, ". . . Whether the money would be dissipated in JBG's residential centers which are notoriously expensive and have huge deficits . . . created a tremendous problem. . . . JFS . . . people had a great deal of concern about that. . . . We had to give guarantees that money would not be touched. While it was to become an asset to [the] new agency, the moral position of the new agency would be to leave those dollars untouched for several years, and not [have it] go toward solving deficits from the old JBG problems. . . ."

Even more anxiety centered on the question of job security. Care was taken, for example, to keep the employees' union informed, beginning with a meeting in July of 1977. Although the staff anxiety was pervasive, both Sherman and Goldsmith agree that the greatest resistance came from middle management—the division chiefs and program administrators who were uncertain about their futures in the new agency. As Goldsmith summarizes it: ". . . The difficulty is not in the top and not on the bottom. It's where it always is . . . in the supervisory group. . . . That's the group that's most resistant to change. . . ." And as Sherman notes, the problem was particularly acute for JFS administrators: ". . . No matter how many times we said that there were no plans to cut anybody's head off, the administrator . . . in JFS looked over at [his counterpart in] JBG, and saw that JBG had a bigger structure . . . [and] felt, 'What the hell is going to happen to me?'"

The issues of job security and redefinition of responsibilities had to be dealt with delicately. There were, as Goldsmith emphasizes, "endless meetings" between top management, supervisors, line staff, and the union. The union was guaranteed that there would be no job loss (layoffs). The administrative consolidation was dealt with in various ways. Sherman explains how the borough directorships were handled: ". . . We solved it in a variety of ways. In the Bronx we . . . have co-directors. In [another case] one of the borough directors was [fired]. . . . In [another borough] one of the borough directors was promoted to another position. . . ."

If staff problems required sensitivity and delicate maneuvering, structuring the board of directors of the new agency required even more diplomacy. Shep Sherman explains: ". . . There were one or two powerful people in the JBG board and similarly in the JFS board [who] if they had been crossed the wrong way . . . could have blocked [the merger]. . . ." Goldsmith observes further that ". . . The board's been very difficult. The sensitivities are much greater. . . ." The problems at the board level involved reconciling reluctance to abdicate prestigious positions, with the need to consolidate and provide for parity between people from JFS and JBG.

The July, 1977 Joint Merger Committee featured a discussion of board structure for the new agency in which JFS trustees insist that the merger be a merger of equals. There was also sentiment expressed by one JBG trustee that greater representation [be granted to JBG] by virtue of its size. What is worse, Goldsmith recalls that JFS trustees were actually insulted early in the summer of 1977 by the "high hattedness" of some of the JBG trustees: "[In June, 1977] . . . there was a crystallized resolution [of] . . . intent to merge. . . . Then the board committees . . . met at the top and everything began to go bad. Until we reached July, 1977, it looked like the merger was going to be dissolved. . . . Several of our board members at JBG offended the board members and trustees at JFS . . . [because] the JBG crowd looked at [JFS] as an addition of an outpatient service . . . [while] the JFS was very sensitive to the fact [that] this was a merger, not a takeover. . . ."

There was sentiment expressed at the July meeting that all present board members should be allowed to participate in the new board, but there was no agreement on how that board should be structured. By November, 1977, the issue of representation appears to have been resolved in favor of equality between the two agencies.

This seems to have been only the beginning of the resolution, however. The question of who would fill key positions on the board generated considerably more friction. Goldsmith explains: [We faced the question of] who was going to be president. . . . We had two presidents . . . and neither was going to step down. . . . Finally, it was agreed that [the JBG president] would step down . . . [the JFS president] would go on for a year . . . and after a year [the JBG president] would then become president for four years.

". . . The former JBG president . . . now has resumed his role of presidency . . . and as the time has gone on since the merger, it's apparent that a lot of strength is in the old JBG. . . . It looked like all the key . . . spots, by virtue of age and power, . . . were emerging as ex-JBG people. . . . JFS people were getting more and more uncomfortable with that. . . . [The ex-JFS president] got very stubborn about that and [insisted that] the Executive Committee [Chairman] . . . which is the [second] most prestigious position . . . had to be an ex-JFS activist. [However, the man] who had been Chairman of that committee for 12 years didn't want to get off. . . . [The president] finally . . . had to tell him to . . . step down and leave room for an ex-JFS person. . . . But in the process, we've had to juggle all the committees, the budget committee, the balance of power. . . ."

Essentially, successful adoption and implementation of the merger meant operating with deference to the sensitivities of people, staff, and board members, whose conflicting loyalties required solutions within narrow bounds of compromise. Goldsmith himself had to work at overcoming distrust of affiliates of the old JFS while attempting to revise the loyalties of the JBG people without offending them.

OUTCOMES

More than a year after the formal merger, the consolidating and deliberating and rearranging were still going on. There were still numerous staff committees and meetings to deal with the issues of program and service delivery. But the ferment seemed healthy. Speaking of experimenting with a new format of disposition conferences, Goldsmith seemed to aptly characterize the whole state of agency affairs: ". . . [There's] still a tremendous number of bugs but what we've got is a sense of openness and candor and battle."

There apparently has been learning and adaptation by staff from each of the former agencies. For example, Goldsmith notes that "there's more psychiatric input into the new JFS cases. . . ." At the same time, ". . . [we're] incorporating a quick response . . . in order to give service to all clients who come to you. That's a new concept for the old JBG people who really shunned short-term therapy and only thought in terms of long-term care."

Not all parts of the two former agencies have been equally affected by the merger. According to Goldsmith, "It touched the [JBG] residential centers least [initially]. But training has been consolidated . . . [and] all the [old JBG] outpatient units have changed dramatically . . . because we've introduced the notion of a quick response. . . . We've [also] introduced priorities into Jewish families [cases], with children having first priority. . . ."

In those parts of the agency where merger was the most visible, reactions were mixed. As Goldsmith sees it: "It's different in different offices. In [some offices] there's a compatibility and excitement that's very good. [Elsewhere] the JFS crowd feels it's being swallowed up by the JBG . . . [or] the JBG crowd . . . feels it's being swallowed up by JFS. . . . It's a function of numbers and personalities of the staff directors. . . . It's more the personality of the people who where chosen to head up each of [the] boroughs. . . ."

ANALYSIS

The merger of JFS and JBG was a venture of mutual interest to executives Shep Sherman and Jay Goldsmith. To Sherman, whose heart was in practice and in scholarship, the merger represented a contribution to his field—a chance to set into motion the development of a comprehensive model of service delivery to troubled families. The merger also solved a potential leadership problem at JFS, and allowed Sherman to retire with a flourish. For Jay Goldsmith, the merger presented a whole new opportunity set. He would be the center in a whirlwind of new activity. And, as the executive of the huge and financially comfortable new agency, he would have the chance to indulge in grandiose new plans for the reform of service delivery to children and families and to develop new institutional affiliations and arrangements for melding theory to practice.

The merger proposal was born into a receptive institutional and professional context. For years, the Federation had encouraged consolidation among its agencies, but with little recent success in the family and children's service field. Nationwide the merger of family and children's agencies was also in vogue. Such movement had both economic and political roots. As in the New York City context in which JBFCS emerged, traditional client populations were shrinking while philanthropic dollars were also becoming more scarce. Consolidation of partially duplicative and complementary systems made sense. Furthermore, social work and mental health thinking about child care was moving away from institutional care and from the "child as patient" model, towards a more preventive, family-focused approach. At the same time, family services were being encouraged to incorporate children into their purview and clinical specialties into their practice. A comprehensive, multimodal family service model represented the current state of the art.

The merger of JFS and JBG succeeded because it was carried out sensitively, with a good sense of timing. The fact that one of the executives was retiring solved a major potential obstacle to merger, i.e., the choice of chief executive. Still, other sources of pride and uncertainty had to be massaged. The two executives shrewdly engaged their boards and staff into early and detailed participation in merger deliberations. They took a back seat, go-slow stance in order to acclimate their organizations to the concept. At the same time, once all the issues were on the table, the executives, Goldsmith in particular, wasted no time allowing the momentum to slow or the merger to unravel. Rather than work out all the details prior to legal merger, the organizations were urged to merge first, and to continue the process of consolidation over time.

The sensitivities and proprietary feelings of members of both organizations defined a set of constraints within which merger could be worked out. Parity was a key guideline. It was to be a merger of relative equals in which power and responsibilities would have to be properly disbursed. Care would also have to be paid to the use of funds. It would not be acceptable for the funds of one agency to bail out the deficits of the other.

The case of the JFS-JBG merger appears to provide some general insights on the character of at least one class of nonprofit organizations. Certainly this merger experience shows some nonprofits to be ones in which power is dispersed. Chief executives are powerful—certainly merger is all but precluded if these men cannot be accommodated—but they cannot alone carry out such a venture. Unlike a profit-making corporation where an executive-owner might easily have his way, the nonprofit director must mollify the personal and proprietary feelings of his board members, as well as deal with staff, union, donor (Federation) and client (government) concerns. In the case of JBFCS, it was a semipublic process in which political as well as executive (management) skills were required.

NEW INITIATIVES BY EXISTING ORGANIZATIONS

Florida Sheriffs Youth Fund, Inc.

PRÉCIS

The Florida Sheriffs Youth Fund (FSYF) is a nonprofit umbrella organization which administers three residential child care programs—a Boys Ranch, Girls Villa, and Youth Ranch—in three locations in the state of Florida. The genesis of FSYF is the Boys Ranch, founded as a nonprofit agency in 1957 by the Florida Sheriffs Association as a facility to help troubled boys. After some initial years of struggle, the sheriffs hired Harry Weaver as executive director of the Ranch. Under Weaver's leadership, the organization has grown from a three-cottage operation with a $100,000 budget, into a thriving multimillion dollar enterprise. Most outstanding of all, the organization runs entirely on privately derived revenues and has become highly sophisticated in the arts of fund-raising, estate planning, and public relations.

THE ENTREPRENEURS

The Florida Sheriffs Boys Ranch was established in 1957, several years prior to Harry Weaver's involvement. By the time of its 20th anniversary celebration in 1977, the organization had enshrined in folklore its modest beginnings, including the sheriffs and early donors who conceived and implemented the idea. There were several key characters including former Sheriffs Ed Blackburn and Don McLeod who learned about Farley's Boys Ranch during a trip to Texas in 1955, and brought back the idea to the Florida Sheriffs Association; Sheriff Hugh Lewis who led the effort to organize the venture, including the securing of land and funds; Tommy Musgrove, a wealthy farmer who donated the land for the ranch; J.L. McMullen who led a committee of Suwannee County civic and business leaders to persuade the sheriffs to undertake the ranch on the site of Musgrove's land; and Sid Saunders, president of the Sheriffs Association during the period the Boys Ranch was begun. These men were instrumental in launching the Boys Ranch, but it was a very small and shaky enterprise when Harry Weaver took over at the helm, late in 1961.

Harry Weaver's early career gave little formal indication of a managerial orientation. Prior to 1956, he was employed as a teacher and counselor at a state training school for boys. From 1956 to 1961 he was a federal probation officer based in Tallahassee. But Weaver's administrative abilities must have been recognized by the sheriffs. He did, for example, organize an industrial arts program at the training school. But his apparent motives for coming to the Boys Ranch in 1961 were very traditional. After being on the corrections end of the spectrum of youth problems, and perhaps being discouraged by it, he wanted to do something on the "prevention side." The Boys Ranch was intended to help straighten kids out before they became seriously involved with law breaking.

Weaver's style is much easier to describe than his motivations. He is very patient and soft-spoken, and also very disciplined. He is extremely meticulous in his attention to detail, whether it be records of children, encounters with potential donors to the agency, or keeping the agency's finances. Weaver is also a crafty and calculating personality who sees precisely how his attention to details fits into an overall managerial strategy. And if Harry Weaver is anything, he is a very skilled salesman.

The salesman in Weaver comes out best when he is describing his approach to getting people, especially elderly donors, to contribute to his agency. It's hard for the outsider, even incredible, to think of getting someone to make a financial contribution as an exercise in *helping the donor*. But Weaver has carefully thought through this approach and seems both sincere and convincing: ". . . I learned . . . [to get] . . . satisfaction [from] . . . helping people to give. . . . In order for a person to give, to give freely, they have to be comfortable in their giving. . . . We encourage visits to our program. . . . People want to be a part of it and see it. They don't want to know the gory details of the kids' lives. They know they have had a rough time. They know the world today is very difficult for teenagers. . . . But they like to be a part of something that's good, wholesome. . . ."

More than just making people feel comfortable about their giving, Weaver sees himself providing a direct service to the donors. Referring to one elderly woman who visited the ranch: "It is obvious that she is in the middle of her estate planning, and that she needs help. She resists help, however, because in fact she and her husband have done quite well through the years with their investments. I have encouraged her to contact the trust officer, but she has stayed still since she has no relatives and no real close friends. . . ."

Referring to another lady who accompanied the first on her visit: "Now . . . I was not unmindful of the lady who stayed off to the side . . . because she had the same problem. So once she started to leave, I thanked her for coming, and I asked her if she was on our mailing list. . . . [It turns out] not only is she alone, no relatives, [but] she's a real estate broker. . . . Never said a word during our conversations. So what have we got? We've got two friends; they have got at least five friends each. They will be our friends.

"Now we don't do that just for the money. We do it because it is the right thing to do. People are very uncomfortable in their approaching death if they do not have their finances in order. They may be prepared for death emotionally from the standpoint of religion or what have you. But if they don't have a will, and if they don't have their finances in order, they are miserable. . . . We work at this, and we are going to do more, because we think it's a service. And we think it's important whether they give to us or not."

If Weaver is the skillful salesman, he is also a patient, pragmatic problem-solver by nature: "I enjoy working with people and some people say I enjoy problem-solving, and seem to thrive on crisis. I don't know that I do. I rather think that I'm a person who thinks that every problem can be solved, or a reasonable solution can be reached. . . ."

Weaver's upbringing in a poor but dedicated family, sensitized him to the value of enterprising and hard work. And as an FFA (Future Farmers of America) member and a student of industrial arts in his youth, he developed a love for building and growing things, which seems reflected in his enterprising behavior later on. Just as important, the care he received from relatives under somewhat adverse economic circumstances, helped develop his sense of responsibility for the welfare of others. As he puts it: "[It's] how we used to do it when the barn burned and everybody pitched in and built the barn back for the neighbor. Or, if the neighbor got sick, everybody pitched in and harvested the crops . . . ." Thus, while Harry Weaver is a product of his particular family upbringing, he is also a product of the general social milieu of the southern United States—a conservative-minded American who advocates the traditional values.

Yet in many ways Harry Weaver is an enigma. He professes little interest in money, or power, or prestige, yet in moderate quantity he has achieved all these. He seems seriously concerned with helping others, yet he is curiously unmindful of the needs of minority children. And, it is difficult to distinguish between Weaver the salesman and Weaver the social worker, especially in his approach to elderly donors.

It is clear that Weaver is an enterpriser and a builder, who enjoys challenges—seeing what he can do—and enjoys seeing the fruits of his labors, be they physical constructs, organizational structures, or programs of various kinds. He is essentially pragmatic, always behaving in a rational, carefully thought-out manner, and in accord with basic conservative principles. In a wider sense, however, he seems curiously value-free: "I don't know what my philosophy of life is. I just live everyday."

THE ORGANIZATION

The genesis of FSYF lies with the Florida Sheriffs Association, the professional group of chief law enforcement officers in the 67 counties of Florida. In Florida, the sheriffs are locally elected and are influential political figures, both locally, and, as a group, statewide. Association with the sheriffs has been a major factor in building the image and the support for FSYF.

The sheriffs' role in FSYF has changed gradually over the years. At the beginning (1957), it was the initiative of the sheriffs that succeeded in establishing the Boys Ranch. Apparently, the notion of sponsoring a ranch that could "straighten out" young boys before they got into serious trouble, by providing a substitute for poor home environments, was attractive to the sheriffs as an image-builder for themselves. The sheriffs' image was a negative (punitive) one with respect to youth—they were the officials associated with juvenile arrests, detention, and referral to state training schools. The ranch would put the sheriffs in a more positive light, trying to help youth and prevent juvenile law breaking.

The sheriffs had little money of their own, but they were able to use their status to generate resources in a manner that was to set precedents for the pattern of future fundraising. They solicited both cash, land, and in-kind labor and goods, and hit upon the ideas of issuing honorary memberships to the Florida Sheriffs Association for $15 fees, and designating generous donors as "lifetime members." In the 20th anniversary issue of The Rancher, State Representative Ed Blackburn, Jr., of Tampa (one of the original sheriffs involved with the ranch), recalls the early activity of the sheriffs: "The Florida Sheriffs Association was broke . . . [but] at the sheriffs' January 1957 winter meeting in Key West, the sheriffs voted that an Honorary Membership Program be made available to a selected group of good citizens in each county. These good people responded.

"Six months later, the 1957 Summer Conference of Sheriffs was held in Sarasota and . . . as a result of the Honorary Membership Program, the Association had a bank balance of $7,000.

". . . the Associated Press picked up the story and Sheriff Hugh Lewis, of Suwannee County, picked up the ball and ran with it. [Farmer] Tommy Musgrove had earlier given . . . some 20 acres . . . to the Elks Club for a youth project; he still owned the 120 adjacent acres to the south. So Sheriff Lewis persuaded the Elks and Tommy to give this 140 acres for the ranch.

"Suwannee County civic and business leaders got together a prestigious committee, headed by J. L. McMullen, to lobby and persuade the sheriffs to name this as the site for the proposed ranch.

"This committee made the formal proposal to the sheriffs' directors in St. Petersburg in August, 1957. The sheriffs accepted, and the idea mushroomed. Adjoining this land to the east were two abandoned farms that were in estates, about 550 acres in all, and $31,000 cash would buy them both. ". . . With the help and advice of the local committee, together with the help of the two friendly Live Oak banks, the sheriffs bought these farms for cash.

"The banks lent the sheriffs $13,000 for a total of $26,000, the sheriffs added $5,000 of their $7,000. . . ."

Blackburn adds, prophetically: "Sheriffs, of necessity, have lots of friends or the badge of authority and honor that they wear wouldn't be theirs, but all of a sudden they found themselves surrounded by a host of new friends who were attracted when they learned that sheriffs had a virtue they had never before seen. . . . Countless friends, both new and old, responded. Money, materials, and labor were donated. Committees were formed in service and civic clubs and churches all over Florida. . . ."

The legacy of these early years remains strong. The sheriffs still play an active role as directors of FSYF. The image of their association with FSYF continues to be a major asset for fund-raising, and much of the style of that fund-raising has been retained. The sheriffs also form an integral part of the intake process. Admissions to the FSYF campuses work through the local sheriff offices. Indeed, Harry Weaver is careful to preserve the close relationship with the sheriffs: ". . . I work through them. [If] I have a speaking engagement in an area, I don't go to that speaking engagement unless I let the sheriff know I'm coming. I invite him to be with me, and he generally is with me. . . . When . . . our social workers . . . go into an area, they go to the sheriff's office, if nothing other than to check with the secretary. . . .

"Each kid comes to the sheriff. That application has to be signed by the sheriff. . . . We like for them [the sheriffs] to stay involved, to know what's going on. . . ."

The sheriffs muddled through the early years of Boys Ranch, going through four resident directors, and floundering financially, before Weaver was hired. Weaver came in 1961, on the condition that changes be made in the organization, including the nature of the sheriff's involvement in administration. Weaver recalls, ". . . We were on a shoestring. . . . If it weren't for non-cash gifts, such as beef and things, . . . we wouldn't have survived. . . . When I came we could go no way but up. . . . We were at rock bottom. . . .

"[The sheriffs] wanted to do something productive . . . and they also wanted to do something to help their own image. If you're for motherhood, you can help your image, so it was a nice combination. Now, what they did not see . . . were the problems they were going to have running the program. The idea was great; it sounded beautiful, but running an under-financed program . . . was very difficult. . . . At the same time that was all they could do, because that was all the money they had. . . . There were certain changes they would have to make in order for me to come. . . . Finally they made certain changes. . . . The board agreed that I could develop a budget and spend money within that budget and I could sign all checks. . . ."

Essentially the sheriffs agreed to take a less direct role in administration, and a more advisory role as directors. The ranch became more its own organization, rather than an extension of the Sheriffs Association. Furthermore, the sheriffs agreed to restructure the board as well. Weaver explains: ". . . In the beginning, by virtue of . . . [the] limited funds, you had to draw on resources from local people [the Suwannee Civic leaders] . . . and they sort of controlled the organization. . . ."

Weaver insisted on a more statewide, representative board structure. The board structure that emerged required a majority of non-sheriffs, with appointments to the board made by the Board of Directors of the Florida Sheriffs Association. The FSYF Board then elects its own officers, and of course, the executive director (Weaver) is responsible to the board.

Despite the continued formal control by the sheriffs over selection of board members, Weaver says, "It's not a problem . . . [although] that probably will change one day."

Weaver is generally pleased with his board members whom, he says, are selected because they ". . . will agree to attend meetings and be involved. . . . That's the main [thing]. The sheriffs have been very good about this. They want to appoint those that will be involved and take it seriously. You don't have to be wealthy. You don't have to be a president of a corporation. . . . We have a CPA. . . . We like to have a doctor on there . . . [but] the main thing is to have a professed interest in child care, and what we are doing. . . ."

Nonetheless, the financial contributions of board members have been important to FSYF. As Weaver recounts: "Let's put it this way. One of our board members . . . built the medical clinic . . . and he built the administration building at the [Girls] Villa. Another one . . . built this [main administration] building and another one was instrumental in building the cafetorium."

Fund-raising has become a science at FSYF. Yet here, too, the roots in the Florida Sheriffs' original efforts, as well as image, remain strong. Amazingly in this era, FSYF operates (except for tax exemption) without a penny of government funds. Large individual donations or estates willed to the organization have been responsible for much of the capital stock (land, buildings, etc.), but Weaver insists that solicitation of small donors, bequests, and in-kind contributions of goods and services are the backbone of the operation. Of all revenues received in fiscal year 1977, 55 percent represented direct gifts, 27 percent were from bequests, 11 percent from income on investments, 3 percent from sale of livestock and farm produce, and 4 percent other. Most of the gifts (roughly 75 percent) were from individual donors, as opposed to organizations, and most of these, Weaver says, are from "$15, $20, $25 donors." (The list of donors numbers some 30,000!) It is in this area particularly that the imagery and appeal of the sheriffs is most effective. As Weaver states in a 1978 speech to the National Association of Homes for Boys: "We are fortunate to have been founded by and associated with the Florida Sheriffs Association. It links us with law enforcement which has a natural appeal to a wide segment of society. The concept of sheriffs helping youngsters with problems to grow into law-abiding citizens rather than following the path that leads to delinquency and crime is even more appealing."

In summary, despite the fact that the sheriffs' direct financial role in FSYF has been minimal (on the order of $80,000 annual contributions in 1979, out of roughly $4 million in total annual revenues), the sheriffs continue to be an integral part of FSYF—through their direct and indirect representation as directors, through their involvement in intake, but most of all through the imagery of "honorary sheriffs" and other public relations aspects of sponsorship.

The corporate structure of FSYF has become considerably more complex, since 1961. But even on this dimension there is a legacy of the early years. Most important is the fact that the Boys Ranch was originally established as an irrevocable trust which meant that the organization could not expand past its original purpose, e.g., it could not accommodate girls. Nonetheless, the organization did expand to a multiple-campus operation, adding a Girls Villa in 1970, and a Youth Ranch for coed sibling groups in 1976. These additions were made by the cumbersome means of setting up separate corporations, each governed by a similar board structure and headed by Weaver as executive director. A separately incorporated Youth Fund was similarly organized in 1973 to carry out fund-raising and administrative coordination. In 1977, through court action, the provisions of the original trust were broken and the various parts of the organization consolidated into a single operation, the Florida Sheriffs Youth Fund, Inc.

At the outset in 1961, Harry Weaver established his firm control of the organization, and this has become increasingly important as the organization grew into a multi-campus enterprise with abundant physical and financial assets and a wide-ranging system of patrons and donors. Weaver is particularly proud of how he modernized management control. The records of some 30,000 donors are automated and "we will have everything . . . vehicles, children's records, inventory, the whole bit . . . on the computer."

CHRONOLOGY OF EVENTS

1957—Boys Ranch is founded by the Florida Sheriffs Association, with 140 acres of donated land and $5,000 in cash. The adjoining 562 acres is purchased with a $26,000 mortgage.

January, 1959—The first cottage is built and staffed, and the first group of boys is admitted.

1960—Two more cottages are added. Total population of boys is now 32, with an operating budget of $114,473.

1961—Harry Weaver is hired as executive director of Boys Ranch.

1960-1970—Boys Ranch expands to six cottages, 100 boys. Many additional buildings are added. The operating budget grows to $400,000.

1970—Florida Sheriffs Girls Villa is organized in Bartow, Florida, 200 miles south of Boys Ranch.

July, 1972—Girls Villa opens with 8 girls. It expands to 24 girls and three cottages by 1978. Ultimate planned capacity is 40 girls and 5 cottages.

1973—Florida Sheriffs Youth Fund, Inc. is established to carry out the administrative, accounting, and fund-raising activities of the Ranch and Villa.

April, 1976—The Youth Fund purchases land and buildings for a third campus, the Youth Ranch. The Youth Ranch opens in 1979 for 10 children (sibling groups). Ultimate capacity is 30 children, housed in three cottages.

October, 1977—The Ranch, Villa, and Youth Fund are merged into a single corporate body called the Florida Sheriff Youth Fund, Inc. At this point the total operating budget is $2.3 million, with a net worth of $12 million. Harry Weaver, previously executive director of each of the separately incorporated units—Boys Ranch, Girls Villa, Youth Ranch, and Youth Fund—becomes president of the merged corporation. The boards of directors of the separate units are consolidated.

CONTEXT

The locale of northern and central Florida provided particularly fertile soil in which to grow an enterprise of the kind that FSYF has become. There are several reasons for this. First, the state is politically conservative. Thus the notion of contributing to an organization associated with the function of law enforcement is a popular one. The sheriffs are a symbol of authority to be respected and admired.

In addition, the idea that FSYF operates without government funding is also particularly appealing to a conservative constituency. As Weaver views his donor constituency: "These people want only to share their responsibilities with other individuals and families. They strongly object to the intrusion of governmental entities into their responsibilities. FSYF cultivated support of the conservative element, by appealing to the voluntary, nongovernmental feature of its operation. As Weaver emphasizes: ". . . Our donor family is . . . pretty much a conservative group of people. . . . By and large it's the person who feels the government has gone too far, that they give too much money away, that they waste money. It's the Proposition 13 people. We tapped [into] them . . . a long time ago. . . . We're extracting from these people funds that make them comfortable in giving to a nongovernmental agency. . . . [We emphasize] sharing, giving, giving of one's self and time, without being forced . . . to do it."

A second relevant feature of Florida is its large and increasing concentration of elderly residents. Weaver himself discounts this factor, but it is clear that the multitude of elderly has provided a lucrative market in which to solicit bequests for FSYF. Such bequests constituted some 27 percent of income in fiscal year 1977. Weaver and his organization have astutely recognized and exploited the fact that many elderly people need help with estate planning. Thus FSYF staff have developed special expertise in this area. FSYF publishes brochures on the subject and Weaver has spent a major proportion of his own time visiting with prospective elderly donors.

A third aspect of Florida that has assisted FSYF is rapidly rising land values. This phenomenon has had two effects. First, it has caused tax problems for older land owners, making the donation of property to FSYF a more attractive proposition. Second, bequests of property have been a source of increasing wealth to FSYF, not only in terms of the value of current assets, but income realized from sale of land and use of land for commercial enterprises such as livestock and timber farming.

The character of Florida's criminal justice and child welfare systems is another contextual factor that influenced the development of FSYF. The early negative association of the sheriffs with the punitive aspects of juvenile justice has already been noted. Part of the difficulty here arose from the dearth of alternatives provided by the State for residential care of children. State training schools (viewed popularly as prisons for kids) were the only formal alternatives for delinquents. State funds for purchases of service from private child care agencies, basically for foster care, were also meager, although many of the 50 or so other voluntary child care agencies in Florida, many of them church-affiliated, did receive such funds.

Thus, in a sense, FSYF stepped into a partial vacuum focusing on older, presumably predelinquent children, more than other agencies, and developing a viable financial means of supporting such a program.

CHOICES

The basic decision to incorporate as a nonprofit organization was made before Weaver's tenure as executive director. Originally such status provided the tax benefits to donors of the land, cash, and other contributions, needed to assemble the campuses and initial cottages. Other alternatives were essentially null. According to Weaver, the public sector was not a viable option in 1957, despite the sheriffs' positions as government officials: ". . . Back then you really had little government funding in this area. It was almost unknown. . . ."

Even after Boys Ranch was established, during the 1957–1961 period when the organization floundered, the public sector option was reconsidered: ". . . When they [the sheriffs] had so much trouble, they thought of all sorts of alternatives. . . . They talked in terms of turning it over [to the state] . . . [but] . . . there were not enough [sheriffs] for it. . . ." It can only be guessed that the sheriffs had insufficient confidence that the state would carry out the envisioned purpose of preventive programming; and indeed they may have been philosophically opposed to seeking government involvement. In any case, many of the sheriffs probably believed there was still a chance that the Boys Ranch could be made viable as a private venture.

According to Weaver, the profit-making sector was also a possible option. But again, this option violated the original intent. Weaver observes: ". . . I could have become a millionaire in profit-making . . . but it would be with a different kind of youngster. It would be for the youngster with parents of means, presidents' of corporations children and this sort of thing. . . . We looked at that [profit-making alternative] very carefully . . . [But with] the kids that we take . . . we don't even discuss finances with a family. . . . First we determine . . . whether the youngster needs to come. Then if we accept it, and the parents can give a dollar a month, we expect them to do that [but only] because that's therapy. . . ."

Within the framework of the nonprofit form, Weaver and the sheriffs made some basic strategic policy decisions which enabled the agency to stabilize and later to prosper. The most fundamental of those decisions was the setting of priorities. It was decided that building the agency's financial base would be the first order of business. Programmatic considerations would take a back seat. As Weaver puts it: ". . . You have to have money before you can do things. You see, that's always the dilemma. . . . This conflict in a human services organization between fiscal people and program people. But you have to recognize that you can have the most beautiful plan in the world, and great ideas, but unless you have the money to put them into effect, they're not worth anything. All you're doing is dreaming."

Given the financial imperative, Weaver's plans were impressive, especially in an era of relative decline in philanthropy. His intent was to build an endowment large enough to insulate the agency from adversity: "We don't want to amass a lot of reserves . . . We don't want to do like Boy's Town . . . but on the other hand, we have to make sure that we are protected in case of an adversity or disaster, or something like that. So we are trying to come up with a formula that will say—with this many children, with this many fixed assets, such as buildings and equipment, and so on . . . the reserve should equal this. And [we would] stay with that formula . . . [and not] over-extend . . . [ourselves]."

Perhaps more impressive than the goal of financial independence is the manner in which the agency chose to raise its funds. Unique advantage was taken of both the affiliation with the sheriffs, the conservative milieu, and the substantial elderly population in Florida, to develop a financing capacity focused totally on private giving. Weaver recalls that latching onto the particular donor groups at the beginning was somewhat ad hoc, perhaps fortuitous, but having done so, the avoidance of government funding became a requirement: ". . . I've always been asked . . . at speaking engagements . . . 'Do you accept state or federal funds?' . . . People like this business of being able to do [things independent of government]. . . . It's bred in them . . . the sheriffs and everybody. . . ."

Asked if racial attitudes have anything to do with avoidance of government funds, Weaver replies, ". . . No, it's deeper than that. It's the being told what to do and how to do it. . . . You know what government funds do. . . . Boy, they get you. As a matter of fact, the racial [factor] has nothing to do with it . . . [although it may have] years ago."

Similarly, FSYF chose to go its own way in fund-raising, independent of organized charities such as United Fund. According to Weaver, "We don't get involved in that. . . . They've wanted us because we would be a good representative in the United Fund . . . a good agency for them to say that they support . . . [but they don't give much money] and . . . first you have to go through a lot of red tape. So it just doesn't pay us."

Having restricted itself to its own private fund raising, FSYF became expert in various techniques, ranging from the collection, utilization and sale of non-cash gifts, to personalized mass solicitation of small donors, organized visits to the ranch, estate planning and solicitation of bequests, setting up memorial funds, cultivation of the large donors by honorary memberships and prominent display of donor names on campus streets and buildings, elaborate coverage of donors in the agency's magazine, and so on.

Significantly, the choice of private giving as the basic avenue of resource development, served to reinforce the basic policy decision to emphasize finances over program as first priority. While the FSYF child care program certainly was more than adequate in terms of activity content and physical amenities, program development played second fiddle. Compared to the planning that went into resource development, program planning was ad hoc. As Weaver describes the program: ". . . We really [do] not have a treatment modality. . . . I like to think of ours as PLT (Practical Living Therapy). We have a little of all of it . . . behavior modification . . . group-guided interaction [etc.]. . . . It's a very practical approach. Had I been able to come up with . . . some definite treatment modality of my own selection and development, I would have been more comfortable . . . but I never did have it clearly in mind. . . ."

Weaver and his staff were, in 1979, first getting around to an organized, systematic evaluation of their child care methodology and program.

Not only was the child care program given a second order of attention, but in many subtle and not so subtle ways it was shaped and influenced by the focus on donors. The physical campuses are a positive manifestation of this. They are kept clean and manicured, and constantly open for visitation and inspection. Just as conspicuously, however, every road and building carries the name of a donor, and a luxurious guest cabin is maintained.

But there are more troublesome influences also. The admissions policy seems very conservative for an agency presumably designed to deflect delinquent behavior. There have been only a few minority group children, forcing one to wonder if donors, some of whom Weaver admits were biased, would be turned off by too many nonwhite faces. And despite Weaver's observation that: "Our youngsters are a little more disturbed than those in most of the other homes. . . . We are geared to the teenager. They're more difficult to work with. . . ." The criteria of admissions, as specified on the intake form require that the youngster ". . . be of average or above intelligence; not have been adjudicated a delinquent; be in good physical health, have no severe personality problems . . . be recommended by the local sheriff." Furthermore, given the size of FSYF's budget, the agency was conservative in the number of children it served. (The agency served under 200 children in a given year.) Weaver says, "We are trying to maintain the right number, for quality. We could care for a lot more kids, but it would be just a mill. . . ."

The intake form also required that a child "agree to receive religious instruction." This stipulation is reflective of the general style of the agency, not only for children but staff as well. Again, it all revolves around the donors. Weaver is quite candid about this: "[Although] we get very little money from churches . . . we . . . have compulsory church times. . . . We . . . require staff who live on campus to attend church. . . . We could not hire anyone with a beard. . . . They'd have to shave it off, you see, because of the people that support [us]. And this has nothing to do with the character of the person, but it's that identification. . . . We can't have extremely long hair. It doesn't have to be as short as mine, but we can never have that. . . . Where you get your money, and how you get it, dictates what you do and how you do things. . . ."

Finally, the whole corporate restructuring from the original Boys Ranch, to the umbrella Youth Fund, was closely related to fund-raising considerations. Essentially, the original incorporation of the Boys Ranch eventually proved too cumbersome and restrictive. This first became clear with the undertaking in 1970 of the Girls Villa, under stimulus of the Sunshine State Women's Chamber of Commerce. At this juncture, it was apparent that broad-based support could be enhanced by service to girls. (Later, programmatic considerations also indicated the need to provide coed care of sibling groups, leading to the Youth Ranch project.) In any case, such constituencies could not be addressed through the restrictive trust of the Boys Ranch, so Weaver and the sheriffs embarked on a deliberate strategy of separate incorporations in order to accommodate these constituencies in the short run, and make a case later, for consolidation and lifting of the restrictions. Weaver describes the circumstances: ". . . People were partial to the Ranch, and there were those who were opposed to starting the Girls Villa [but] . . . we had some real dissension within the donor family as to whether to give to boys or girls. . . . And I sensed that early. Of course, what I wanted . . . at that point [was to] have one legal entity, [but] it [was] complicated by the fact that the Boys Ranch was established under a charitable trust . . . [a] very difficult trust to break.

". . . The Sunshine Women's Chamber of Commerce gave us $70,000 to get [the Girls Villa] started. . . . Then [when] we received [donated] funds we kept everything separate. We had duplication of everything. We wrote separate checks, had separate bank accounts, and the whole bit."

Part of the problem was solved in 1973, with the establishment of (another) separately incorporated Youth Fund. As Weaver notes in his 1978 National Association of Homes for Boys (NAHB) address: ". . . In 1973, we established a third organization (or legal entity) to provide 'an umbrella of support' over the Boys Ranch and Girls Villa . . . The Youth Fund . . . took on the responsibility for all major administrative, accounting, and fund-raising activities of both the Ranch and Villa.

"With three organizations (the Boys Ranch, Girls Villa, and Youth Fund) in operation and a fourth (the Youth Ranch) on the horizon, some type of move toward unification seemed wise. We already had three separate boards of trustees, three executive committees . . . and three separate sets of minutes. . . . We were doing three of everything . . . in spite of the Youth Fund organization that we had established to eliminate duplicated effort. . . .

". . . I had an ulterior motive in all of it. I saw eventually that the Youth Fund would be the umbrella. . . . [So] we [had] three sets of everything . . . cumbersome and bulky, and the circuit judge went right along with [our arguments for consolidation]. . . . [Had] we tried to do that . . . with just the Boys Ranch [he] would not have gone along with it."

RISKS AND CONSTRAINTS

Harry Weaver describes himself as a risk-taker. Indeed, his coming to Boys Ranch in 1961 is evidence of this, as he gave up a secure, well-paying job as a federal probation officer, which promised an early retirement and a good pension, to lead an enterprise which was on the financial ropes. Having come to the Ranch, Weaver continued to take gambles.

For example, during his early days at Boys Ranch, Weaver directly supervised FSYF's child care program, and he believes that perhaps the riskiest decision he has made at FSYF was to move himself out of direct programming involvement and into the fund-raising function: "I had trouble with it for a while. . . . I was very possessive of the kids and the program. I probably thought that nobody else could do it like I could. . . . [But] we had to . . . make a choice. We had to have money. . . . [Nonetheless] I felt uncomfortable because it might have an adverse effect on our income [too] . . . if we had problems, or some crisis."

As noted earlier, another of Weaver's gambles was the gambit of separately incorporating the Villa and the Youth Fund, in the belief that the courts would allow ultimate consolidation with the Ranch. He might have been stuck permanently with the cumbersome multi-corporate structure.

Overall then, FSYF under Weaver undertook a number of significant risks in the short run, in order to build a stable base and hedge in the long run. It has been the basic corporate strategy of FSYF to build an efficient organizational structure, backed by a sufficient financial reserve, to buffer the agency from whatever changes in donor behavior or governmental regulation (e.g., tax exemption policy) may obtain in the future.

From the beginning of Weaver's tenure (1961), corporate decisions had to conform to various institutional constraints. Some of these have already been noted or implied. For example, the restrictive trust under which the Boys Ranch was originally incorporated, required some organizational acrobatics to accommodate and eventually circumvent it. Prior to consolidation, for instance, funds could not be easily moved between the Ranch and the Villa, restricting overall flexibility in program and resource development.

Similarly, in the funding area FSYF had to live with certain restrictions, emanating from three sources—the marketplace, the sheriffs, and the donors.

The marketplace has always been viewed as a source of fiscal discipline by FSYF. At the beginning of Weaver's tenure at FSYF, it was a matter of avoiding bankruptcy ("It takes money to operate . . . you have to pay your staff.") Later on, despite some calculated risks, expenditures at FSYF continued to be rigorously justified.

While on balance, association with the sheriffs has by far been a net asset, this relationship also imposed constraints. For example, care has continually been taken to preserve the wholesome, law abiding image. In the fund-raising area, Weaver explains: ". . . We have to be very careful in gifts to us. We can't let anybody of an underworld nature give to us. . . . We have had to refuse money . . . send some money back. We can't let a known criminal element be seen with one of these [FSYF] bumper stickers on his car."

The greatest source of restriction remained the donor population, however. The overall shaping of FSYF's program and style by the preferences of the donor population has already been discussed. More specifically, despite the consolidation of the Youth Fund, donors were able to designate particular usage for the funds they donate (e.g., building, scholarships, etc.). This, of course tended to reduce the agency's flexibility in expenditures. But FSYF was extremely creative in recognizing, indeed appealing to, the tendency of donors to try to earmark how their dollars are spent. The theme which FSYF adopted—"Something for Everyone"—meant just that. The organization developed elaborate lists of items and programmatic needs that donors could "buy" for the agency, as well as a variety of general purpose memorial and other funds to which they would contribute.

Still the donor influence at FSYF has been profound. For example, FSYF became a fairly expansive agency in terms of multiple campuses and intake services, and ranged far and wide for donors, around the state; but it was restricted to Florida. Weaver says, "There's too much to do here. . . . I think [expanding outside Florida is] going too far. . . . The needs are just so great . . . in the state.' Why do that? . . . There's no reason. . . ."

This seems a curiously modest position for an enterprising, risk-taker of Weaver's caliber. But the reasons may have something to do with the donor base. Going interstate would involve overview, perhaps interference by governments in other states, or perhaps even by the federal government under the guise of interstate commerce. FSYF would also risk losing the "take care of one's own" community flavor of its operation, and its special association with the image of the local sheriffs. Such a situation would be anathema to the conservative element that built FSYF.

OUTCOMES

To the outside observer, FSYF is a hugely successful physical and financial operation. Under Weaver's direction, the agency moved from a $114,000 operating budget in 1960 to a $2.3 million budget in fiscal year 1979—all of it from private sources. Just as impressive, the agency generated a substantial surplus of revenue over current expenditures (e.g., $836,000 in fiscal 1977), permitting it to amass a net worth of more than $12 million in assets. These assets include substantial holdings of real estate and marketable securities, as well as commercially viable timber and livestock operations. The intent was to build a self-sustaining endowment.

Managerially, FSYF is a highly professional business operation. It utilizes modern techniques of data processing, and is meticulous in its accounting and management control, ambitious in its investment program, and streamlined and constantly self-evaluating in its internal organization. Its fund-raising operations were most innovative, meticulous, and diversified. FSYF was highly sophisticated in its approach to estate planning, personalized solicitation of large numbers of small donors, appeal to large donors, and utilization of non-cash contributions.

Based on its affiliation with the sheriffs, and its careful study of the psychology of giving and special attention to its own image, FSYF emerged as a public relations masterpiece. In Florida, the Boys Ranch became practically a household word—representing a good, wholesome, popular, charitable cause. Strategic, professional use of the media—television, films, literature—broadcast this word in an eminently successful way.

The reality of FSYF's child care program was somewhat less clear. No doubt, it had a wholesome program, with marvelous physical facilities and a well-paid staff. But the notion that it was making a serious impact on preventing delinquency is unproven. Although one may argue that prevention requires taking in a youngster before he becomes seriously involved with law-breaking, FSYF's intake policy seemed particularly timid. The emphasis was on the deserving child of unfortunate circumstances, rather than any demonstrated risk of delinquency.

Furthermore, considering the scope of FSYF's financial success, the agency did not extend itself very far in terms of the number of children served. While there was expansion to additional campuses and a conscious widening of orientation from local (Boys Ranch) to statewide, the total population served less then doubled in the 1970s while the operating budget (not counting accumulated surpluses) increased fivefold. Rather the emphasis was on establishing a firm financial base for the future of the agency by building up assets.

ANALYSIS

The chemistry which resulted in the spectacular development of the Florida Sheriffs Youth Fund appears to have had three essential elements: the entrepreneurial talent of Harry Weaver, the special imagery of the sheriffs, and the fertile environment of conservative and elderly donors.

Clearly Weaver was a driving force. Before his tenure the Boys Ranch was headed for failure. Weaver was the master builder and salesman who turned the operation around. He seemed to be motivated largely by the satisfaction of experiencing the fruits of his building efforts, seeing what he could do in constructing, physically and organizationally, a viable enterprise almost from scratch.

But Weaver is not simply a builder by instinct and motivation; he is also a social worker. Possibly as a result of his upbringing, he needed to feel that he was "helping people." Perhaps that is why he was such an effective salesman. When the organization required that he become a fundraiser rather than be directly involved with the children, he transformed this role into one of counselor for the elderly. He convinced himself that he was performing a service for his donors, and exuded the sincerity that came with this resolution. Thus he could not be easily dismissed by potential donors who may have suspected that it was simply their money he and the Youth Fund were after.

The imagery of the sheriffs played a very special role in the evolution of FSYF. The sheriffs "law and order, helping" image certainly assisted the agency to develop the required philanthropic base of support and make the ranch a public relations man's dream.

The social environment of a conservative, elderly population of potential contributors in Florida was the third element of FSYF's success. Surely, the Florida of the 1960s and 1970s was one of the more fertile fields in which to solicit such a group. But this is probably more a matter of degree than kind. Other states have similar populations, perhaps in smaller numbers. Essentially, it was the genius of Weaver and his staff, in organizational design and public relations, that enabled the tapping of this resource in such a spectacular way.

Given the essential chemistry, the "flashpoint" was the decision in the early 1960s to put financial development as the agency's first priority. This decision influenced not only the corporate, financial success but profoundly shaped the style and program of the agency itself. The donor reigned supreme at FSYF, his influence seen and felt in the physical facilities, administrative operations, staffing, programming, and intake policies. Weaver claims that by giving primacy to the agency's sources of support, FSYF put the horse before the cart—establishing a firm organizational base to facilitate carrying out the agency's mission. The reverse may also be argued. Over time, the approach may become more balanced. According to Weaver, ". . . I believe that we have a good program. . . . Of course, it is not what we want it to be one day, but we each day work towards excellence in these areas.

"I like to think that we put equal emphasis on our children's programs and our public relations and fund-raising. I am convinced that we cannot survive without placing equal emphasis in these areas."

Greer-Woodycrest Children's Services

PRÉCIS

In 1961 the Greer Children's Agency was in deep trouble. It was running a large operating deficit; its physical facilities were in disrepair; its staff was aging, overworked, underpaid and underqualified; and the agency was under attack by the State for shoddy care. In that year Dr. Ian Morrison, a former college dean and businessman, was engaged as executive director. Over the next seven years, under Morrison's leadership, Greer's books were balanced, its physical facilities rebuilt, its budget tripled, its endowment and asset values increased severalfold, its services reoriented toward minority group children from New York City, and its performance commended by the State. Greer has since continued to expand under Morrison's guidance into a multicampus, $10 million operation, having absorbed (merged with) two other child care agencies, in 1971 and 1977, and has been acclaimed as the largest nonsectarian not-for-profit residential child care program in the United States. This case study focuses largely on the turnaround of Greer in 1961 and immediately thereafter.

THE ENTREPRENEUR

Ian Morrison came into leadership of Greer almost by happenstance and without a full appreciation of how bad things were. The agency was in great difficulty in 1961, although it still had $2 million in assets, and a well-to-do board of directors, to fall back on. Nonetheless, there is no doubt that the revival and subsequent thriving of Greer is largely a product of Ian Morrison's leadership and enterprising behavior.

Ian Morrison has had a varied career in higher education, private business, and child care. From 1948 to 1956 he served as Dean of Men and Dean of Students of Wagner College.

Morrison was reasonably happy with his career in higher education; but he grew restless at Wagner largely because the salary scale was so low and he saw opportunities for advancement and greater remuneration elsewhere: ". . . The hardest decision in the world was . . . to leave the college faculty. . . . I was 32, I had a child, I was trying to finish a doctorate, I had run out of money, and I went into an area that I knew nothing about

. . . in [to] a highly competitive world . . . a very large company . . . that manufactures institutional furniture. . . ."

Although Morrison's tenure in business lasted only two years, it was, by measurable standards, successful. He formed a college and school division for the company, and took division sales from $100,000 to $5,000,000 per year. Nonetheless, he seized the first respectable opportunity to get out.

In 1957, Morrison had some choices to make—alternative offers: to return to Wagner as a Vice President or to join Greer as executive secretary for fund-raising and public relations. He took the Greer job to expand his skills and give him a chance to finish his doctoral studies.

Morrison's four-year tenure as executive secretary for Greer was a preamble for his subsequent success as executive director. In particular, he substantially increased contributions to the agency (50% by his account) and succeeded in bringing favorable media coverage to Greer. By 1961, Morrison had become the prime candidate to fill the top administrative post when the current director left to become president of a small college.

THE ORGANIZATION[1]

The Greer School, originally called Hope Farm, was established in 1906 by the Bishop David Hummel Greer, as an institution to care for Protestant children from broken homes. The school was located on property in Dutchess County, New York, which is still called Hope Farm. From its beginnings, board members and contributors to Greer represented a cross-section of New York "society." Revenues were obtained through a combination of charitable contributions, marketable services (it actually was a farm), and fees paid by families of the children it served.

The agency thrived as a boarding school, with its commercial, farm-related enterprise, through the 1920s. But the depression of the 1930s, and the war decade of the 1940s took their toll. According to Morrison: "The years [after 1932] . . . were difficult for Greer . . . since it was almost entirely dependent upon contributions of donors to maintain its budget, and at the onset of the Depression donations rapidly dropped so that in two years contributed income had decreased by almost 30% from what it had been in 1930. A loyal staff accepted salary cut after salary cut with little grumbling since they knew that in some respects their lot was better than much of the general population. Greer was still to some extent independent because it raised a great deal of its own food and all the staff lived in shelter provided by the institution. All accounts indicate that despite the pressures, the care of children continued with undiminished quality, although maintenance of facilities was postponed time and again.

---

[1]The early history of Greer is based on a draft by Ian A. Morrison, dated September, 1974.

"At a time when the board of directors felt that the Depression was over, and the institution could catch up with delayed maintenance, World War II began and the resulting shortage of supplies and skilled manpower delayed the proper maintenance of the facilities even longer. . . . The end of the war did not diminish the problems. Dislocations caused by wartime increased the numbers of children seeking care, and Greer was hard put to provide space for those that needed it since many of its facilities were suffering from overuse and undercare."

Through the 1950s, the management of Greer was never really able to grapple with the problems of rebuilding. Not only were the physical facilities deteriorated, but staff long affiliated with Greer were aging, poorly paid and undertrained, donations were falling off, and the farm operation was becoming uneconomical. In 1952, the State Board of Social Welfare issued a report highly critical of Greer's operations, citing among other things a lack of professional staffing to deal with emotional problems of children.

In 1961, Greer was still a single-campus facility at Hope Farm (plus a New York City office) although substantial acreage had been accumulated at the farm site since the beginning (from less than 400 acres and a few buildings in 1906 to 1500 acres and 45 buildings in 1961). Greer served approximately 160 children in 1961, not much more than the 130 children in its first year of operation, and comparable to its capacity of 175 in 1910. Similarly, the population of children was still basically white Protestant boys and girls aged 5 to 16: only 20 of the 160 children were charges of the (New York City) Department of Public Welfare. Overall, 56% of Greer's children came from New York City, the rest from Connecticut, New Jersey, and upstate New York.

The revenue structure in 1961 is also revealing of Greer's constituencies. Only 13% of total revenue was derived from private payments for children, indicating a continued use of tuition (on a sliding scale) and very substantial service to indigent children. The bulk of revenues was derived from individual contributions and foundation gifts (42%) and from investments (14%).

The financial picture in 1961 was clearly a troubled one. Morrison recalls, "We had 160 kids with an average payment of $30 a month . . . and the board was writing off each year about $150,000 rather than harass anybody for it." Indeed, operating deficits had been consistently experienced over the previous decade with recent shortfalls on the order of 25%.

Nonetheless, the picture was not completely bleak. Specifically, ". . . in the years since 1957, more money was added to the endowment fund by means of bequests than was withdrawn to cover operating losses. In addition, the inflated investment market increased the market value of Greer's securities by several hundred thousand dollars. . . . In terms of total annual income for all purposes Greer, in recent years, has obtained more money than it has spent" (Morrison, 1962).

Despite appreciation of the endowment fund, the financial problems were serious. Apart from possible lack of fungibility of endowment monies, the operating deficits were greater than they appeared to be on the surface. Morrison recalls, "We had a new state minimum wage law . . . we had new regulations by the State Department of Social Services. . . . In contrast we had house parents who were working seventy hours a week . . . married to a teacher working a teacher's week and then covering on the weekends for the spouse. There were people who had one day off a month, no professional staff, not a psychiatrist or psychologist to be seen. No counsellors, poor bedding, dirty houses, difficulty in buying equipment and supplies." In sum, staff salaries, working conditions, and capabilities needed upgrading, and facilities required rehabilitation and proper maintenance. Morrison concluded at the time that ". . . if Greer is to do nothing more than it is presently doing in the way of program philosophy, then sixty to seventy thousand dollars more a year is needed in order to implement correctly that philosophy. Such a sum is necessary to attract and keep competent teachers, to add the minimum counseling services deemed necessary, and to compete for houseparents. Another $120,000 is needed in a three-year period merely to correct serious deficiencies in the existing physical plant in order that henceforth plant maintenance can be maintained on a suitable level" (Morrison, 1962).

From its beginnings in 1906 until 1960, Greer had also changed little in its philosophy, governing board, and management structure. The board still reflected an economic and social elite of New York society, the school was still considered a refuge for (white) Protestant children, it remained oriented to education rather than social service, and operations were still based on a single campus under direct supervision of the chief executive officer. Much was to change in the next two decades. A reorientation towards the public foster care system of New York City shifted the agency heavily in the direction of minority group children and clinical and rehabilitative services. This shift did not sit comfortably with some long-standing board members but caused only minor change at this level. Morrison recollects: "[There was] a tremendous board loyalty. . . . The core of the board, probably over a third of the board, had been together for a long time. It was inconceivable to them that it [Greer] would close. . . . Most . . . were anxious to keep up with modern times and do what was necessary. Some of them would say, 'I don't like what you're doing, but I know why you have to do it.' . . . [One board member] . . . was a widow of an extremely prominent industrialist. . . . She said, 'I'm getting off . . . I know what you're doing and I agree you have to do it, but I don't have to be part of it.' And then she gave me a hundred thousand dollars! Her [late] husband had been president of the board for years. . . ."

Once Morrison took over the reins and the renewal program began, the agency's structure changed substantially. Greer grew to a million dollar operation in 1968, and a ten million dollar operation in 1978, with a shift to over 80% dependence on public welfare payments for operations. The number of children served has increased to more than 600 (1977). As a result of two mergers, the agency operates three major campuses as well as a differentiated program that includes foster homes, group homes, adoption services, and institutional care. Board representation has been broadened to reflect the constituencies of the agencies with which Greer has merged, although it is still a board which commands significant economic resources. Administratively, authority has been delegated to resident directors of the major campuses, leaving the executive director the freedom to deal with larger policy issues. As Morrison describes the changes, ". . . There was really no relationship between the program in 1961 and the program in 1968. In 1961 . . . [we were] serving direct parental placement children on a sliding scale which usually meant $20 to $30 a month . . . half of them teenagers in high school, there for no other reason [than] that they were from a broken home. There were no clinical services, no social workers . . . houseparents and teachers were often comingled, and it was really a very cheap, not too well-run prep school for poor children who happened to come from single parent families By 1968, it was serving children referred by public authorities from three states, children who had not only . . . sociological problems . . . but personal or emotional problems . . . that called for clinical services, counseling, case management, that kind of thing.

"By '72 or '73 it had changed even more. . . . [We] were moving . . . to provide a cafeteria of programs. . . . We had . . . a family service in New York (City). . . . We had moved into group homes for children who could make it in the community. We had . . . an agency operated boarding home (program). . . . We were about to move into foster [family] care and . . . into adoption services. . . . In . . . '71 we merged with another agency and expanded our program. And in '77 we merged again and that caused a major expansion of programs and somewhere in between we changed the management structure. . . ."

CHRONOLOGY OF EVENTS

As previously indicated, the changes in Greer in the early 1960s were rooted in problems that accumulated over the previous three decades. Yet, in 1961, events began to move rapidly. The following is an outline of key events and developments.

1952—The New York State Board of Social Welfare issues a report highly critical of Greer's operations.

1957—Ian Morrison becomes executive secretary of Greer, for fund-raising and public relations. (Significantly, Morrison operates out of Greer's New York City office and remains substantially unaware of the conditions on the main campus at Hope Farm.)

1961—Morrison becomes executive director of Greer, combining the positions of director and executive secretary. He immediately insists on a total reassessment of Greer's status and future options. In September, 1961, Morrison and his staff begin "an exploratory investigation to determine strengths and weaknesses in the program, to relate the findings to the board with possible alternatives if it was determined that the Greer program should be changed." The board itself organizes a Committee on Future Operations chaired by retired Army General and board member, Paul E. Peabody.

1961—The State Board of Social Welfare is due to make another evaluative report. In view of the change in leadership, Morrison succeeds in getting the State to postpone its survey.

April, 1962—Morrison submits his report to the board, assessing the status of Greer's program, facilities, financing, staffing, and operating philosophy. Five basic strategic options are presented for the future of Greer (see below), one of which is Morrison's preferred alternative.

July–October, 1962—The Peabody committee submits its assessments of Morrison's recommendations, generally endorsing the director's preferences.

Fall, 1962–1968—A major rebuilding and restaffing program is undertaken. Services are fundamentally reoriented towards New York City public welfare foster children.

Summer, 1966—The oft-postponed Board of Social Welfare report commends Greer for modernizing its program of child care services.

CONTEXT

To a substantial extent, the changes at Greer in the early 1960s were responses to change in the outside world as much as responses to internal problems. External changes in the economy, in the field of social welfare, in governmental support of social services, and in the demography of children requiring care were all important. These changes were acutely observed by Morrison and his staff, in his report to the board in 1962.

One development was the inclusion of nonprofit organizations under the minimum wage law in New York in 1960, under which "Greer houseparents for the first time obtained a wage of $1.00 an hour and a realistic work-week." (Morrison, 1962). More generally, changes in the labor market applied pressures to agencies like Greer: "With increased unionization of labor and a strong economy, the problem of acquiring suitable houseparents is one we share with most other institutions. . . . The type of people once generally available now enjoy skills learned in high school and union education programs. Social security, unemployment insurance, and other mandated benefits have reduced the urgency of finding employment and persons formerly available need not seek employment in this particular market." Similar remarks apply for teachers in the Greer school. Better opportunities elsewhere made it difficult for Greer to attract and hold competent personnel.

Labor market conditions were one source of economic pressure, but the changing standards of governmental regulation were another. In the 1960s, the New York State Board of Social Welfare (BSW) developed a set of "Rules and Recommendations" for child care institutions which emphasized physical standards which Greer's facilities could not have met. Furthermore, the BSW was beginning to emphasize staffing for social services, such as a suggested standard of one caseworker per 25 children.

But even more fundamental changes were taking place in the child care arena that would affect the future viability of Greer and its decisions regarding program and clientele. Institutional care was no longer viewed as desirable for most children requiring out-of-home placement. Morrison clearly recognized this in his 1962 report to his board: ". . . As more insight developed into the needs of children in distress, the entire concept of child care changed. . . . Wherever possible orphan children are placed for adoption and dependent and neglected children are placed in foster homes where more individual attention can be provided in a fairly normal family setting. . . . As a result . . . large numbers of dependent and neglected children are being cared for without the high annual costs incurred by institutional children and without the tremendous capital investment. . . . With such an avenue open . . . it is no wonder that the type of children once placed in an institution . . . are [now] sent to foster homes."

Morrison goes on to note that if Greer wants to continue to run an institutional program it will have to respond to the changing pattern of need, and to reorient itself to a different clientele: "There are, of course, many children for whom it is difficult to find such foster homes, and they are the ones that all public and private agencies attempt to place in institutions. The Negro, the Puerto Rican, the physically and mentally handicapped, the troublesome, the predelinquent, the emotionally disturbed, the dull—they are difficult to place."

The in-migration of nonwhite minorities into New York City and other urban centers during the fifties and early sixties was of course of great magnitude, and concomitant social problems caused demands for care of children in these groups to run high. Correspondingly, government began to put more money into foster care programs and in a way that provided incentives for Greer. As reviewed in Morrison's [1962] report: ". . . New York City, within the past year, established a reimbursement formula to pay child-care institutions 100% of the cost of care of children referred by the City. The formula is established in such a way that those institutions which accept the largest number of New York City children and which provide the necessary social services obtain the largest per capita reimbursement.

"It has been impossible for Greer (under its present policies) to benefit much from this reimbursement formula. In 1961 our per capita cost of care was $7.50. New York City paid $6.14 on reimbursement. To increase our services to obtain higher reimbursement was impossible since only 20 of our 160 children were New York City Department of Public Welfare charges. With 140 children for whom *we* had to find the major support, any move to comply with welfare requirements would merely send us further into debt."

CHOICES

The choices that were made by Morrison and his board in the 1961–1962 period can be roughly separated into three parts: (1) the decision of Morrison to undertake the rebuilding once he realized the condition of Greer; (2) selection among strategic options for Greer's future; and (3) selection of options for financing and organizing the preferred strategy.

It seems ludicrous to consider that having been executive secretary for four years and then accepting the directorship in 1961 that Morrison was not fully aware of Greer's condition when he took the helm. But in fact, Morrison worked out of the New York City office, and solely on fundraising and public relations, and was not intimately familiar with the problems at the campus. He was knowledgeable about Greer's finances (which, as previously discussed, were troubling but not apparently hopeless), but not its cost structure or program and facility requirements. Furthermore, Morrison was not a child welfare professional and not close to current thinking in the field of institutional care. He was hired for his management skills and the finance-related accomplishments of his tenure as secretary.

Finally, as it turned out, members of the board of directors—who hired Morrison upon notification of the previous director's resignation—were themselves somewhat in the dark about Greer's true state of affairs. So it is not absurd to consider that upon becoming familiar with Greer's real condition, Morrison might have felt surprised and betrayed and might consider abandoning the enterprise. It would have been completely uncharacteristic of him to carry on "business as usual" without trying to repair the damage, but he did consider quitting early in 1961. It was only at the beckoning of the board president and a commitment to ". . . back you a hundred percent . . . whatever you want to do" that convinced Morrison to stay on.

Morrision took some six months to prepare his report. In it, five major wide-ranging strategic options were identified for Greer's future:

(1) Remove Greer from the social welfare field and become a private educational institution. This option would require giving up charitable contributions and social welfare payments, raising tuitions, and reorienting the program to students whose families could pay. According to Morrison's report: ". . . We are confident that, utilizing current plant and endowment, a private educational institution could be self-supporting within four years."

(2) Meet another type of current social need other than that of dependent and neglected children, e.g., "exceptional" children such as the mentally handicapped. By Morrison's reckoning: "A program fulfilling this purpose would be expensive, but in light of current practices such programs more than pay for themselves and have considerable public appeal."

(3) Develop a "closed" school for unmarried teenage mothers and girls who have exhibited sexual promiscuity. Judges of the New York Children's Court were cited by Morrison as solicitors of such a facility.

(4) Create a foundation to help children, from the Greer endowment and proceeds from selling the physical plant. It was estimated that this "might net . . . in slight excess of $100,000 per annum" for foundation grants.

All of these options were considered feasible by Morrison, but his preferred alternative (No. 5) and recommendation to his board, consisted of an eleven-point plan to enable Greer to effectively fulfill its original chartered purpose of service to unfortunate children from broken homes in the New York City area. The eleven-point plan involved consolidation of Greer's school program and use of the community high school, increased admissions of public welfare children, strengthening of social service staff, development of group homes, experimentation with new programs including one for preschool children, new construction of children and staff facilities, sale of some of Greer's real estate, and lowering of the age bracket of the Greer population (Morrison, 1962).

With little exception (sale of the land being one), the board's Committee on Future Operations accepted the thrust of Morrison's proposal and elaborated on the details. Five years was considered to be a reasonable transition period over which the changes could be implemented. The next problem was financing, especially for construction and physical improvements. Mass fund-raising was considered, but found to be a marginal proposition compared to soliciting a few wealthy donors or foundations: "Greer has never been able to afford the initial high cost of obtaining new donors [through mailings] . . . particularly since the program is of a social welfare nature with a limited hinterland of service. The process of gaining new donations from the general public . . . is for Greer a slow, selective, limited process.

"On the other hand, the support to be obtained from interested wealthy individuals depends to a great extent upon the number of such persons the board of directors can involve in the program.

". . . Foundation support when given for social welfare purposes, is given for bricks and mortar or experimental short-term programs" [Morrison, 1962].

Greer managed to successfully solicit wealthy donors and foundations. Morrison amusingly writes about how some of this happened: "In 1962, a recently elected board member [Mr. Dyson] . . . and the executive director lunched in New York to discuss the possibility of . . . a sizeable gift. The executive director explained that he visualized a number of new cottages . . . and that a suitable, low maintenance, comfortable cottage for twelve children could be built for about seventy thousand dollars. After this discussion, Mr. Dyson said, "I'll give you the money for one such cottage if you can get the other board members to provide the money for four more. Then you ought to be able to find funds for another five.

"When the board convened . . . the proposition was made. . . . Several minutes of silence prevailed. . . . As the meeting progressed, a note was passed on to the executive director; it read, 'I will give a cottage.' A short while later, another note: 'I can give half a cottage.' Another two notes: 'I'll give a quarter of a cottage.' . . . [Ultimately] . . . three cottages had been promised and within a week the money for five cottages was available from individual board members! Within a month a foundation, upon hearing of this participation by a volunteer board, granted Greer's request for funds for three cottages, and within three more months other board members had provided funds for the remaining two cottages" (Morrison, 1974).

In considering the global choices that were made for Greer's resurrection, it is interesting to note that changes in the corporate status, from nonprofit to something else, e.g., to a profit-making corporation or to takeover by government, were never considered, perhaps for the same reason that alternative No. 4 (to sell the assets and convert to a foundation) was rejected. In its report of October 1, 1962, the Peabody Committee states: "The Committee feels that this is a last ditch stand and as Mehitabel was prone to remark, 'There's life in the old girl yet.'" A loyalty of purpose and long-time association seemed to persist among members of the board.

RISKS AND CONSTRAINTS

In 1961, when Morrison took office, events were closing in on Greer. Operating deficits were continuing to mount, and endowment funds could not be expected to bail out operations indefinitely. Child care practices were behind the times, staff was aging, facilities were inadequate, and the Board of Social Welfare was due to make another report in the near future, whose results could be devastating. In the long run, these programmatic and economic failings could lead to the agency's collapse, and certainly to a smeared reputation in the interim.

Greer was Ian Morrison's first major opportunity for executive leadership. As such it was essential to him that such a tenure be viewed as a success. Thus, when the full dimension of Greer's difficulties became apparent, it was important for Morrison to move quickly—either extricate himself from a hopeless situation or mobilize the support to turn that situation around. No caretaker regime (waiting for the axe to fall) would do. This is why Morrison, immediately upon assuming leadership and realizing the situation, insisted on the board's full backing to make changes. Although it would have been a "second best" alternative, Morrison would have resigned had he not received that support.

Any sort of major change faced institutional constraints, of course. The board of directors had many long-time members who were reluctant to allow radical departures from the agency's original intent. In addition, changes would require new financial resources. Perhaps surprisingly, however, these factors seem less constraining than that of reconstituting Greer's staff. Morrison reflects: "The staff is a difficult barrier. . . . Unless one has a board willing to go along with you, it could be cold-blooded. . . , just fire everybody . . . over a period of time . . . people who gave a number of years to an organization. . . . If those people have even given five years, let alone ten years and they're 63 or 64 or even 60, it's very hard for you to be the one to throw them out, when they were really not at fault. . . . Somebody was at fault for hiring them and letting them believe that they could stay there forever. . . ."

Once the options for Greer were spelled out in Morrison's 1962 report, two main factors seem to have influenced the choice. In the first place, the accepted course of action was essentially Morrison's preference, and the board promised to back him. Secondly, although the recommended course represented major change, it also was closest in spirit to Greer's chartered purpose. The latter was apparently very important to the board, which would have resisted a more radical shift. As noted earlier, for example, closing Greer and converting it to a foundation was anathema. The Peabody Committee's reasoning for backing Morrison's preference was similar: "The committee, for financial reasons and because it would substantially change the original concept of Greer, recommends that we do not accept the physically and mentally handicapped children nor the troublesome, pre-delinquent, dull, nor teenaged unmarried mothers. The committee is [also] not in favor of leaving the welfare field and becoming a private educational institution."

OUTCOMES

The post-1961 changes in Greer and for Ian Morrison were impressive. Both went from relative obscurity to national recognition. Morrison grew from a struggling, ambitious, would-be executive looking for an opportunity to prove himself, to an accomplished chief executive of one of the largest and best-managed child care agencies in the country. Greer itself was transformed from a relatively small, static, run-down, deteriorating, residential school into a thriving, dynamic, multi-campus, multi-program child care agency.

While statistically Greer was most changed by the mergers of 1971 and 1977, the basic turnaround occurred in the years 1962 to 1968. In this period, the campus was rebuilt, the admissions policies were redirected, the staff overhauled, the operating deficits eliminated, and modern management procedures instituted. By 1968, Greer could be described as a well-run, though still fairly modestly sized agency, with a quality child care program. Perhaps most significantly, the quality of its management was beginning to be recognized, and Greer became a candidate for other struggling agencies to approach with offers of consolidation.

ANALYSIS

It was inevitable that change would ultimately come to Greer. The processes of organizational deterioration, economic and social trends, and the intervention of government would eventually catch up with the agency. But change was not inevitable in 1961 nor was the precise nature of Greer's redevelopment an obvious outgrowth of structural, environmental, and internal forces. Under alternative leadership, Greer might have scraped by for several years in the old mode, and when the inevitable crisis came, might have gone under or been shored up or redirected in some other, less impressive way (as happened to a number of other such agencies in similar circumstances).

Having, under Morrison's direction, "grabbed the bull by the horns," however, Greer's choices reflected both an opportunistic response to environmental trends, and a sentimental attachment to tradition. To an extent, Morrison may have read the conservative bent of his board well in advance, when he set up, almost as "straw men," four alternative strategies that would have taken Greer farther afield from its chartered purposes. Although he himself had no sentimental attachment to Greer's history, he knew that many of his board members did. Thus in proposing alternatives to the historical direction, he made his own preferred recommendations seem less drastic.

Morrison's own preferences were not sentimental, but more a realistic response to changes in the social welfare field and the economic environment. The needs to place minority group, welfare-dependent children, especially Protestant children for whom no strong sectarian agency system existed, were building rapidly, and so was government's willingness to pay for that care. By moving in this direction, Morrison could retain, indeed exploit, the support of his current board, while maneuvering into position to secure public funds. This strategy could extricate Greer from its current doldrums and establish a solid operating base for the future.

This set of developments allowed Morrison to fulfill a number of personal objectives that had troubled him in the past. A solid record of performance at the Greer helm would allow him to achieve the material well-being he had sought, but in a field that was honorable in its objectives and mores. More than this, however, Morrison sought to excel—to prove himself as a management executive and to gain recognition for his accomplishments. His preferred course for Greer was among the best from this viewpoint. It put Greer on the ground floor of a dynamic and expanding field, compared to the more limited-scope alternatives—such as a foundation, a private educational institution, or a closed school for unmarried mothers. Nor was the preferred alternative completely foreign to Greer's previous experience, as service to the mentally handicapped would have been. Morrison had in mind not only to put Greer back on its feet but to reconstruct it as a staging area for future accomplishment.

REFERENCES

Morrison, I.A. (1962). *A report to the board of directors of Greer, A children's community.*
Morrison, I.A. (1974). *History of Greer.* Unpublished.
Peabody, P.E. (1962). *Memorandum of the Greer Committee on future operations, July through October, 1962.*

Pleasantville Diagnostic Center
(Jewish Child Care Association)

PRÉCIS

The Pleasantville Diagnostic Center is a unit of the Jewish Child Care Association (JCCA), one of the largest voluntary child care agencies serving foster children in New York City. The diagnostic center operates as a short-term residential facility for boys referred by the New York City Family Court or Bureau of Child Welfare and judged to be "hard to place." The center provides intensive diagnostic evaluations for the purpose of developing appropriate child care plans, including possible long-term placement and treatment.

The Pleasantville Diagnostic Center was established in 1973, as the culmination of an initiative by Jacob Trobe, chief executive of JCCA, and Paul Steinfeld, director of JCCA's Pleasantville Cottage School, in cooperation with the staff of New York City's Office of Special Services for Children under Assistant Commissioner Barbara Blum.

THE ENTREPRENEURS

The Pleasantville Diagnostic Center resulted from the combined efforts of a few key individuals. Jacob Trobe, Executive Vice President of JCCA and an avowed social entrepreneur, seized an opportunity to respond to the articulated needs of the City and to implicit criticisms of his own agency, by stimulating, encouraging, and negotiating the project. Paul Steinfeld, a career social worker administrator and director of JCCA's Pleasantville Cottage School on whose campus the diagnostic facility would be housed, developed the proposal, and carried it through to implementation. In the public sector, Barbara Blum, Assistant Commissioner for New York City's Office of Special Services for Children (in the Department of Social Services), helped create the environment in which the proposal arose by articulating the city's need for diagnostic services and by responding expediently to the JCCA initiative; her Associate Deputy Commissioner, Henry Rosner, is credited with the specific ideas for helping to finance the proposal with Medicaid funds.

Seen from outside of JCCA, the Pleasantville project is one of a good number of entrepreneurial ventures undertaken by JCCA under the stewardship of Jacob Trobe. Mr. Trobe is a charming, energetic, stubborn yet compassionate, fast-moving and fast-talking man who is proud of his characterization as an entrepreneur: ". . . I've always been a social worker who thinks entrepreneurship . . . [is] a very honorable thing . . . but, you know, social workers . . . very often think [negatively] of every term that isn't part of our jargon; they're concerned [about] the word [entrepreneurship]. . . . I don't feel that way at all. . . . If I'm . . . proud of anything, I'm proud of my entrepreneurship. . . ."

What Trobe means is creative, enterprising, risk-taking behavior—garnering resources and developing new programs and organizational arrangements, negotiating with government, and working with other outside agencies. Indeed, Trobe says, "Hell, I could be doing the same thing for Esso International. . . ." He sees his whole career in child welfare as evolving in this mode, having moved quickly into administrative positions in Jewish child care agencies following his completion of graduate school in 1937 and early field placements in the Jewish Board of Guardians and the Jewish Family Service.

Jake Trobe appears to derive great satisfaction directly from the rough and tumble of the action arena, the organizing of people and resources and pursuit of new ideas, the process of problem solving in "a constantly moving and changing situation." This kind of involvement excites him and keeps his juices flowing. But aside from the basic enjoyment of participation, Trobe reflects a sense of personal responsibility: "This city and this nation have served the Jews well, and we owe it to give something back."

Paul Steinfeld was trained in social work and has devoted the bulk of his career to child welfare. Having received his MSW from Columbia in 1947, Steinfeld served as a social worker and caseworker for two different agencies prior to joining JCCA in 1952. Like Trobe, Steinfeld has had a long career at JCCA rising from caseworker to supervisor to resident director of the Pleasantville Cottage School Division and more recently (1974) to Associate Executive Director of the agency. If Trobe is the lifelong entrepreneur, wheeling and dealing at the top, Steinfeld is the career administrator, rising steadily as manager to positions of more and more scope and responsibility.

Together the combination of "Mister Outside" (Trobe) and "Mister Inside" (Steinfeld) succeeded in conceiving and implementing the Pleasantville Diagnostic Center in relatively short order. Memories of the two men, in terms of who conceived the idea in the first place, seem to differ. Trobe describes the diagnostic center as his own notion (a Mayo clinic for child welfare), for which he recruited Steinfeld to carry the ball, as he had done for other programs at Pleasantville. Steinfeld remembers suggesting the diagnostic center idea to Trobe after the latter passed through to him a memo on program needs offered by the City. The actual sequence is probably of little consequence. The fact that both men claim credit attests simply to the pride each takes in the venture, and the strong motivations each brought to it. Once the idea had surfaced, both agreed on the division of labor. Trobe was the agent of negotiation with the outside world, namely city government, while Steinfeld put the pieces into place on his campus at Pleasantville.

THE ORGANIZATION

The Jewish Child Care Association is one of the largest and most diversified Jewish foster care agencies in the U.S., and one of the biggest of all the eighty-odd voluntary child care agencies serving New York City in the 1970s. JCCA represents the consolidation of some eighteen Jewish child care agencies, some dating back to the mid- and early nineteenth century, which have merged together since 1940.

In fiscal year 1973, the year in which the Pleasantville Diagnostic Center was conceived, JCCA had a total operating budget of some $9.7 million of which $7.9 million consisted of revenues from government (per diem payments for foster care). The remainder was financed by contributions of the Federation of Jewish Philanthropies (almost $600,000); the Greater New York Fund; some direct fees ($150,000); and various contributions, endowment income, and drawing down of reserves ($890,000)

In fiscal 1973, JCCA served some 2,000 children, 1,600 of these in its six residential divisions. In addition to the latter, JCCA also administered four-day treatment programs and a scholarship program. In such a large, multi-campus organization, it is necessary to decentralize and to delegate authority. Indeed, the 1973 annual report lists some thirty directors and assistant directors of various divisions and programs. Nonetheless, as chief executive, Mr. Trobe maintained a level of effective central control partly through wise selection of loyal deputies and by inculcating them with his own enthusiasm. He claims to be satisfied with nothing less than excellence and is impatient with those that "just want to sit and live on the past." His technique was to challenge and enthuse his lieutenants, describing JCCA as a flagship agency that should lead others. Those under him (like Steinfeld) who rose to the challenge and showed talent would be rewarded.

There were also more mundane means of control. Steinfeld elaborates: "Almost all (official) correspondence [to JCCA] comes to the Executive Vice-President [Trobe]. . . . [Furthermore], there are certain central controls. . . . For example, no division can hire people [by itself]. . . . Central control of personnel is very important. Where there *is* a degree of autonomy it is [with] the administrator who has the responsibility, ultimately, for the care of the youngsters. [He or she] does have the last word [as to] whether she can serve a particular youngster."

The budget is a negotiated business between the divisions and central office. For example, according to Steinfeld, ". . . If you [think] you . . . can't staff the cottages any more with four people, [say you need] five people, well then you'd have to make a case. [You'd] have to convince [the Assistant Executive Director], the personnel director . . . [but] it could be done. . . . Part of the responsibility centrally . . . is to be sufficiently aware of what's going on and how programs operate so that [one] can make some judgement and exercise some discretion . . . [or suggest] another possible way to do it. . . . So, you know, it's hard to say precisely that we are highly centralized or that we are decentralized; there are mixtures of both, I would say. . . ."

The board of trustees of JCCA is very large, consisting of some 52 regular members, plus 19 honorary trustees, and nine additional "members of the corporation." It is a diverse group, reflecting strains of the various Jewish agencies that have merged into JCCA in the past as well as more recent appointments. Attorneys, businessmen, and those with specific child care interests are represented, as well as generous donors.

The financial relationship of JCCA to the Federation of Jewish Philanthropies has already been noted. Another tie of JCCA to other Jewish social agencies was through the Joint Planning Service (JPS). JPS, a semi-autonomous unit, served as a central intake division for both JCCA and a sister child care agency, the Jewish Board of Guardians (JBG). As a matter of procedure, JPS would receive (from various sources) children in need of services, and refer them into the various JCCA and JBG divisions. The proposed diagnostic center at Pleasantville, however, would supercede this function for a specialized population of children. A similar facility called Geller House, already operated within JBG. (After 1979, JPS was later disbanded and each agency handled all of its own referrals directly.)

The Pleasantville Cottage School is one division of JCCA and the site of the new diagnostic facility. Paul Steinfeld, director of Pleasantville in 1973, would eventually oversee both the school and the diagnostic center as separate units. The school (a residential treatment center) dates back more than 60 years, serving some three hundred emotionally disturbed children of normal intelligence in 1973. (One time residential capacity is 140 boys and 40 girls, living in cottages of 12–16 children.) The campus itself is 150 acres and is also the site of a day treatment program for 35 seriously handicapped children, and a day care center for 30 preschoolers.

Steinfeld describes the relationship of the school to the new diagnostic center: "They are on the same campus . . . [but] segregated from the other programs. . . . [The children] may see one another in passing . . . but they have their own staff and their own programs. . . . It happened that the administrator, when [the diagnostic center] began, was just part-time in that program and part-time in the regular [school] program, but all of the child care staff and all of the clinical staff were hired just for that program. . . . We [also] set up a [separate] advisory board [for the center] which represented the consumer groups like the court and Department of Social Services. . . ."

One fact worth noting is that, roughly at the time the diagnostic center opened, JCCA decided to undertake a major rebuilding and modernization program, including a $6 million building fund drive. Renovation of the Pleasantville campus was one target of this program. According to the Fall 1973 *JCCA Journal*: "Although well constructed when the [Pleasantville] School was opened in 1912, the 15 cottages now require extensive renovation, from the repatched 60 year old plaster to the antiquated plumbing and electrical systems. In addition, the children and staff will benefit from redesigned living units affording greater privacy and improved work and play areas."

It seems likely that the intent to mount a major building fund drive may have facilitated the decision to undertake the diagnostic center. The drive would make capital funds available, and rehabilitation of the center would amount to a relatively small part of the overall renovation agenda.

CHRONOLOGY OF EVENTS

1971–1972—JCCA commits itself to complete modernization of the physical plant of its Pleasantville Cottage School, part of an overall $6 million building fund campaign to renovate JCCA residential facilities.

1972—The Committee on Mental Health Services Inside and Outside the Family Court of New York issues the report "Juvenile Justice Confounded," which documents the needs of children involved in the juvenile justice system and is critical of the voluntary child care agencies' response to these needs.

Late 1972—New York City's Office of Special Services for Children issues a list of priority projects for improved services. Diagnostic services to facilitate placement of older behaviorally difficult children is one identified need. Jacob Trobe encourages Paul Steinfeld to investigate the feasibility of establishing a diagnostic center on the campus of the Pleasantville Cottage School. Steinfeld selects a committee of Pleasantville staff to do so.

December 13, 1972—The JCCA Board of Trustees approves a recommendation of the Pleasantville Committee to establish an emergency diagnostic shelter in a building on the Pleasantville campus to serve children referred by the Family Court, with the understanding that operating expenses would be covered "almost entirely from public sources."

Early 1973—Trobe approaches Barbara Blum with the concept of the Pleasantville facility, and a meeting is arranged.

April 20, 1973—Jacob Trobe and Paul Steinfeld of JCCA meet with Barbara Blum, Steven Hochman, and Henry Rosner of New York City's Department of Social Services. There is substantial agreement on JCCA's proposal to open a diagnostic center at Pleasantville, and discussion centers on financing. Mr. Rosner suggests that the status of the Pleasantville Cottage School's Day Treatment Program as a contractor to the Westchester Community Mental Health Board can be used to justify "piggybacking" a high Medicaid per diem rate onto the City's regular foster care per diem rate, to finance the diagnostic center at a near break-even level of operation. Substantial agreement is reached on this strategy.

April 23, 1973—Jacob Trobe writes to Barbara Blum formally indicating JCCA's willingness to undertake the new program, based on the suggested arrangements for Medicaid financing. Barbara Blum and Henry Rosner countersign the letter, indicating the City's approval.

April 24, 1973—The JCCA Board of Trustees formally approves the diagnostic center, on a one-year pilot basis, and indicates it is prepared to spend $10,000 to renovate a building on the Pleasantville campus for that purpose.

May 29, 1973—JCCA formally announces plans for the center in a press release.

June/July, 1973—Various correspondence and meetings take place between staff of JCCA and New York City to work out rules and procedures for placement in the diagnostic center. It is agreed, for example, that 60 percent of referrals will originate from Family Court, and 40 percent from the Bureau of Child Welfare. An advisory committee consisting of representatives from the New York Family Court, Department of Social Services, the State Office of Court Administration and JCCA is set up. Provisions are made for progress reports and evaluations of the center during its pilot year.

August 13, 1973—Pleasantville Diagnostic Center begins operations.

1973–1975—The center operates at full capacity (10 beds, 4 to 6 week stays) with a continual waiting list.

September, 1975—The center's capacity is expanded from 10 to 22 beds.

CONTEXT

1972–1973 was a period in New York City in which the voluntary child care agencies, some eighty in number and responsible for approximately 85 percent of the 28,000 children in foster care, were beginning to come under attack from various quarters. The nature of the criticisms were severalfold, but a strong undercurrent was the fact that the population of children in the City requiring out-of-home placement was changing rapidly—becoming older, behaviorally more difficult (even violent), and more handicapped—and that the voluntary agencies were not changing their admissions policies and adapting their programs sufficiently to meet the new requirements. Another important crosscurrent was that of racial and religious discrimination. On the horizon (1974) was a class action suit called *Wilder vs. Sugarman* which would charge the New York foster care system and its voluntary agencies (of which the Catholic and Jewish agencies were proportionally the strongest) with discrimination against black and Protestant children in need of care.

One dimension to the controversy surrounding the voluntary agencies was the fact that systems parallel to the traditional child welfare/social service system, particularly the mental health and juvenile justice systems, looked increasingly to the foster care system for placement services. Of special relevance here, the Family Court was a source of referrals for so-called "Persons in Need of Supervision" (PINS), children who have committed "status offenses" such as running away, truancy, or general "incorrigibility." In a 1972 report entitled "Juvenile Justice Confounded: Pretensions and Realities of Treatment Services," the local juvenile justice system was criticized for providing inadequate diagnostic and treatment services to PINS children, and the voluntary agencies were chastised for refusing to open up their services to these children.

For various reasons, JCCA seems to have been particularly sensitive to the thrust of "Juvenile Justice Confounded." Some of this sensitivity can be attributed to Jacob Trobe's own sensibilities regarding the problems of minorities, and his personal antennae on trends and current issues. More than this, it must be recognized that JCCA was a very large agency compared to most. As such it would be a particular target for criticism, especially as Trobe was a part of various committees and task forces concerned with these problems in the city. Whatever the reasons, both Trobe and Steinfeld made special efforts to emphasize the social context in which the Pleasantville Diagnostic Center proposal was conceived, and Trobe specifically recalls the previously noted report as a stimulating factor. Indeed, the news release announcing the diagnostic center reads, in part: "In announcing the new program, Mr. Trobe said: 'The Jewish Child Care Association has designed the Diagnostic Center in accordance with several of the recommendations of the report of the Council on Crime and Delinquency's Committee on Mental Health Services Inside and Outside the Family Court of the City of New York. The report ("Juvenile Justice Confounded") called for a study of important trends in the characteristics and numbers of children for whom placement is sought by the court; the type of treatment they require; a review of the problems of children found to be in need of supervision; and development of special programs and facilities for them."

In developing the diagnostic center, JCCA could be seen as responding in a constructive and responsible way to the changing demands facing the voluntary foster care system. And there was good precedent for their proposed approach. In 1968, the Sisters of the Good Shepherd, a Catholic voluntary agency, had successfully pioneered the first such diagnostic center. Later, JCCA's sister agency, the Jewish Board of Guardians, had opened Geller House. By 1973 the City itself was toying with the notion of setting up its own centers, or encouraging others. JCCA was in good company at the forefront of the diagnostic center movement.

It is interesting to juxtapose the social realities of changing populations and demands for placement, with the internal issues these trends raised at JCCA. For herein lie some clues as to the reasons JCCA and other agencies may have been a target for criticism, and to understanding how the diagnostic center could serve to diffuse these criticisms.

JCCA, and the Pleasantville campus in particular, were subject to two sources of internal pressure—a reluctance of staff to risk involvement with more violent, acting-out children, and a traditional leaning toward maintaining a balance of Jewish clientele. (After all, an important slice of JCCA's support still came from Jewish philanthropic sources.) Paul Steinfeld explains the reluctance to extend services to more and more difficult children: "We were . . . aware . . . that voluntary agencies such as ours were being roundly criticized . . . that we would only take on the blonde, nice, blue-eyed, easy-to-manage children. [But] here, sitting in an institution where often you feel that you're on a powder keg, and at any moment it's going to erupt . . . you see numbers of children . . . including black faces . . . kids who were violent . . . kids who were hard to manage . . . from various ethnic backgrounds. . . . [Yet] we were told [we were] taking the easy way out. . . . We wanted to put more [study] into this apparent discrepancy between who we are . . . what the community impression was, and our own impression of what's good here.

"The reality [an institutional manager] . . . sees very often is that if he takes violent, aggressive children into a caring system, where a certain number of children are getting reasonably good care . . . [he] imposes as it were the wolf on the lamb. . . . [Actually] there are very few lambs in institutional care today, [but] if you put into an [institution] an individual who . . . manifests aggression . . . of one kind or another . . . exploitation or shakedowns . . . or whatever, there is a limited amount of [such] inflow . . . the institutional apparatus can absorb. . . . The institutional administrator is responsible for helping . . . the kids, and must protect them."

In any case, it is clear that JCCA, and the Pleasantville School in particular, were subject to internal stresses caused by the changing social scene. As Barbara Blum puts it: "If you look back to that period, it was generally presumed that (a) severe retardation and (b) racial factors could negatively influence admission at Pleasantville. . . . I think Pleasantville [was] . . . still heavily weighted toward the white [Jewish] child.

"There had been questions raised about the nature of the population served in Pleasantville, in relation to the cost of the service, and in relation to the city's needs. There was a lot of conservatism among staff. When you run a large institution, you have a staff with certain [established] ideas, particularly when you've got one that is respected in the professional world as Pleasantville had been. I think there existed a great reluctance to change."

CHOICES

Once conceived in concept, the diagnostic center fell into place very quickly, perhaps because it seemed like an eminently logical and satisfactory solution from various points of view.

In the first place, proposal of a diagnostic center was a good way for Trobe to deflect criticism and respond positively to the salient concerns for treatment of the new breed of child now entering the foster care system. Trobe talked in global terms of a Mayo-type clinic for children with behavioral problems: "I said, let's really put together the most thorough diagnostic inpatient diagnostic center, and let's get it all the tools . . . [and] an adequate staff. . . . Let's strip the kid nude, in effect, to find out what makes him tick, what the nature of his problem is. . . ."

Of course, the idea of a diagnostic center was already in circulation, but Trobe and Steinfeld grabbed the initiative and claim to have been little influenced by the earlier centers. According to Steinfeld: "I knew of the concept of a diagnostic center because I had heard of Geller House . . . and because I had heard that the City of New York had either the plan or were in the process of developing some diagnostic centers. So I knew that concept, but truly . . . I was more in tune myself to what I had learned about the admission of kids or their failure to be admitted. . . . [This] meant more to me than the little I had heard from far away. . . ."

Given the notion of a diagnostic center, why should it be located on the campus of the Pleasantville School rather than some new location, or at the site of some other JCCA facility? The Pleasantville site was a "natural" for several reasons. First, as previously observed, the school was a particular target of criticism regarding the nature of its population. Steinfeld claims that another factor was the difficulty Trobe might have had in finding a resident director to take up the project: ". . . To be honest, I think the reason that it took the form it did, and [in] the place it did, was that I was the only administrator who had any enthusiasm for doing this. . . . The fact is that . . . very often the administrator [of an institution] becomes attuned just to keep the thing going. [It] often takes everything he has got just to keep the existing thing going: to develop something new [with] more headaches . . . is usually not . . . attractive. . . ."

Be that as it may, the Pleasantville campus was also the most sensible site from an economic point of view. As noted before, a renovation program was already contemplated, and all of the physical facilities and administrative apparatus were essentially already in place. As Trobe notes: ". . . It seemed to be very simple. I . . . felt . . . we've [already] got a great residential treatment center. . . . All I had to do is imbed it [the diagnostic center] on physically. Then I really basically . . . have a multipurpose service [center]. . . ."

Paul Steinfeld elaborates, "[There are] advantages of spinning-off a new program from an existing program. . . . [There] is an existing plant, land, buildings, and above all, an experienced staff . . . caring people, clinical people, and administrative people. . . . You could recruit their expertise. Actually in the beginning . . . there was [little] cost. . . . I didn't have to go out and rent a building and pay rent in advance of the children's occupancy. I had the building there. . . . I did have to relocate staff, but we played checkers. . . . We moved a person from this building to that building. . . . It began very modestly. . . .

"In fact . . . in the beginning we didn't want to go out and hire a full-time administrator for 10 kids [so] we took one of the middle management resident administrators [at the school] . . . [paid him] a little more and [asked him to] work longer hours . . . and be available more weekends and holidays."

Given the logical concept and logical site, the diagnostic center was a creative, perhaps brilliant, strategy for easing the tensions thrust on JCCA and for precipitating a movement toward long-run policy change. As Paul Steinfeld indicates: "We thought . . . that there might be certain side benefits or by-products for JCCA because . . . people who were critical [were] saying, 'Why don't you care for this kid? Why don't you care for that kid?' We felt that we were in the best position to decide which kids we could care for and not care for. And if as a result of the diagnostic center's work, the hypothesis was that Pleasantville or Edenwald [both JCCA treatment centers] or a group home could best care for them, then we would rely on that. We wouldn't have to be skeptical that we could do it. . . . Because [the] position [of] institution managers [would be]: 'Look, you tell me that this kid lived in the cottage [diagnostic center] for four weeks or six weeks, and was kept in school for that time, and he didn't murder anyone. . . . If you tell me this, and we believe you, we are going to take this kid.' Well, I could say the same thing to my own staff [based on] an honest report of what happened to this kid *in the* [diagnostic center] residence. . . ."

Barbara Blum elaborates on what she perceived as some very creative leadership by Trobe and Steinfeld to effectively initiate change at JCCA: ". . . I think there existed a great reluctance to change . . . [but] I think that both Paul Steinfeld and Jake Trobe . . . felt a professional responsibility to respond better than Pleasantville then was, to the city's needs.

They recognized that they couldn't just turn an institution around overnight. So that they really were very creative. They figured out that [if a] certain number of individuals [children] came to a part of the campus, which was discrete but professionally staffed with respected persons from the psychiatric or social work field, and if those children were carefully and accurately diagnosed and evaluated, then two things . . . would happen. One, the staff on the campus would become more familiar with the children in residence at the diagnostic center, and that more and more of those children would begin to be placed on campus. Second, for those kids who couldn't be placed on campus, or for whom there wasn't an appropriate response on the campus, the fact that they had a sign-off and evaluation from Pleasantville staff would make it more likely that a referral could actually be effected to another agency. I found it a very interesting way to bring [about] incremental change. And that's what they were doing. And I think they succeeded. When you look at the statistics of where those kids eventually ended up, for the most part they ended up a lot better off than if there hadn't been a diagnostic cottage development. . . . If they had started just a routine change in their intake for . . . long-term care on their campus, I don't think that we would have seen the same number of kids helped. . . ."

Certain design parameters of the diagnostic center proposal were crucial to making it palatable within JCCA. One such aspect was the choice of a discrete unit, separated from the rest of the Pleasantville campus. As Steinfeld explains: ". . . All along we were saying, 'We can't have the sheep and the wolves together.' . . . Suddenly we were going to do it. They are there on the same campus. Well, my response was we would do it by discrete programming. The program of these aggressive or delinquent kids . . . would be . . . segregated from the other programs. . . . It is designed [separately] for this group of kids. They may see one another in passing. Regular kids may be in one corner of the ballfield and they [the diagnostic center kids] may be in the other, but they have their own staff and their own program . . . [and] their distinct play areas. . . ."

Another very important parameter was the financial arrangements for the diagnostic center. Although the JCCA trustees historically have taken risks to undertake major projects, including invasion of endowment capital, they were naturally somewhat reluctant to see the center become a significant drain on the JCCA treasury. Mr. Trobe recalls that when the diagnostic center was proposed, "we were running deficits . . . I think we actually had a deficit [of] three quarters of a million dollars. . . ." (According to the treasurer's report for the year ending June 20, 1972, the difference between expenditures and revenues from government, the Federation, United Fund, and other fees, was almost $900,000, financed by additional voluntary contributions, income from investments, and drawing down reserves.) That there was concern over operating funds seems to be confirmed in the minutes of the board of trustees meeting of April 24, 1973, which state: "It is the understanding of the trustees that operating expenses for this project [the diagnostic center] would be met almost entirely from public sources. . . ."

JCCA had determined the operating cost of the center upwards of $50 per day while the normal institutional per diem payments for foster care services were more like $30 per day. The gap was closed in the key meeting of Trobe, Steinfeld, Blum, and Henry Rosner. Steinfeld recalls, ". . . Hank fished around for us for a moment and discovered that we did have a contract with the Westchester Community Health Board on the campus at Pleasantville, and that provided for a Medicaid rate; I think it was $21 per day . . . and he was sure that it was legitimate to charge the clinical component of this program to that. And that enabled [the City] to finance the difference between the total cost . . . [and the regular foster care rate]. . . . And it [the idea] took. That was one of the remarkable things about it. . . ."

The projected arrangement satisfied the JCCA trustees. As Steinfeld remembers: "They [the trustees] were certainly concerned about it, and we indicated that we had a reimbursement rate which we thought would be adequate. It might cost a little. We did project a little deficit. At that time [however] the board was accepting programs, whether there was a [small] deficit or an expectation of Jewish communal funds supplementing the public funding. . . . The prospect for a *moderate* deficit was not too big an issue with the board because they could expect a certain amount of earnings [from investments], also stipends from the Federation of Jewish Philanthropies and from the United Fund. . . . We more or less knew what the capital that was coming in would cover. We felt that we were within reason here. . . . [If the proposal had come through two years later] . . . it would have had rougher sledding. . . ."

As noted in the trustees' minutes of April 24, 1973, the final arrangements provided ". . . that in addition to reimbursement from the City for this diagnostic shelter at the current Pleasantville Cottage School rate of $30.50 per day for institution care . . . an additional $21.00 per day [would be provided] for covering psychiatric clinic services . . . making for a total of $51.50 per day. The actual cost of the program is estimated at $51.75 per day, leaving the very small deficit of $.25 per day per child."

The estimated cost of $51.75 per child per day was based on full utilization (an assumption which proved correct). Even so, aside from initial capital costs (estimated at $10,000), the diagnostic center could be viewed at the time as at least a break-even proposition, considering that various cost items were estimated simply by prorating existing Pleasantville expenditures over additional children.

RISKS AND CONSTRAINTS

Jake Trobe ascribes individually to a professional philosophy of responsible risk-taking: "I always . . . [had] a slogan . . . for myself: 'If an individual in an institution hasn't the courage to fail, he doesn't have the right to succeed.' . . . It's better to fail in the project than not to try at all [although] that doesn't mean trying foolhardy . . . schemes. . . ."

He feels similarly about his organization: ". . . We didn't . . . ever say . . . you can spend X% a year of your endowment. . . . Basically, we took the philosophy if you go broke doing the job . . . [i.e., the organization goes bankrupt] at the end of 20 years . . . well [at least it's] because it's blown its money for good causes. . . . [However] I'm not saying [we] didn't have . . . lump[s] in [our] throat[s] all the time . . . when the tough times came in the city."

As far as the Pleasantville project was concerned, Trobe saw it as a pretty straightforward thing: "So I undertook this and it seemed to be very simple." Steinfeld, however, in contrast to Trobe's almost cavalier attitude, admits to a bit more anxiety: ". . . I was always anxious that we might have underfunded it. [But] both Mr. Trobe and I were very eager to get this off the ground, and we didn't worry [too much] . . . about whether we had ensured its financial solvency on a long-range basis. We weren't even sure it would go long range . . . [that] it would continue to be in demand. . . ."

There was some chance of financial trouble, however, as indicated in the trustees' minutes of April, 1973: "Mr. Trobe pointed out that if the court makes the fullest use of this program throughout the year, as we anticipate, then the operating deficit will be only 25¢ per child per day. However, he wished to point out that we have no guarantee of its fullest use and based on the guestimate of the number of children coming into care, we will run the same risk here with respect to full capacity as in other programs. . . ."

There was also concern among the trustees that if the diagnostic center were aborted, JCCA would remain obligated to the newly hired employees. The minutes continue: "Mr. Deitch [a trustee] stated that he assumed we will be hiring additional staff and asked about the possibility of hiring them as project people rather than regular JCCA staff so we need not get involved with severance payments. . . .He urged that we make a real effort to protect ourselves against financial consequences in the event the project is terminated. . . . Mr. David Roth [Associate Executive Director] . . . added that we are exploring the question of using the project clause under our union agreement, but the only problem is that after a period of nine months, such personnel become regular employees and we do have some obligations."

In addition to financial risks, there were programmatic risks, despite the plan to segregate the diagnostic center from the rest of the Pleasantville campus. These risks also gave Steinfeld some anxiety: ". . . Our attorneys are careful about legal responsibilities that they incur. . . . They want to be adequately protected to make sure the agency's reputation, and also finances, are not damaged by negligence in any form. . . . [For example] if you bring in delinquents, let's say . . . are you able to protect the other kids from delinquencies? . . . Would . . . [you] be comfortable in placing a kid in Pleasantville Cottage School . . . [if] there is a kid [next door] who stabbed someone and killed him? We had such a kid. Is it safe to enter the diagnostic center? Is it safe for [other] kids? . . . [There] were many of these questions . . . that have to do with the health and safety of children. . . . It was the board people who knew me, who knew of my job performance, who thought, 'Well, this guy knows what he is doing.' [But], when it came to the protection of children, I couldn't give them an iron-clad guarantee. I said that I thought the risks were not too severe . . . [but] there are hazards in doing a job of this kind, which the board recognizes. . . ."

Clearly the financial and programmatic considerations, the need to break roughly even, and to avoid a precipitous mixing of children from the diagnostic center with those of the school, were the most crucial constraints surrounding the proposal. There was also concern that the diagnostic center might begin to strain the general systems of the Pleasantville campus, such as the education system, which had to make separate provisions. But the capacity of the center was very small compared to the overall campus so the latter did not loom large. The convenient logistics of the campus permitted the segregation constraint to be observed. And the proposal to supplement financing through Medicaid allowed the break-even constraint to be honored.

OUTCOMES

Programmatically, the Pleasantville Diagnostic Center succeeded. Almost immediately, it was oversubscribed, so that fears for less than full usage were, in retrospect, needless. Indeed, according to the JCCA newsletter of summer, 1975: "During the first 17 months of operation, the Center admitted 109 children, and has had a waiting list for service almost since its opening."

Thus by summer, 1975, plans were laid to more than double the center's capacity, from 10 to 22 beds, by that September. For this purpose an additional cottage was renovated through a special gift, and age requirements for admission were widened from 10 to 14 years to 9 to 15 years of age.

The center also was instrumental in bringing changes to the population served by the Pleasantville School and JCCA at large. In a 1974–1975 Annual Report, JCCA boasted that the center "has a record of 85 percent success in finding facilities able to serve its children for at least one year." Many of the placements were in the facilities of JCCA itself. Specifically, of 117 boys placed from the center by December, 1975, some 30 were placed with JCCA, 24 of these at Pleasantville Cottage School. Thus, the strategy of incremental change which Trobe and Steinfeld had envisioned, had begun to take hold. As Barbara Blum was wont to comment: "When you visit Pleasantville [School] now, there is quite a difference in population."

Perhaps another sign of success is the fact that Paul Steinfeld rose within a year of the time that the center was implemented to become Associate Executive Director of JCCA. This was possibly a vote of confidence in the project as well as the man. Yet, despite the operational success, the financial problems which JCCA had sought to avoid were not completely averted. Steinfeld explains: ". . . It soon became apparent that we had underestimated our costs. We [were] locked into the per diem rate, which wasn't covering our costs. For one thing, since 1973 we have had a union contract with the staff. They have built-in raises in salaries [but] . . . the [per diem] rate was from it [by the City]. . . . So we didn't build in much of a margin for escalation of costs. . . . We are now running a very big deficit in our program. . . ."

ANALYSIS

The diagnostic center at Pleasantville was an inspired solution to a problem created at JCCA by external pressures. The changing nature of New York City's population of children requiring foster care brought JCCA, as a prominent voluntary child care agency, under attack for lack of response. The inertia of JCCA could be attributed to its roots in Jewish service and its traditional sources of support in the Jewish community, and to a natural anxiety of staff to expose the current clientele and program to the potential risks and disruption of a more handicapped and in some cases violent group of children. The diagnostic center was a way of introducing change to JCCA, particularly to the Pleasantville campus, incrementally weaning it towards a new population in a deliberate and controlled manner.

The diagnostic center project reflected the combined efforts of two executives of complementary styles. Trobe, the energetic problem-solver and negotiator, was "Mr. Outside," immersed in the global concerns of his city and profession and charged with defining and setting into motion appropriate policies for his agency. Steinfeld, the career administrator, was "Mr. Inside," taking on the task of translating the proposal from idea to reality and solving the practical problems of implementation and operation. With each content in his own role, the combination worked well.

The Pleasantville case also illustrates the constraints on executive leadership in a large decentralized agency such as JCCA. Success required that a division director (like Steinfeld) be found who was willing to risk the potential turmoil that such a new initiative might entail. Moreover, ways had to be found to overcome the natural conservatism of professional staff and careworkers concerned with the uncertainty and possible volatility of introducing a new clientele mixture. Finally, the financial and programmatic concerns of trustees had to be duly considered and attended to. Thus, the decentralized regime of administration which facilitated JCCA's large and diverse operation, also required its executive to trade some of his skills as battle commander for the skills of a politician.

The Pleasantville case also illuminates the barriers to organizational change and the requirements for successful innovation. While staff conservatism, financial worries, constituency pressures, and fear of the unknown inhibited change, the confluence of environmental pressures and internal leadership motivation was eventually responsible for bringing change about. Much had to do with the fortuitous timing of events and identification of acceptable solutions to problems that had been allowed to build up over the years. In particular, the diagnostic center was the correct solution to JCCA's problem of external criticism on grounds of unresponsiveness to the city's needs. And Pleasantville was clearly the logical site. Indeed, the proposal for a center and the choice of the Pleasantville site seemed to be conceived simultaneously. The Pleasantville campus was already the lightning rod for external criticism, yet all the pieces were in place there for synthesis of the new program.

Once conceived, the diagnostic center moved rapidly from idea to reality. The timing was just right. Building funds were already being raised by JCCA. Just as fortuitously, however, a single idea—using Medicaid to finance the additional clinical costs—was proposed. This was the missing piece that, when added to the basic elements of entrepreneurial motives, contextual issues, and organizational tensions, led to the solution.

Seabury Barn
(Smith Haven Ministries)

PRÉCIS

Seabury Barn is a short-term group home for adolescents in Suffolk County, located in Stony Brook, New York, and administered under auspices of Smith Haven Ministries, Inc., an "ecumenical" social service agency sponsored by several major religious denominations and based in a large indoor shopping mall in Suffolk. The Barn program began operations in January, 1973, on the basis of an LEAA grant which funded the Barn as well as an ongoing youth program of the Ministries.

Establishment of the Barn was an outgrowth of the Ministries' effort in 1970–1972 to fund its existing youth program, in order to bolster current staffing capacity, and to help relieve financial pressures on the agency as a whole. Securing of the grant took almost two years and required persistent and skillful political negotiations at the state and local levels. Success in this effort is largely attributable to the entrepreneurial activity of Father Peter Ryan, then Associate Director of the Ministries.

THE ENTREPRENEURS

There are several people who were important to establishing Seabury Barn. Among these are the Rev. Paul Hanson who developed the Ministries' original youth program (a "drop-in center" in the shopping mall, where teenagers could come to socialize or get help); Carol Tweedy, the first program director of Seabury, who helped secure the physical facilities and translate the Barn from plans on paper into an operational unit, once funding was established; Larry Bracken, Chairman of the Suffolk County Criminal Justice Coordinating Council who helped to negotiate the proposal through government; and Andrew Casazza, Director of the Youth Board of Huntington Town, who provided some of the original ideas for the proposal. But the key character was Father Peter Ryan who wrote the proposal, shepherded it through government, hired the staff to implement the program, and supervised the implementation period.

Father Ryan is a soft-spoken, wryly humorous Catholic priest of the Rockville Centre Diocese (which covers much of Long Island). He was trained in theology and philosophy, and has long been active politically in causes of social justice and civil rights.

Through his involvement in public affairs, and with ecumenism, Ryan learned the arts of political negotiation and lobbying, both within government and within the structures of his own (Catholic) and other church establishments. "Convincing people" is the keystone to his ability to get things done. As Carol Tweedy observes, "He is the most marvelous political genius I've ever run into. . . . He doesn't play party politics, he knows how to do it on both sides. . . . He was able to make a great deal of social connections. . . . When you become a priest you get access to social connections. (He could call on) this incredibly complex network . . . and he's very judicious about when he asks a favor. He knows just the right time. . . . A lot of times he would let us struggle and deal with an issue and it would only be when it was really bad . . . that he would move in and do something for us. . . . The way he used himself was appropriate."

Ryan views political and administrative skills as necessary and useful, but *not* the essence of his career. Fundamentally, Ryan sees himself as a priest whose functions are to help and counsel those in need and to advocate on behalf of the oppressed. He sees the priest's position in society as especially advantageous to carrying out these functions in two senses: (1) as one who is skillful and trusted in dealing with people, he can more easily gain access to them and be more effective in getting them to change their behavior, and (2) as clergy, he is better able to take on "hot issues" because of the sincerity and moral basis attributed to his position.

THE ORGANIZATION

The Seabury Barn is a program unit of the Smith Haven Ministries (SHM), an unusual nonprofit social service agency with roots in ecumenism and the social service thrusts of particular Christian denominations. A brief history and description of SHM helps account for the proposal leading to the Barn program.

The original initiative for SHM came from the Presbyterian Church, which in 1964 called for "bold and creative forms of ministry." In the same period of time, the local Presbytery of Long Island was exploring possibilities for a new congregation in the vicinity of the site of the proposed, large new (indoor) Smith Haven shopping mall. In 1967, the Reverend A. David Bos took up the initiative and proceeded under supervision of the Church Extension Committee of the Long Island Presbytery to develop the idea of an ecumenical ministry in a shopping mall designed to "benefit directly or indirectly . . . the poor in the broadest sense." An interfaith proposal committee was formed, which under the joint leadership of Bos and Father Ryan, then assigned to a local parish of the Rockville Catholic Diocese, met for over a year to develop goals and priorities and to formulate the proposal.

The Presbytery of Long Island began renting a former model home near the construction site of the new mall for meeting space and "trial programming," using the name "Nesconset Experimental Ministries." One such trial program was a coffee house for teenagers of senior high school age, (the genesis of SHM's youth program). Meanwhile, Rev. Bos negotiated a lease for space in the new mall, and financial support was elicited from the local Catholic, Episcopalian, Methodist (and later Lutheran) dioceses, some local congregations and parishes, as well as the Presbytery. Most notably, the principal denominations undertook four major forms of financial commitment, several of which were to influence the future of SHM in important ways: (1) they guaranteed a ten-year lease for SHM in the mall; (2) they provided $150,000 in capital loans for finishing and furnishing the facility; (3) they paid the salaries of participating clergy including the Rev. Bos, Father Ryan, and Rev. Hanson; and (4) they provided some operating funds for programmatic activity.

As originally planned, SHM was to derive an important fraction of its income from "marketable services," including a bookstore and a shopper's child care service in the mall, plus substantial volunteer labor, as well as denominational and congregational financial support. But from the time of its incorporation in June, 1969, and its move into the mall in February, 1970, the agency was continually on the financial ropes. The bookstore and child care services operated at a loss, and rental and other bills went unpaid. The May, 1970 issue of SHM's newsletter had a frantic tone: "Smith Haven Ministries is in the midst of a financial crisis. . . . We have overestimated income AND underestimated expenditures in regard to both rental and capital expense. . . . Unless we can find a solution . . . within the next few months, we are liable to be thrown out of the Mall in a year's time. . . . The short term capital funds crisis . . . endangers our credit standing. . . . Three (denominations) together with the Long Island Council of Churches are guaranteeing our lease and, should we fail, would be liable for the unpaid rental. Four (denominations) have loaned funds for building and, should we fail, will probably not be able to recover very much of that. . . ."

While some short term palliatives were found, e.g., a short-term loan from the United Church of Christ, a trimming of the expense budget, a renegotiation of the lease and move into smaller quarters, and closing of the loss-making marketable services, the next couple of years continued to be financially unstable. Meanwhile, the demand for services, especially in the youth program, grew. Location in the shopping mall became a magnet for kids to congregate, and staffing (largely volunteer) became inadequate to the task. The confluence of these factors—oversubscription, understaffing, and financial difficulties—motivated development of the proposal that led ultimately to Seabury Barn.

Over the years, the organization of SHM also changed considerably. Originally it consisted of the interfaith proposal committee, chaired by Rev. Bos. In 1968, the committee disbanded and formed various task groups (reporting to Bos) responsible for developing various aspects of the SHM proposal. Upon incorporation in 1969, a tripartite board structure was adopted which included a board of governors (or trustees) on which the denominations and other participating agencies were represented according to the size of their financial commitments, an advisory council which was a consultative body with a single representative from each participating agency, and a steering committee which included representatives from the advisory council plus "at-large" representatives. Essentially, the executive director (Bos) consulted with the steering committee on matters of goal formulation, and through the steering committee, reported to the advisory committee for examination and change of existing program policies and to the governors on corporate matters. Staff, of course, reported to the executive director through various program directors.

This structure was found to be cumbersome and was simplified in early 1972 by having the advisory council absorbed by the board of governors, having the steering committee serve in an advisory capacity to the board, and having the director report directly to the board. These changes were among several structural and program alterations designed to make SHM more efficient in light of its tenuous position. For example, board membership was also broadened to reflect a wider cross-section of the Suffolk County community, a professional business manager was hired, and an organized effort was undertaken to solicit "membership" contributions by individual citizens and businesses.

The relationship of the board to the executive director is especially interesting in the SHM case. On the one hand, Ryan, and Bos before him, used the board in an advisory capacity, but the agency's program thrust was "very much David Bos or Peter Ryan." On the other hand, it seems clear that until 1972 at least, accountability to the denominations was important. For one thing, SHM was financially beholden to the denominations, and these denominations were concerned about their capital loans and lease and debt obligations incurred on behalf of SHM. Secondly, the executives had been drawn from the denominations themselves. David Bos was a Presbyterian minister who ultimately left SHM for another ministerial assignment. Peter Ryan was a Catholic priest who would take on other diocesan posts in the future. It seems clear that these executives had to operate partly with denominational interests in mind. Ryan, however, points to the crossroads he faced after six years with SHM—a decision point where his allegiance to the diocese vs. SHM had to be decided. A decision in favor of the latter (which would probably have to be funded by external grants) would make him ever more independent of the diocese especially as SHM's board structure had been broadened. The same issue will arise with future clergy in his position, or to a lesser degree with a lay administrator paid directly from denominational funds.

A number of other interesting points concerning SHM's (post-1972) organizational structure should be mentioned. First, routine administration is handled by a professional administrator leaving the director more free to pursue program development. Second, major divisions such as Seabury Barn, the youth program in the mall, and advocacy activities such as housing services, are each headed by a program director reporting to the executive.

Third, and very important in light of the agency's overall difficulties, the housing program (Suffolk Housing Services or SHS) is separately incorporated with its own board, although it functions within the SHM structure. The separate incorporation protects SHM in terms of its liability under litigation. But it also reveals the tension that exists within SHM between its dual missions to provide "direct services" as in the youth program, and its advocacy programs for oppressed groups (as in SHS). Although Ryan perceives this as a "creative tension," there is some feeling among SHM board members that advocacy stirs up community resentment which inhibits the agency in securing funds and other support. Indeed, as discussed below, the antipathy towards SHM's radical image was responsible for considerable difficulty encountered in the implementation of the proposal for Seabury Barn.

CHRONOLOGY OF EVENTS

The following key events marked implementation of the Seabury Barn:

March, 1968—Coffee house opens in temporary quarters.

February, 1970—Opening of SHM facilities in the new mall, including the coffee house "drop-in center."

Spring, 1970—Suffolk County conference on youth problems, run by SHM under a grant from the Sears Foundation. There is a discussion here with Andy Casazza who provides ideas for the proposal, including LEAA as a possible source of funds (through the State Office of Crime Control and Planning).

July, 1970—Rev. Paul Hanson joins SHM as Youth Program director (funded by the Lutheran Church).

July–August, 1970—Father Ryan and Larry Bracken of the Suffolk County Criminal Justice Coordinating Council work out a $175,000 proposal for SHM youth services program called Operation Bootstraps, which includes the mall "drop-in center" and Seabury. The Seabury component is an "addition" suggested by Mike Silverman of the State Office for Crime Control and Planning to secure State Division for Youth (DFY) backing. (DFY is engaged in promoting group homes at the time.)

September, 1971—The grant is approved by the State, but Suffolk County sign-off is also required. This is a problem because local politicians object to a direct state to private agency arrangement, bypassing the County; also, there is local distrust of SHM by conservatives in the county legislature.

January, 1972—The grant is approved by the Suffolk legislature (which has just changed from a Republican to Democratic majority) under a compromise arrangement wherein funds are channeled through the Suffolk County Youth Board, and an advisory committee of Suffolk officials is set up to supervise implementation and initial operation of the Barn.

June, 1972—The grant officially begins: $175,714 over 14 months, plus in-kind contributions of $61,856 from SHM.

Summer, 1972—Carol Tweedy is hired to implement and direct the Barn program; a director, Jack Ericksen, is also hired for the youth program in the mall.

September, 1972—Rev. Hanson is recalled by the Lutheran Church, leaving Ryan primary responsibility for overseeing the implementation of the Barn under Tweedy. During this period Ryan is also active in securing certification from the State for Seabury as an official child care facility, formally permitting the admission of children and making the Barn eligible for state social service per diem funds.

Fall, 1972—A facility for Seabury is rented and furnished, and staff is put in place.

January, 1973—Seabury Barn opens and receives its first clients.

Summer, 1973—A second full year of funding is secured for Bootstraps, i.e., the Barn and mall youth programs.

Fall, 1973—State certification as a child care facility is received, making Seabury officially able to receive children and eligible for state social service payments.

CONTEXT

The chronology of events leading to the successful funding of Seabury, and the history of SHM, reflects the general social context in which these developments took place. The key elements are the rapid growth of a suburban county, the growing social consciousness of churches, the problems of youth in the turbulent late 1960s, the dearth of local youth programs and facilities, newly available federal funding, and the fears of a conservative political constituency. These developments established the backdrop within which SHM, its youth program, and Seabury itself, could be entrepreneured by Bos and Ryan, and significantly affected the shape of these activities.

Since the late sixties, Suffolk County has been the most rapidly growing county in New York State. Development has followed a classical suburban pattern of single family tract housing, auto-based transportation, and large commercial shopping centers. Although there are pockets of poverty, both older and newly arrived residents are generally conservative, and social services (governmental and voluntary) were slow to follow the migration.

Suffolk had a growing young population, for which the suburban context presented special problems. Transportation was difficult and facilities, especially for youth outside school, were few. There were no street corners or candy stores, and shopping centers became the new hangout. The idea for services in a mall grew out of this realization, and indeed the success of the drop-in center, in terms of "demand" for service, is testimony to the accuracy of this perception.

Nationally, the sixties were also a turbulent time for youth, a time of runaways and flower children, hard rock music, experimentation with drugs, and alienation from the establishment spurred by concerns over civil rights and Vietnam. In reaction, scattered residential programs for runaways and drug treatment, such as Huckleberry House in California, began to appear. Federal and state funding became available for group homes and other youth-oriented initiatives. And while individual clergy first became involved in front-line social activism, the church establishments began to search for ways to make themselves more relevant to social problems. These developments created mandates and opportunities for agencies like SHM to be created by the churches and local activists, and for youth programs to be funded by government. Indeed, the state thrust toward group homes was basically responsible for attaching the Seabury component to the concept for the original proposal (see below).

On the local scene, the new social activism and the rebellious behavior of youth came into conflict with a basically conservative political community, part of Nixon's "(not so) silent majority." An agency like SHM evoked distrust with its advocacy activities, e.g., litigation and agitating for desegregated housing. And a proposed residential facility like Seabury stirred opposition from community members who saw it as a potential magnet or haven for delinquents and drug abusers, and a disruptive influence on neighborhoods. At the same time, the availability of federal and state funds enabled youth advocates to involve local governments in youth programs. Youth boards were established and the money and shape of programs they influenced became politically sensitive issues. In and out of government, the new resources and burgeoning problems stimulated youth-oriented groups, such as SHM and the youth boards, to confer and coalesce over strategy.

Despite the conflicts between youth-oriented groups and a conservative community, the late sixties and early seventies were times that could be described as relatively "receptive" to the needs of youth. Father Ryan observed that the thrusts which brought SHM and Seabury into being would have been much more difficult in the recession-ridden and more disillusioned Suffolk County of the late seventies.

CHOICES

Alternative forms that the Seabury venture might have taken must be understood in the context of SHM's financial condition and service demands in the 1970 period. As noted earlier, SHM was in difficult financial straits. At the same time, the essentially volunteer staffed drop-in center in the newly opened mall facility was becoming overwhelmed. Overall, there seemed to be four broad choices: (1) close-up shop (and perhaps ultimately disband the Ministries); (2) fashion a proposal to government, designed to suit the particular programs and purposes of SHM at the time, and stick to this position; (3) remain flexible in developing a proposal which would compromise SHM and governmental objectives; (4) divest the youth program to local government.

Of course, other actions were taken to bolster the condition of SHM. But Father Ryan admits that "the fact that the grant was in the offing was one of the strongest forces that kept us alive" as it "offered the hope of stabilization and the ability to meet expenditures."

In essence, alternative number three was the only reasonable one, given a desire of SHM to survive. Closing up shop would not only mean frustrating the growing clientele of youth and other groups that had come to depend on SHM, and the volunteers who had devoted their energies to it, but it would also require the founding denominations to write-off the capital loans to SHM and to cover other SHM debts. In view of board member and staff loyalties and associations with the denominations, this represented a very distasteful outcome.

Nor would option number four suffice. During the time (late in 1971) when the Suffolk legislature was sitting on approval, the idea of giving the program over to the Suffolk Youth Bureau was considered. But this might have radically altered the program, and in any case would not have relieved SHM's debt problems.

Given the decision to seek government funding, the preferred design of SHM was simply to find and professionalize the existing drop-in center at the mall, and to do this via a direct grant or contract with the State. One alternative, number two, would have been to hold to this concept inflexibly. However, approval of a direct contract still required local (county) sign-off and it was doubtful that the County would permit such a precedent, bypassing local politicians in the allocation of state funds.

The addition of the Seabury Barn component to the original proposal is a different case. This component was added to facilitate support from the State, whose State Division for Youth was pushing the group homes concept and also attempting to confine future allocation of LEAA funds to "new" programs rather than existing ones. The new (Seabury) addition to the existing drop-in center proposal represented a compromise for the State. It also involved trade-offs for SHM. While it greatly improved the probability of state funding, the Barn would be an additional responsibility for which the Ministries was not especially prepared. Secondly, a residential facility would undoubtedly arouse local opposition.

These implications may not have been perfectly clear at the time, however. In the initial stages of negotiations, the prime concern was getting the State Office for Crime Control and Planning behind the proposal. The operational implications of the Seabury addition were not spelled out until the grant was actually in-house in June, 1972. According to Carol Tweedy, the Barn's first director, who was responsible for implementation: "It was really incredible . . . how I articulated that program. . . . We had no clients. . . . I was shown a proposal. . . . I didn't have a facility. The proposal was *very* sketchy. I wish I still had a copy of the proposal because I'd frame it, I swear!"

Similarly, it may not have been fully appreciated that the addition of Seabury would further arouse local fears, and that the County would infringe on SHM autonomy by requiring close governmental supervision. All this is not to say that SHM opposed the Barn in concept. Such a service was consistent in principle with the intent to be of service to Suffolk youth; indeed, the need for such a facility had been recently demonstrated in a study carried out at the State University at Stony Brook. Nonetheless, the necessity to get the proposal funded was the overriding concern of the moment, and the first step was to get a commitment from the State. Loyalties to SHM and its founding denominations required flexibility to attain state funds. Administrative problems and local frictions would be dealt with later.

RISKS AND CONSTRAINTS

To summarize, the risks associated with remaining inflexible in the design of the proposal which led to Seabury Barn, or in curtailing SHM and its youth proram, were both concrete and intangible. Failure to fund the program would raise the specter of imminent collapse for the agency, and concomitant financial losses for the founding denominations. Other less-measurable losses would also result from the disappointments of volunteers, clientele, and staff who were committed to the concepts of ecumenical social service and advocating for social justice.

There were, of course, costs to flexibility. The addition of Seabury meant more administrative responsibility at a time when SHM needed to get its existing programs in order. And it meant stirring more local antagonisms, when feelings had already been stirred up by SHM's advocacy activities. There was also the risk that Seabury would turn out to be a powder keg of volatile juveniles, which SHM might not be able to control. As Ryan notes, "You are always walking on eggshells with this kind of program." Certainly, demands for more control by the County threatened a loss of autonomy for SHM, and possibly curtailment of its advocacy work on behalf of social causes.

Thus, the entrepreneuring of the Bootstraps proposal was an exercise in constrained choice. Governmental mandates at the state level counseled the addition of a new, residential program component. Local political pressures required acceding to demands for greater overview by local government.

SHM's own needs dictated making the best of it. The risks of lost autonomy, administrative burden, and program volatility seemed outweighed by the prospects of bankruptcy and loss of confidence of the denominations in the people and principles behind the Ministries. The Seabury program, given its initial survival, offered not only short-term financial salvation via the initial (federal) grant but also long-term stability by tying into the State's own system of payments for residential (foster) care. Hopefully, this would be achieved without severe compromise of the agency's ideals.

It is interesting to note that technically Seabury was prohibited from opening its doors, i.e., receiving children, before state certification was obtained from the Board of Social Welfare. However, problems with BSW procedures delayed certification. In the interim, however, with no license, but grant money in hand, Seabury opened its doors—helping to force the hand of BSW. According to Tweedy who says she pressed for this decision, this was a risk which Ryan was somewhat reluctant to take; if the word got out, enemies of the program could destroy it and Ryan was sensitive to this. But the step seemed necessary because grant renewal in the following year would require having "something to show for the money."

OUTCOMES

In all apparent respects, Seabury Barn is a success story. The Bootstraps proposal was competently implemented; indeed, the initial LEAA grant was renewed. Opposition to the program was diffused by the Suffolk Advisory Committee to the Barn, which helped supervise the first year. The committee liked what it saw and indeed became an ally; eventually, it disbanded when it determined that committee overview was no longer necessary. In 1975, the Barn's state certificate was also renewed on a long-term basis (until 1986). More significantly, the Suffolk Youth Bureau picked up the Barn's (and mall program) funding after the renewed LEAA grant expired. Thus the youth program became stabilized on long-term state and local funding.

The success of the Barn was instrumental in achieving stability for SHM as a whole. Subsequent annual reports, although solicitous of private contributions, no longer had a frantic tone. The agency succeeded in continuing its advocacy work in a workable, if not comfortable, balance with the direct services that provided the economic foundation for agency operations. Services of both varieties were also diversified over a wider range of social needs in the county. And, while long-term loan obligations were still outstanding, the agency began to cover the cost of its current operations and chip away at the debt. Meanwhile, the size of the operating budget increased more than fivefold from under $100,000 in 1971–1972 to over $500,000 in 1976–1977, with the youth program accounting for well over half.

Although the Ministries changed in the process of achieving stability, it still retained the flavor of ecumenism, social justice idealism, and "street corner" social service that stimulated its founding. For Father Ryan, the outcome was also satisfactory. His actions helped absolve his diocese and other founding denominations of financial burdens, and in the process preserved his own effectiveness in diocesan and community affairs, and kept the concept of ecumenical cooperation, in which he believes, viable.

ANALYSIS

The establishment of Seabury Barn was part of an exercise in rescue of an unstable, small and young organization, whose failure nevertheless would have entailed significant financial losses and collapse of a cherished institution. The men who established SHM, including Peter Ryan, were idealistic, with strong beliefs in social justice, ecumenical cooperation, and service to the oppressed. But they were also pragmatic, recognizing that if SHM failed, it would have far-reaching implications for themselves, and for the concepts and modes of action they espoused. Thus, when pressed, they were willing to accommodate state and local program modifications in order to secure a solid base from which the Ministries could operate. Loyalties to the new organization (SHM) and to the founding denominations prevailed, so long as compromise did not blatantly undermine the concepts on which the enterprise was originally founded.

PUBLIC SECTOR VENTURES: CASE STUDIES

Brookhaven Youth Bureau

PRÉCIS

The Brookhaven Youth Bureau is a department in the government of the Town of Brookhaven in Suffolk County, Long Island. The function of the youth bureau is to comprehensively plan, coordinate, contract for, and in some cases directly administer, youth services throughout the town. In New York State, youth bureaus are the conduit for special state funds allocated for these purposes.

The Brookhaven Youth Bureau was established in 1977 after a year of planning by a special advisory committee appointed by the newly elected town supervisor. However, the initiative to establish a youth bureau in Brookhaven dates back to 1973. At that time, the proposal failed to make inroads with a Republican town administration, but supporters of the concept waited patiently and exploited a new opportunity in 1976 when the town administration changed hands in the election.

THE ENTREPRENEURS

Establishing a new program in the public sector normally requires the organization of an effective base of political support. This is true for the Brookhaven Youth Bureau. From various quarters interest existed in the town for the development of more effective and comprehensive services for youth. Representatives of these interests were eventually brought together into a working committee. Ultimately two town councilpersons, Karen Lutz (Democrat) and Joel Lefkowitz (Republican), became strong advocates for the initiative. But even in this political environment, the role of the individual entrepreneur can be crucial. In the case of the Brookhaven Youth Bureau, that entrepreneur was Tom Williams, a college professor who spearheaded the ill-fated activity in 1973, picked up the ball again in 1975, and ultimately became director of the new agency.

THE ORGANIZATIONS

The Brookhaven Youth Bureau is a department of the Town of Brookhaven, which is governed by a seven-member town board consisting of six councilpersons plus the town supervisor. A council majority was required to establish the youth bureau. For many years prior to 1976, both the supervisor and the council majority were Republican, and opposed to the youth bureau concept. In 1976 the Democrats won a majority, creating the opportunity for the youth bureau initiative.

The youth bureau is one of some 22 town departments, each with a department head who reports to the supervisor and the town board. In some ways the youth bureau is lowest on the departmental totem pole, with the lowest-paid department head, and total budget and staff very small compared to other units.

Thus, interdepartmental conflicts are potentially dangerous to the youth bureau. One source of sensitivity and latent friction is with the recreation department, a natural rival for youth programming in the town. Tom Williams explains why this was an initial source of opposition to establishment of the youth bureau: ". . . Most departments in the town really didn't understand what the youth bureau could do, or why one was needed. I think the recreation department in many ways was somewhat threatened by the interest [in] a youth bureau. . . . The [State Division for Youth's] regulations say that youth programming that is funded [for the] recreation department, which this Town has had for a long time . . . fall(s) under the youth bureau. So that was sort of an administrative consideration, although the recreation department here is so well established that it didn't affect them at all. But I think they had resisted a youth bureau in the past, and might have recommended against it [in 1976]. I don't know about it for sure. But they were never very positive. . . ."

It is not difficult to understand why the town recreation department was leery of the youth bureau. Nor is it hard to appreciate the especially tricky mandate of the youth bureau to build its own program primarily by coordinating the efforts of other agencies, both internal and external to the town government. Still, this is a cornerstone of the youth bureau mandate. Indeed, Tom Williams participates in almost a dozen interagency committees at the county and state levels, in his role as coordinator and youth advocate. But as far as other town departments are concerned, Williams (in 1979) observed: ". . . No other departments [except recreation] really knew much about [the youth bureau] or really cared. . . ."

A very crucial organization to the establishment of the Brookhaven Town Youth Bureau, and to its continued development, was the Division for Youth (DFY), an executive department of the State of New York. DFY's programs are basically divided into two functions, direct service programs (such as correctional institutions and services) and local assistance. Youth bureaus are the primary vehicle through which the State, via DFY, carries out the local assistance function, by providing funds to counties and municipalities for the purpose of supporting and developing youth-related services.

DFY's "carrot" to localities, to encourage the establishment of youth bureaus and their associated functions, is primarily financial. Youth bureaus allow localities to receive funding for which they would not otherwise be eligible. State aid is essentially provided on a one-to-one matching basis with town funding, up to a maximum of $2.25 per youth living in the town (as of 1979). However, only $1.20 of the $2.25 can be spent on recreation. The youth bureau permits the Town to receive the additional $1.05. Furthermore, participation of town youth boards in comprehensive planning with the Suffolk County Youth Bureau permits town bureaus to directly receive an additional $0.75 per youth through the County, or a total maximum of $3.00 per youth of state funds. Finally, comprehensive planning within the town itself permits an increase in this figure up to $4.50.

Aside from regular state aid through DFY, the Brookhaven Youth Bureau has been able to pick up other avenues of financial support. New state funds for runaways support its Sanctuary program, while CETA funds through the County Labor Department were used to staff special projects. Another grant from the Suffolk Youth Bureau supported Brookhaven's participation in the county's comprehensive planning process.

Consistent with the youth bureau's purpose to primarily coordinate rather than directly administer youth services, the bureau uses its funds to contract for various projects, taking advantage of both a local project's community base, and state aid matching provisions: "If they can raise some [local] money, I can match it. In other words, if the [local] group is . . . able to raise $1,500, they will give that to me, and I will use it as a local match [to] get $1,500 from the State, so I can boost their budget. . . ."

The Brookhaven Youth Bureau does centrally administer some direct services, such as the Sanctuary program for runaways but primarily its function is coordinative and its style is decentralized. Use of the contract mechanism is illustrative. Indeed, the contractual model is the genesis of plans for a much more extensive decentralization of youth bureau activity throughout the sprawling suburban town. Tom Williams explains: ". . . We have a scheme whereby the town would be divided into 11 regions and . . . that with each of those regions there would be some sort of a community-based development program and then, as needed, counseling . . . and family intervention services would be brought into the area . . . through an agency such as the Y or Catholic Charities . . . or our [own] Sanctuary program. . . ." (See Choices below.)

It is in the nature of a youth bureau that its director has plenty of "advice." In a town such as Brookhaven, the director is accountable to both the town board and to his own board of directors or youth board. In addition, individual projects or programs within the orbit of the youth bureau have advisory committees, while the youth bureau as a whole has a special advisory council composed of youthful members.

The DFY imposes certain requirements on the composition of a youth board. For example, the board must contain from 13 to 28 members. Furthermore, according to DFY regulations: "Lay citizens shall comprise at least 50 percent of the total membership . . . and be representative of such key interests as social agencies, business, youth organizations, industry and labor. Public officials may comprise the remainder . . . and should include representatives of disciplines directly concerned with the welfare of youth such as the Family Court judge, superintendent of schools, and the commissioner of health, mental hygiene, police, and social services."

In Brookhaven, the youth board is a direct descendant of the advisory committee appointed by Supervisor Randolph to establish the desirability of a youth bureau. Its composition is balanced politically (i.e., bi-partisan) and geographically within the town, and reflects a variety of local youth-related interests including the county police, schools, voluntary organizations, the YMCA, two youths (persons under 21 years old), and so on. The delineation of public from lay members is vague, as in the case of a policeman employed in the juvenile section who is on the board simply as a town resident. Furthermore, potential conflicts of interest are avoided by the creation of a category of ex officio (non-voting) membership. This applies to members of the town board (to which the youth board is accountable through budget and power of appointment) and to a member of the recreation department.

Tom Williams describes his board as extraordinarily effective, with this effectiveness rooted to its history in bringing about the youth bureau at the beginning: "There is always the question as to whether the . . . board is advisory or policy-making, and that sort of tension . . . exists. [But] to the extent that they make deliberate, thoughtful, and respectable recommendations to the Town Board, I think they [make] policy. . . . I think the fact that they are able [i.e., have the power] to recommend to the Town Board [who shall be] the director of the agency, is unprecedented. That's [normally] a political appointment from . . . year one.

"They recommended my budget for this year, which is an increase of $100,000 over last year. The Town Board accepted it with no cuts. I think that's extraordinary."

Of course, the effectiveness of the youth board vis-à-vis the Town Board is hard to separate from the effectiveness of the youth bureau director himself. Indeed, the director has a dual accountability to his own board and to the Town Board, and must effectively combine with his board to produce a united front. Williams explains, "I am accountable really to both groups . . . although the youth board is accountable to the Town Board. . . . It's sort of a triangle. . . . [But] it's very hard . . . for the Town Board to distinguish between me and my board because we work very closely and I don't do [things] my board doesn't know about and doesn't approve."

In short, the youth bureau, despite its consciously nonpartisan design, came into existence and continues to operate in an essentially political organizational environment. Geographically, bureaucratically, and in terms of partisan politics, the youth bureau must maintain a delicate balance and sensitivity.

CHRONOLOGY OF EVENTS

May 3–4, 1973—The Long Island Conference on Youth Services is held at the Suffolk State School, sponsored by various state and local social service-related agencies interested in youth services, especially the organization of youth bureaus and "comprehensive youth service systems." Sponsors include the Association of New York State Youth Bureaus (Long Island Region), the Suffolk Youth Services Coordinating Committee, the Suffolk Community Council, the Nassau County Health and Welfare Council, and the New York State Division for Youth. Attendees include Professor Martin Timin, a professor of psychiatry deeply involved in local youth programming; Milton Luger, Director of the State Division for Youth (DFY) which provides state funds for youth bureaus; Charles Merwin, Director of the Suffolk County Youth Bureau; and Andrew Casazza, Director of the Huntington Town Youth Bureau (the pioneer bureau on Long Island).

Approximately 20 people from the Town of Brookhaven coalesce at the conference and establish a Youth Service Study Committee. Tom Williams assumes the chairmanship of this committee.

Mid-May, 1973—Tom Williams exchanges correspondence with Charles Barraud, Brookhaven Town Supervisor on the results of the Long Island Conference, and the proposal to establish a youth bureau in Brookhaven. Barraud rejects the idea as unnecessary and duplicative of the town's recreation program.

May 30, 1973—The study committee holds its first meeting subsequent to the conference, and continues to meet over a period of several months. However, the political environment remains unreceptive, no major initiatives are taken, and the effort becomes dormant.

November, 1975—John Randolph (a Democrat) is elected Town Supervisor of Brookhaven. In addition, Karen Lutz and two other new Democratic candidates are elected to the Town Board. This is the first time since 1961 that the council majority and supervisor of Brookhaven are Democratic.

Williams approaches Randolph and later Lutz with the idea of establishing a youth bureau in Brookhaven. Randolph is uncertain but Lutz takes up the cause.

Spring, 1976—Under prodding from Lutz, Randolph establishes a bipartisan youth advisory committee to study the youth bureau proposal. The committee contains 12 members including Lutz, Williams, and a key and initially skeptical Republican councilman, Joel Lefkowitz.

May, 1976—The Youth Advisory Committee begins to meet on a bi-weekly basis through Spring, 1977.

June, 1976—Tom Williams is laid off from his position as director of the Experimental College at the State University at Stony Brook, as a result of university budget cuts. Williams goes onto unemployment insurance to support himself.

May–September, 1976—The advisory committee is very active. Its members meet regularly, and make numerous visits to community groups, schools, and agencies in an effort to collect information and develop ideas. Tom Williams is the engine. He personally visits and conducts interviews and collects data from nearly all 17 school districts and many other agencies and groups. Under committee auspices, Williams authors "Brookhaven Youth," a comprehensive and carefully written report documenting the significant needs and problems of youth in Brookhaven Town. The report is formally issued in December.

September, 1976—The advisory committee prepares a draft proposal for the Town Board to establish a youth bureau, recommending a first year budget of $50,000.

October, 1976—The committee formally recommends, and the Town Board accepts, creation of a youth bureau. $39,700 is appropriated for that purpose, in the 1977 budget.

December, 1976—The advisory committee formally submits the "Brookhaven Youth" report to the council, calling it a feasibility study required as a prerequisite for State Division for Youth recognition of a new youth bureau.

The Town advertises for the position of youth bureau director. The board asks the advisory committee to set up a screening committee to review applications.

January, 1977—Sixty applications are received by the screening committee, which selects three names to recommend to the Town Board. Tom Williams is included in this group. Simultaneously, the committee makes recommendations to the board for members of the youth bureau's advisory board. (All willing members of the advisory committee are included in the recommended group.)

February, 1977—The Town Board interviews the three candidates for director, and hires Williams.

April, 1977—The Brookhaven Town Youth Bureau is officially established by local law. The bureau begins to operate in a planning mode.

1978—The first local service contracts are issued to nonprofit groups in two school districts. Other services including a cable TV project, and a sanctuary project for runaway youth are organized. Comprehensive planning continues.

CONTEXT

Establishment of the Brookhaven Youth Bureau was a logical culmination of two social currents. First, the Town of Brookhaven was undergoing major population growth and its burgeoning youthful population was experiencing serious social difficulties. Second, there was a growing general interest, in the state as well as Long Island, in the coordination and development of preventive youth services through youth bureaus. In 1976, the local political circumstances were right for youth bureau proponents to ride these waves to a successful conclusion.

The demographic situation in Brookhaven was carefully documented by Tom Williams in his 1976 report "Brookhaven Youth," on behalf of the youth advisory committee established by Supervisor Randolph. The report highlights the fact that Brookhaven was by far the fastest growing town on Long Island, experiencing a 33 percent population growth over the 1970–1976 period, compared to 15 percent for Suffolk County as a whole, and 8 percent for Long Island (Nassau and Suffolk Counties). By 1976, the population of the town had reached almost 330,000, some 43 percent of which was under 21 years of age. Compounding these dimensions, Brookhaven is also the largest township on Long Island in terms of area, having almost 29 percent of the land in Suffolk County. Given Brookhaven's sprawling suburban development pattern, service delivery is thus hampered by low density and long distances as well as a fast-growing and youthful population.

Brookhaven is basically a white middle-class town, although the Williams report identifies pockets of racial minorities and indicates a relatively higher incidence of poverty in Brookhaven than Suffolk County as a whole. But perhaps what the Williams report did best was to dramatize the seriousness of youth problems in the town. According to the report, "The number of juvenile delinquency arrests as well as the arrest rate in Brookhaven is the highest for the county. There are many young people involved in drug and alcohol use and abuse. There is an alarming rise in the rate and numbers of teenage pregnancies. . . . Divorce figures, child abuse, the rising number of single parent homes, and out of wedlock births are all indications of the difficult times children are facing in their family situations. . . . The lack of employment opportunities, vocational guidance, transportation, recreational opportunities, and early childhood education are common throughout the town."

The Williams report, which utilized newly available (1975) census information, helped bring the problems of Brookhaven youth into public consciousness as never before. As Williams puts it: ". . . [The] statistics showed that the town was in trouble with its kids. . . ."

The general social context of Brookhaven made a youth bureau seem, in Williams's words, "theoretically a good idea." What was also helpful was a slow, but definite movement in the state and locally, towards the establishment of youth bureaus. For some time the State DFY had been generally encouraging of this movement. Fifty-eight youth bureaus already existed throughout the state, with the oldest ones such as those in New York City and Rochester, dating back several decades. In nearby Huntington, the first township youth bureau was established in 1968 and its director, Andy Casazza, has continued to be active in the youth bureau movement on Long Island. In 1970 Suffolk County established its youth bureau.

Williams describes DFY activity on behalf of establishing local youth bureaus as passively supporting: "They're looking to develop youth bureaus in all municipalities throughout the state, so they were for us from the very beginning. . . . They have always supported me and given me information. . . .[Nonetheless] the DFY leaves it mostly up to the locality. . . . DFY didn't come down and say, 'All right, it's time for a youth bureau.'"

Still DFY was an active sponsor of the Long Island Conference on Youth Services in 1973, from which the Brookhaven effort began to emerge. Indeed that conference whose "central focus is on youth bureaus which can be a principal coordinating and funding agency to advance the efforts of all agencies dealing with youth problems," revealed considerable interest in youth bureaus by various social agencies on Long Island and seemed to crystallize an underlying momentum in this direction.

Given the demographic imperatives, and the momentum of the youth bureau movement in the state and on Long Island in particular, advocates in Brookhaven required the right local political climate. Despite the Democratic majority achieved in 1976, the town was still basically conservative (see discussion of Constraints below). There was continual worry about expanding government and adding "duplicative" programs. People viewed the youth bureau idea from conflicting perspectives. Tom Williams recalls, "I remember a public hearing where they talked about a youth bureau. There was a fellow from a civic association who got up and said, 'I don't think we can afford it. My taxes are too high.' . . . Other people joined in on that. . . .[On the other hand] somebody from the League of Women Voters . . . said that she had quickly calculated how much a youth bureau would cost her, and she said it was probably 44¢ per family and . . . she'd be willing to pay at least 88¢. . . ."

It seems fair to say that while fiscal conservatism was strong, that 1976 was a relatively opportune time for pushing the youth bureau. The Democrats had taken over a surplus in the Town's budget, and Proposition 13 fever was not yet rampant. As Williams puts it: ". . . When Randolph took over, there was a surplus. . . . There was no tremendous fiscal crisis, and it was still a year in which there was growth, and an increase in taxes . . . didn't evoke crazy actions." Such an environment, if not supportive, at least did not seriously inhibit discussion of a new town department.

CHOICES

The organizational format of the youth bureau, as a separate department of municipal government, was pretty much dictated by state legislation and policy. As Tom Williams explains: ". . . In order to get state aid, you have to have a youth bureau that stands apart. In fact, there has been a lot of controversy . . . within the state about [having] youth bureaus under [a] human resources administration. . . . They will not give state aid to a youth bureau within that [type of] structure."

Neither can youth bureau functions be entirely contracted out to private groups: "[One] can't contract out the bureau [itself], but [one] can contract out everything else." On the other hand, ". . . the County has a youth bureau, and the County could contract [with a private organization] to provide all youth services to Brookhaven, if there wasn't a Brookhaven Youth Bureau . . . but a [private] agency cannot apply directly to the State for that money. It has to come through a municipality. . . ."

One option of Brookhaven youth advocates was simply to rely on the County, or an alternate means of supporting youth services. But as Williams recalls such services were already in place, but apparently not satisfactory: ". . . Before there was a youth bureau, the recreation department simply did its recreation [program] and got . . . state aid. . . They could get some youth services without a bureau." Furthermore, several agencies provided services in Brookhaven under contract with the County Youth Bureau: ". . . There were a number [of agencies] who were already doing that. . . . The County spends approximately . . . $300,000 in the town, so it is significant. . . . [But still] I really felt that the Town needed the youth bureau." One reason, as noted earlier, was that the combination of county and town bureaus working in concert would maximize state aid for Brookhaven youth services. Furthermore, a town youth bureau could more effectively articulate, stimulate, and coordinate *local* service needs.

In short, the (municipal) youth bureau framework had been long operant in the state, as the sanctioned (and funded) means for coordinating and expanding local youth services. It was the natural rallying point for youth service advocates. And having chosen to establish a youth bureau, its proponents in Brookhaven Town were fairly limited in their discretion of organizational format. Nonetheless, a number of clear decisions were required by Tom Williams and others in order for the youth bureau proposal to reach fruition.

Perhaps the first key decision was Tom Williams's determination to commit his energies to this project. The commitment passed through two stages. The first stage, from 1973 to early 1976, could be characterized by a consistent but low-level interest and exploration. The second stage, from early 1976 until the youth bureau was established in early 1977, was an intensive effort.

The second key decision was that of Supervisor Randolph to establish a youth advisory committee. This was the first official step, and provided the opening which youth bureau advocates needed to establish a foothold.

The third key decision was the strategy of the advisory committee itself. Undertaking an intensive information-gathering and analysis effort would allow the committee to make a strong case to convert skeptics and to demonstrate a high level of commitment by town constituents. (Williams himself made an explicit point of "donating" his services as "consultant" to the Town.) Finally, the choice of internal organization for the youth bureau would be crucial in its development. For example, the plans to develop services by contract with local nonprofit groups was a key decision.

Tom Williams's interest in the youth bureau dates back at least to the 1973 Long Island Conference. As a faculty member in the newly developing School of Social Welfare at Stony Brook at that time, this interest was consistent with his professional activities. As Williams recalls, "I was working . . . to develop a program to train social workers and youth workers, and . . . it was part of our effort to get the School [of Social Welfare] involved in the community, and provide a training ground for [students] . . . to learn about communities and to learn about young people, and how one could provide youth services to kids and families. So . . . that is why we got involved in that conference." But Williams took more than a passing interest; indeed, he assumed leadership for a Brookhaven task force.

Despite Williams's leadership of a 1973 Brookhaven study committee and subsequent advocacy of the youth bureau idea with politicians over the 1973–1975 period, nothing happened. Possibly this was related to strategy, and to the level of commitment Williams himself was willing to devote: "I became chairman of that group for Brookhaven, and we met with a large variety of people [but] we just weren't able to get anywhere. What we could have done, perhaps, was to do a massive community organizing job . . . but I didn't have the energy at the time. But my interest was there, and it was stimulated at that conference, and I kept in touch with people. . . ."

At one point following the Long Island Conference, Williams corresponded with Brookhaven Town Supervisor Charles Barraud in an effort to get the proposal moving. After Barraud's rejection, Williams considered approaching the town Republican Party boss, but later thought better of it: ". . . I spoke to several people about going to Richard Zeidler . . . who, as I could see, controlled most everything. . . .I felt that if there was an outside chance . . . [then] why not? . . . But I also think that if he said no, then that would absolutely close the door, so I decided not to do that. . . . I think I was right. . . . It would have become a political thing, and it would have become a Republican bureau, and when the Democrats came in, it would have been subject to [pressure]. . . ."

In 1976, the political situation changed and so ultimately did that of Tom Williams. With the initial success in getting the town supervisor to appoint a youth advisory committee, Williams began to sense not only the chance for establishing the youth bureau, but also the chance that he might become the bureau's director. By June, 1976, Williams had both an extra incentive and a need to commit himself to the project one way or another. He was laid off from Stony Brook and was faced with the choice of vigorously pushing the work of the committee (while living on unemployment insurance) or looking seriously for alternate employment. By that time the lure of the potential youth bureau directorship had become too strong, and he chose the former: ". . . It was a voluntary thing, and I did it both because I thought the Town should have a youth bureau . . . and then the more I did it, the more I realized that this would be a job that I'd love to do. . . . I can't say that I didn't have that idea from the very beginning, but the more I worked on this project, the more I liked the idea of implementing it. . . ."

The decision of Supervisor John Randolph to establish a youth advisory committee was a crucial step. That committee was one of several created by Randolph when he came into office, the others including committees on the handicapped, on shell fishing, and other issues. Still, the designation of the committee was by no means automatic. Randolph himself seems to have been ambivalent about the need for a youth bureau but was willing to consider it. Considerable prodding by Tom Williams, enlisting the crucially important aid of Councilwoman Karen Lutz, was required to get Randolph to agree to the committee. According to Williams, "I spoke with Karen and Karen really, in many ways, pushed John into the advisory committee. But it was John's creation. . . ." Indeed, the committee did reflect Randolph's caution. He balanced the committee with Republicans and Democrats. A key member was Joel Lefkowitz, a Republican councilman who was initially skeptical of the need for a youth bureau. He is quoted in a local newspaper as saying, "The town has for years had an excellent recreation program, and I was of the belief that if you kept kids busy and tired out, they wouldn't get into trouble. But I'm willing to believe I'm wrong."

Nonetheless, Lefkowitz's service on the committee converted him to an advocate, and his support became crucial to establishing the bureau and preserving the bipartisan and professional environment in which it operates.

The initial ambivalence of Randolph and Lefkowitz made the choice of the committee's strategy a very critical one. People both internal and external to the committee had to be convinced that a youth problem existed in Brookhaven and that a youth bureau was the proper approach to the problem. An intensive study was needed, and Tom Williams, with his own commitment now solidified, energized the committee to do so. And that study process, which involved interviewing of citizens and officials throughout the town, also helped build a constituency for the youth bureau concept. Councilwoman Karen Lutz explains how important the report which Tom Williams wrote on behalf of the committee was to galvanizing support for the bureau: " . . . The report was really a big selling point because there were people on the [board, including Councilman Lefkowitz, who weren't] . . . quite convinced about the definite need for it. . . . When some of the statistics came in that Tom was gathering . . . statistics on criminal activity of the youth, juvenile delinquency . . . I think it did a lot to change . . . people's minds. You know, kids aren't staying around with their little hands folded . . . because . . . they needed some sort of services. . . . I think Tom's report certainly did a lot to change some people's minds."

With the youth bureau having come into being in 1977, organizational planning was the order of the day. The planners started with fairly vague normative concepts and principles. As Williams describes it, it reflects some of his own values about youth and community: ". . . I always saw the youth bureau [as] . . . an umbrella under which youth services could develop through the Town. . . . It would be an advocate for youth. . . . It would be providing community education . . . [and] organizing programs where they were needed. . . . It's really based on community, and . . . on the fact [that] if kids don't feel a part of it, it has no role to play . . . The way to provide good services is to build communities as a developmental model, . . . to work with all existing groups, and try to get youth involved in decision making. . . ."

Translating these concepts into practice involved various considerations of management control and flexibility, political equity and constituency building. Early on, such concerns came to the fore on the question of contracting out. Williams generally favored contracting out for services, but there were exceptions: ". . . The youth bureau really is not a direct service agency, so I wanted to contract out my youth service program, but I decided to keep the runaway program [in-house] because I felt that as a direct service that had town-wide application, that it would give me a network to gain information in terms of planning and providing other services. . . ."

Direct youth services were indeed contracted out, but here the political factors came into play. In particular, local contractor groups had to reflect local constituencies (through their own advisory councils) and contracts had to be equitably distributed geographically in the town. Williams talks about the first such contract: "The one in Three Village has a community board and is incorporated [as] not-for-profit, and they have been planning

. . . for a long time. . . . On a local level, they did what I did on a town level. . . . So they came to us . . . and we considered it. [But] we felt that we shouldn't fund one program without seeing proposals from another area. So we held off on it . . . [until] we finally got another proposal from William Floyd [School District]. . . ."

RISKS AND CONSTRAINTS

To Tom Williams, the risks involved in the youth bureau enterprise have been straightforward and very real. He invested enormous time and effort, with no assurance that the gamble would pay off. The crucial period was late in 1976 when Williams decided to work on the youth bureau, while unemployed, rather than look seriously for another job. His economic well-being was on the line, and there was good reason to doubt if Brookhaven would ever approve a youth bureau or make him the director: "At that point I suppose . . . it was . . . a financial sacrifice in the sense that I probably should have gone out and gotten another job, paying more than unemployment [insurance]. . . . But the more I worked on it [the youth bureau] the more delighted I became with the prospect . . . [but] it was a risk for me to put [all] my eggs in this basket . . ."

Indeed, even after Williams's efforts had resulted in establishment of the bureau, there was a real chance he would not be appointed as director. "The board advertised the job position of youth bureau director . . . and . . . received about 60 applications for the job. . . . A screening committee was set up, and they submitted three names to the Town Board, one of which was mine. And then the Town Board interviewed those three individuals. . . . And I must say I had invested so much that I got really nervous. . . . I went through a whole application process, and emotionally I thought they were absolutely unfair. . . . There should be no question whatsoever about my getting the job. But, on the other hand, I was really glad that they did that, because that made the appointment much more significant. . . . I feel that if they hadn't gone through that process for my position, it would be much more shaky."

Nonetheless, a less-secure position, especially in government, is hard to imagine. Initially, Williams's appointment was provisional: "I had no security for the job, at first. I was appointed in January, and . . . they could have terminated me . . . at any time. . . . I had no permanent civil service status . . . . no contract, no nothing. Yeh, it was a risk, but I wanted it enough. . . ." Later, in 1979, Williams did receive a permanent civil service status, however.

Establishing a youth bureau in Brookhaven required surmounting serious obstacles. These constraints were all essentially political. Partisanship, geopolitical distribution of services in sprawling Brookhaven, and philosophic and fiscal conservatism all had to be faced up to, in order for the youth bureau proposal to succeed. This was a major challenge for Williams, whose own apolitical image was a limiting factor because he was viewed as "a naive professor" whose ability to work in the real world, with politicians, was questioned. On the other hand, the fact that Williams was a "political nonentity" also worked to advantage in projecting an unbiased and untainted point of view.

To begin with, the youth bureau was not attractive to Republicans who controlled the Town prior to 1976. As Williams recalls, "We tried to approach public officials in the Town, [but] they were not receptive to it. They didn't think we needed one in the Town at that time." The resistance was a combination of philosophical and fiscal conservatism. The youth bureau would cost money, and was viewed as duplicative of existing school and recreation programs. Furthermore, there was some antagonism to an indulgent social services approach to youth. Youth problems were viewed as essentially a family matter, and a firm hand plus sufficient recreation was all that was needed. In a letter to Williams, Town Supervisor Barraud noted that: "The Town of Brookhaven is very proud of its recreation programs . . . [which are] . . . attempting to keep our young men and women active and a part of the community in which we all live."

Barraud went on to note: "There are too many overlapping governmental units and I, personally, believe that part of the problems facing this country is too many units of government performing the same service. If each school district would take care of the problems of youth programs, there would be no need for a duplication by another group. . . ."

Even with a change to a Democratic administration, the conservatism lingered. Randolph, the new supervisor, may himself have had his doubts about the need for a youth bureau, and in any case was cautious enough to require bipartisan support before he would move on it. Achieving that support was another political obstacle, although this exercise may have helped ensure a more professional nonpartisan bureau in the long run. Williams recalls the role of Councilman Joel Lefkowitz, the key Republican figure on Randolph's youth advisory committee: ". . . He is Republican and the Republicans in this town had not really wished that there be a youth bureau. They felt that it wasn't necessary, that recreation was taking care of all that. I think that Joel came to the advisory committee . . . with that same feeling. But he saw this information (compiled by the committee), and he began to look at it and read it and realize its significance. . . .He turned around and . . . said he fully supported the youth bureau, and that was a very significant step. . . ." In a basically conservative town (and with only a 4–3 Democratic council majority), the support of a verified conservative was necessary. It was not an issue for which the supervisor (nor perhaps other Democrats) would be put out on a political limb.

Once the bureau began operating, its decisions appear to have been constantly shaped and channeled by another type of political constraint—the necessity for geographic equity. It is no accident, for example, that the youth bureau's head office is in Port Jefferson, on the north side of Brookhaven Town, while the runaway program is housed in Patchogue, on the south side. As Williams puts it: "Everybody in Brookhaven is paying for the youth bureau. So if . . . people in Sachem get upset [because they] don't have any [local services], that's a real problem. . . ." From the initial awarding of contracts to the ultimate plan of youth bureau decentralization, geographic equity has been a byword for decision-making.

OUTCOMES

As of 1979, the Brookhaven Youth Bureau was a small but functional department of town government. Its budget had grown from an initial $40,000 in 1977, to $53,000 in 1978 to some $150,000 in 1979. Such a limited budget supported only a small core staff, but the bureau stretched these resources considerably by using its funds as seed money for local (contracted) projects, and by recruiting additional staff under the CETA program. Thus the bureau has been able to implement a sanctuary program for runaway youth, an innovative cable TV project (which provides a means to educate youth in television technology and to broadcast youth-related and other public interest programs to town residents), and to engage in youth services planning. Yet the resource base for the Brookhaven Youth Bureau remained tenuous. As Councilwoman Karen Lutz observed: ". . . That budget is a very low budget. Tom gets paid less than any other department head. . . . He has one staff member, really . . . I mean we [the Town] have put out a little bit of money, but it is getting a lot . . . back. . . . [On] a very little bit of budget . . . they have done . . . a lot of good things. . . ."

ANALYSIS

In the larger historical perspective, it seems inevitable that Brookhaven Town would eventually have had a youth bureau. Other towns in the region have moved in this direction and most have already established such departments. Nonetheless, the timing, professional quality, and organizational shape of the Brookhaven Youth Bureau resulted from particular local elements, including the nature of the town itself, political events, and the special motives and dedication of the primary entrepreneur, Tom Williams.

Williams tries to isolate his own contribution: ". . . If I had not gone to Randolph and said we needed a youth bureau . . . he might [still] have created a committee on youth. And if he created a committee on youth, I think they might have made a recommendation, but I don't think they would have made it as quickly. I don't think there is any way . . . they could have gotten their materials together. . . . It would have been delayed. . . . They might have one now, but I don't know. . . . I was the one that got the data and the statistics and wrote the report [but] I can't say that nobody would have done it. . . ."

However, in retrospect, a significant delay might have been fatal. Early 1976 was an especially opportune time, with a change of town administration, a budget surplus, newly available census data highlighting the burgeoning growth of Brookhaven and so on. A year or two later, the proposal might have been cut down by the backlash of tax-cutting fever.

Williams's dedication was fortunate not only for its timing but its quality. In order to succeed, the bureau needed to generate bipartisan support. This required convincing evidence of a problem, which Williams as a professional could produce. It also required entrepreneurship of an apolitical, conciliatory and non-threatening nature. Williams's style and motives were a good match for these requirements. He was not seeking partisan political or bureaucratic power, nor personal aggrandizement. He sought a meaningful job and he sought to establish youth services consistent with his own beliefs in youth and in the local communities. Those motivations served not only to energize Williams's own timely initiatives (and personal risk-taking), but also to establish a constructive tone in which the enterprise could go forward. While there was some initial skepticism about his pragmatism in a political world, his idealism and professionalism served well to build confidence in the concept and need for a youth bureau and to allay fears of political empire building.

The shape of the emerging bureau is also witness to the successful admixture of personal motivations and political requirements. The Brookhaven Youth Bureau is projected as a very decentralized regime. This suits the sprawling nature of Brookhaven Town and the need to be "fair" in dispensing resources and attention across the spectrum of local constituencies. But a more power-seeking entrepreneur might have sought more centralized control. Williams was comfortable, indeed happy, with the more decentralized scheme—which enhances his own predilections for interaction and local community building. Such a confluence of motives and requirements seems especially fortunate and perhaps necessary for long-range success. Similarly, the preservation of bipartisan support, which Williams's own apolitical motives helped to enhance, was particularly important to the development of the youth bureau for two reasons: It has in the past hedged the risks politicians faced in supporting the bureau, and it permitted the youth bureau to develop in a professional mode, outside the patronage system of local politics, and protected from the ax that threatens partisan programs when elections turn their supporters out of power.

Sanctuary Program
(Huntington Youth Bureau)

PRÉCIS

Sanctuary is a program for runaway youth in the Town of Huntington, Long Island, operated by the Huntington Youth Bureau. The program provides counseling and crisis intervention services including a 24-hour hotline and temporary shelter for runaways in the homes of volunteer families. Sanctuary began formally in 1976 with the receipt of an H.E.W. grant to the youth bureau. The grant culminated an evolution begun in the early 1970s by youth workers in the youth bureau's satellite Youth Development Associations, who provided services to runaways on an informal basis.

THE ENTREPRENEURS

The enterprising behavior that led to the establishment of the Huntington Sanctuary program took place in distinct stages and was distributed among a number of key figures. Initially, the Sanctuary model grew as an informal response by youth workers in the local Youth Development Association (YDAs) which operated under contract to the youth bureau, as a way of coping with runaways in their districts. Eventually, one youth worker, Jim Novotny, tried to formalize the program for two of the YDAs by promoting official certification of volunteer foster homes by New York State's Division for Youth. The actions and importuning of Novotny and other youth workers prompted the Huntington Youth Bureau itself to become involved in coordinating the Sanctuary efforts of the YDAs and promoting the program as a whole. At this level, Youth Bureau Director Andy Casazza directed his staff to develop proposals to the federal government in support of Sanctuary and was instrumental in eventually getting a proposal funded. Of special interest, Casazza arranged for a CETA worker, Sandy Booth, to be hired to assist with the efforts to coordinate and fund the program. Sandy, who eventually became Sanctuary project director, mobilized the research effort that led ultimately to the successful proposal to U.S. H.E.W.

It is difficult to pinpoint the beginnings of the informal efforts by youth workers to house runaway youths temporarily in the homes of volunteer families. Such efforts may actually predate the YDAs, which emerged as part of a youth board reorganization in 1972 or even the youth bureau itself which was established in 1968 as a successor to Community Development for Youth (CDY), a program begun in 1965 focused specifically on delinquent youth. There were several youth workers, located mostly in the Northport and Half Hollow Hills areas of Huntington Town, who worked with runaways and developed informal networks of volunteer homes to house them from time to time. These included Jim Boyle, Bill Nash, Jim Novotny, Chris Fedorowitz, and Paul Lowry.

Jim Novotny, who as youth worker reporting to Paul Lowry at the Northport YDA in the 1972–1973 period, was instrumental in working out the concepts for a formal runaway program. According to Lowry, "Essentially I worked with Jim . . . [but] it was mostly his idea. I was the supervisor. We would talk over what to do. . . . We wrote together the first little draft that got put in the file and eventually . . . was the basis for the . . . grant. . . ."

It is testimony to the loose and open structure of the YDAs in the early 1970s that Jim Novotny could play such a large role is researching the legal issues and shaping on a preliminary basis, the arrangements for certification of homes by the State Division for Youth. In terms of formal qualifications and organizational rank, Novotny had little in the way of credentials. He simply took it upon himself to see what he could bring about.

Much of the credit for the successful funding of the Sanctuary program by H.E.W., and the subsequent organization of the program at the youth bureau level, is attributed to Sandy Booth. With Mary Boyle providing the guidance and expertise on proposal writing, Sandy gathered and synthesized the information for the successful bid. According to Jim Novotny, ". . . Sandy was able to put it together. When she was hired [in 1975] she came to me and asked me for information [on] what I had done before. And I gave her . . . some proposals I had done . . .[and] the contacts I had made . . . Sandy took it from that point. She obviously took it well beyond that point. . . ."

Sandy Booth was a bit unclear of her assignment when she was hired as a CETA worker in 1975: ". . . When I came here it was clear that I was to develop a program, some kind of coordination [of] the YDA's [Sanctuary efforts, and] . . . to pursue certification [of foster homes] and to coordinate and maybe recruit homes or whatever, but I didn't have the concept of a separate project. I had only the concept of . . . coordinating services, of making a central service for runaway kids with what was available. . . ."

The individual entrepreneurial activities of the early youth workers, the particular exploratory efforts of Jim Novotny and culminating activity of Sandy Booth, are singular, albeit connected, threads in the fabric that ultimately resulted in the Sanctuary program. But the weaving of these threads is no mere happenstance. There was a master weaver behind the scenes, setting the tone and the context, citing opportunities and providing strategic stimuli. That person was Andrew Casazza, executive director and founder of the Huntington Youth Bureau. Sanctuary was one of several entrepreneurial ventures of the youth bureau during Casazza's administration, and in many ways the program developed in a manner consistent with Casazza's organizational plans. As Sandy Booth observes, Andy sets the tone: "Andy is an unbelievable person. I think one of the reasons this [youth bureau] system gets so much money is that it is prepared most of the time. It is two or three years ahead of other places. So all of a sudden things fall into place and people say, 'Oh, there it is.' But that's not really [how it happens]. . . It's been step by step by step. . . ."

Before his tenure at the youth bureau, Andy Casazza was a social worker for a variety of organizations in the public and nonprofit sectors, including Catholic Charities, the New York City Youth Board, and public schools in Suffolk County. Organizing the New York State School Social Workers Association was one of a continuing series of enterprising ventures for Casazza. He also founded the private nonprofit Community Development for Youth (CDY) and later CDY's successor, the Huntington Youth Bureau. Since 1968, he has directly or indirectly stimulated a series of new programs within the youth bureau structure. Casazza was also one of the founders of the Association of New York State Youth Bureaus, one of a number of involvements in community and professional activities.

THE ORGANIZATION

The development of the Sanctuary program parallels the evolution of the Huntington Youth Bureau itself. The first step came in 1965 when the private, nonprofit Community Development for Youth, Inc. (CDY) was established in Huntington. According to a 1972 youth bureau document: "CDY was created . . . in response to the emergence of fighting gangs modeled after those to be found in the worst of inner city ghetto areas. Their appearance shocked community leaders into recognition that the benign atmosphere of suburbia was in itself no protection against the development of anti-social behavior among its youth population. . . ."

The CDY operated three youth centers and developed a number of notable programs including the Teen Volunteer Corps, the Black Cultural Arts Project, and a drug abuse control and prevention program. Funding was received from the Town and the State Division for Youth, and from various other (specialized) sources.

In 1968, Huntington established its youth bureau. While there are perhaps 90 municipal and county youth bureaus, some of which date back several decades in New York State, Huntington was the first (suburban) township to have a youth bureau. The youth bureau is a department of town government, whose director reports to the town supervisor and council. The basic purpose of the bureau is to coordinate and develop youth services throughout the town. Basic funding for the bureau comes from the State Division for Youth, matched by local expenditures.

Paul Lowry observes the difference between the old CDY and the intent of the youth bureau: "[CDY] was an agency designed to deal with the drug abuser, the kid on the street, with the gang member. It was really oriented towards the troublemaker. . . . I thought we did great work [but] everyone hated us because all we did was deal with bad kids. No one wanted to know about bad kids. . . . [And we ran] . . . a . . . drop-in center [where] they became very visible. . . . [The youth bureau] . . . would be more sensitive to local needs and deal with a whole range of youth issues . . . [not] just the drug abuser, the gang member, the school dropout. . . ."

From 1968 to 1971, the youth bureau and the CDY operated as technically separate, but closely interrelated organizations. They had separate boards and staff, but shared physical facilities and an executive director (Casazza). CDY was more or less an action arm while the youth bureau administered and coordinated townwide youth functions. In 1971, the youth bureau developed a comprehensive plan which was to fundamentally change both organizations.

The plan, which was implemented in 1972, called for a decentralized system of (ultimately) eight private, nonprofit Youth Development Associations (YDAs), each assigned to a particular geographic area (school district) in Huntington Town, and each under exclusive contract to the central youth bureau. (The YDAs also raise some funds privately.) The youth bureau's 1977 Annual Report outlines the structure and operations of the YDAs: "The foundation upon which the decentralized youth service network rests are the eight Youth Development Associations. Each YDA has its own charter and each is committed to its local community. Policy is developed by a board of directors composed of youth and adults acting in partnership. Each YDA has a program coordinator and professional youth workers.

". . . The YDAs are encouraged to operate with a great degree of autonomy. They are regarded as in the best position to judge the needs and services most appropriate for their own communities. . . . At the same time . . . they are tied in with the centralized programs offered by the Huntington Youth Bureau [see below] . . . Most often this is achieved by the direct assignment of workers from those programs to the YDAs. . . .

"The YDAs are funded under an annual contract with the Huntington Youth Bureau. . . . Under this arrangement the YDAs must subscribe to the goals and guidelines . . . [of] . . . the Town's Comprehensive Youth Plan. Coordinators submit a bi-monthly report to the Youth Bureau . . . Field visitations are made by . . . contract managers from the Youth Board office. Such supervision assures the greatest degree of communication and coordination between the Youth Bureau and the YDAs."

As a result of the Comprehensive Plan, CDY was dissolved and its facilities and staff turned over to three of the new YDAs. Thus, at the youth-worker level, there has been a continuity since 1965, a circumstance pertinent to the evolution of Sanctuary. Just as relevant, however, is the decentralized structure of the youth bureau that emerged in 1972. According to Andy Casazza, the "bubbling up" of the Sanctuary idea from the local YDAs to the central bureau, illustrates exactly how the system is supposed to work: ". . . the basic idea was to get [the YDAs] to funnel needs into us . . . when we would assess those needs and then do a town-wide program. So what we saw in . . . Sanctuary was that concept . . . beginning to work. . . . A need was established—a need for a runaway program. The YDAs were beginning to see that the best way to approach this was to [recruit] volunteer foster parents. . . ."

The central youth bureau picked up the ball from that point, but Casazza credits the overall "system": ". . . We have a youth-service system We don't have projects and programs. We have a system , . . which . . . allows . . . that creativity to develop at a lower level [and] to come through. . . , If you don't have this system, then you go off with a fragmented approach and . . . that's not what we want. . . ."

That system Casazza talks about does not run without substantial management diligence. Negotiating skill is required to accommodate the competing demands of the eight YDAs in dividing up the youth bureau's budget. Considerable emphasis has been placed, for example, on the use of formal program evaluation procedures to assess YDA performance. In addition, the contractual arrangement between the YDAs and the youth bureau provides important leverage. In particular, the franchise of a particular YDA is not permanently guaranteed; indeed, on a couple of occasions the youth bureau has refused to fund a YDA. According to Paul Lowry, "It has been done. We have defunded agencies. They were just not performing. . . . We replaced them. . . . It's only been done twice and the second time . . . the agency simply picked itself up by its bootstraps and reorganized . . . and then it was refunded."

The contract leverage played a significant role in the case of the Sanctuary program. In an admittedly naive fashion, Jim Novotny began (in 1973) to independently pursue a sanctuary program proposal with the State Division for Youth, on behalf of the Northport YDA. Andy Casazza candidly asserts, "I smashed that one. . . . They were going to do that on their own. . . . My job here as director . . . is to work for the entire town. I saw those same basic needs for the entire town and not just for Northport. . . . So I put a provision in the contract that we have for all the YDAs . . . that . . . they cannot seek outside funding without the approval of the youth bureau. We didn't give them any approval. What we did do is say, 'We'll take your project . . . if we think it is a good one and make it go townwide.' . . . [So] sure [they could] go . . . all the way . . . to the [State] DFY, but then [they would] lose the rest of the money because of violation of the contract. . . ."

Casazza's style of handling the Sanctuary proposal is the rule, not the exception: ". . . For every proposal that comes out of here, I have to give an okay on it. . . . So I . . . make an input into all that stuff. . . . [That's] how it's done. . . . [Our] staff write it up and discuss it, and if there is something we don't like we'll change it. My big thing is that I want to see this program run professionally. . . ."

Since 1971, the Huntington Youth Bureau has been unusually successful in funding proposals, from a variety of sources. As Paul Lowry notes, there is a general atmosphere within the bureau that writing grants is essential to maintaining organizational viability: " . . . You want to maintain what you have. Obviously . . . that takes money . . . grants. . . . I think there's a certain amount of pressure. You have to be competitive. I think you have to write grants to survive. . . . It's like making profits. . . ."

The grant writing posture shows up in terms of the diversity of funding sources supporting the youth bureau's million dollar annual budget. Rather than depend solely on State Division for Youth and local (town) matching funds, the bureau raises half its revenues from other sources.

The Huntington Youth Bureau remains a bureau of town government, with its director serving by appointment of the Town Council. But, the diversified funding base, the dependence of the decentralized YDAs on youth bureau contracts, and the wide involvement of town constituents in the programs project advisory committees, YDA boards of directors, and the advisory board of the youth bureau itself, seem to have given the bureau a fairly stable base of operations. Perhaps more to the point, the Huntington Youth Bureau has been a leader in its field and has brought returns to the Town in terms of both external revenues and recognition for exemplary programs. Sanctuary is an integral part of that picture.

CHRONOLOGY OF EVENTS

1971—The Huntington Youth Bureau develops its Comprehensive Plan for youth services in Huntington Town. Emphasis is placed on local community involvement through eight nonprofit Youth Development Associations that contract with central youth bureau for local services.

1972—The local YDAs are established. Youth workers in some of these agencies work with runaway youth and develop an informal network of volunteer homes.

1973—The Sanctuary idea catches on, and is undertaken in most, if not all, the eight YDAs in Huntington.

Summer, 1973—Jim Novotny, a youth worker in the Northport YDA, researches the feasibility of certifying volunteer homes, and proposes a contractual boarding home/foster care program for the Northport and Half Hollow Hills YDAs. Novotny's efforts to negotiate this proposal directly with the State Division for Youth, on behalf of the YDAs, is quashed by the Town Youth Bureau, but a dialogue is begun between the latter and the YDAs on ways to improve and coordinate the informal runaway services.

1974—The youth bureau submits an unsuccessful $250,000 proposal to U.S. LEAA which encompasses services to runaways, including a residential facility called Harbor House.

1974—The federal government passes the Runaway Youth Act.

Early 1975—Program coordinators of the eight YDAs meet to attempt to develop common procedures for handling runaways, to clarify the legalities of overnight placements, and to develop a pool of knowledge on the runaway issue. The youth bureau becomes the coordinating agent.

May, 1975—The youth bureau submits an unsuccessful proposal for funding of a sanctuary project, to U.S. H.E.W., under the Runaway Youth Act.

February, 1976—Sandy Booth is hired by the youth bureau under the CETA program to coordinate the runaway program efforts. With Mary Boyle, Sandy develops documentation for a new proposal to H.E.W.

May, 1976—A second proposal is submitted to U.S. H.E.W.

July, 1976—The H.E.W. proposal is funded. Sandy Booth is appointed coordinator of the Sanctuary program.

August, 1976—Sanctuary formally begins operations. Over an eight-month period over 30 volunteer homes are certified.

1978—H.EW. renews its grants to run through 1981.

CONTEXT

Since the late 1960s, the problems of youthful runaways have received considerable national attention. Concern has been expressed over the number of youthful runaways (perhaps 1 million per year under age 18) and the declining average age of this group. There have been several notable phases of the recent youthful runaway phenomenon, over time. Attention first centered on the "flower children" who drifted to the Haight-Ashbury section of San Francisco during the heydays of the drug culture and anti-war protests of the late sixties. In the early seventies, concern shifted to the flow of runaways into the sex industry in places like the Minnesota strip in New York City. Later, the phrase "urban nomad" was coined to describe adolescents who roamed the streets and lived in abandoned buildings in places like the South Bronx. Attention also began to focus on the religious cults under Rev. Moon and others, which many young people ran to join.

The raising of national consciousness over youthful runaways led in 1974 to the passage of the federal Runaway Youth Act. This legislation provided for a national information exchange on runaways and funding of runaway programs through U.S. H.E.W. It is noteworthy that the national attention to runaways has been essentially urban-focused, if not on urban youth per se, then on the the urban destinations to which many runaway youth ran. The staff of U.S. H.E.W. appears to have assumed a parallel posture. Huntington is, of course, a suburban township, albeit a large one (population 218,000) and a fairly dense one (16 persons per acre). Thus the youth bureau in suburban Huntington Town, recalls in its (1977) Annual Report: ". . . considerable effort by HYB to convince H.E.W. that the problem of runaway youth was not exclusively an urban one. . . ."

Indeed, the youth scene in Huntington closely parallels national developments. The 1960s and 1970s, recalls Paul Lowry, were a time of restlessness for local youth: "Pretty much the same things . . . were happening everywhere. . . . People were running away on a day-to-day basis . . . in . . . the [late] '60s. . . . The drug scene was out of control. . . . There was a lot of heroin [in] the early '70s when I came here . . . in the parks, in the streets. The police were busting everyone in sight. There was a great deal of friction between the 'freaks' and 'jocks' and the whole hippie scene. . . . [In] '71 and '72 you have . . . the Jesus movement and kids were running away to that type of situation. . . ."

Given this general background, the circumstance of the local runaway appeared from the youth worker's viewpoint to be a mix of topical and conventional forces. Jim Novotny observes, ". . . There were a lot of things going on in kids' lives other than what was happening in school. . . . [Things were] happening right in their own homes causing them to run away, to leave home . . . to get out at the first opportunity they could. . . . Also, I was dealing with a lot of emergency [case] kids who were thrown out [of their homes] for a night or a weekend. . . . The same kids who were thrown out often . . . were the same kids having trouble in school. . . ." Indeed, the youth bureau's first Sanctuary proposal to H.E.W. cites five types of circumstances for which temporary housing was needed for runaways in the town. These included: immature independence-seeking behavior; flight from parental alcoholism, conflict, or other pathology; flight from direct parental abuse; parental expulsion from the home; and long-term hostility between parents and children, requiring temporary disengagement.

Quantitatively, the magnitude of the runaway problem in Huntington was estimated by the youth bureau in its 1976 proposal to H.E.W.: Out of a total population of some 27,000 youth between the ages of 13 and 18 (47,000 between ages 10 and 19), approximately 330 were reported each year to the Suffolk County police as missing persons. This figure appeared to have been fairly stable over the 1973–1975 period. The youth bureau estimated, on the basis of a local study, that for every juvenile reported missing there was at least one other that was unreported, yielding a figure of 660 runaways per year in Huntington.

Alternatives for servicing runaways in the town, other than Sanctuary, were meager. In the surrounding county, there was a county children's shelter with 70 beds, and a County Department of Social Services system of nonsecure detention with 21 beds, but these were all primarily for children processed by the Family Court. In Brookhaven Town 20 miles to the east, there was a residence for runaways called Seabury Barn which had 12 beds. None of the foregoing services were located in Huntington.

CHOICES

The development of the Huntington Sanctuary program was spurred by a number of critical choices made over a period of more than seven years. These choices arose in various ways. Some were solutions to problems developing in the context of current program operations. Others were responses to new opportunities (e.g., for funding) to which the organization was attuned. Still other choices represented the resolution of potential conflicts within the youth bureau framework. Overall, through a staged, evolutionary sequence of decisions, the rationale for Sanctuary's current design and organizational format slowly emerged in clear perspective.

The first critical choice in this evolution was the decision of youth workers, Bill Nash and Paul Lowry at first, and others like Jim Novotny a bit later, to set up their own informal networks of foster homes in which they could temporarily house runaway youth. As Jim Novotny explains, it was a creative act born of desperation: "I started . . . working with kids who were getting thrown out of their houses . . . [or] who left their houses, who didn't get along with their parents too well . . . or [would] have constant fights [after] which they ended up spending a night or weekend over their friends' [houses]. . . . Or they would have no place to stay for a weekend, or maybe for a week. . . . I was constantly being put into a position of . . . trying to get the kids back into their homes. . . . In some cases I actually could provide services [but for] a great [number] of kids I couldn't. . . .

"So I . . . tried to devise some sort of mechanism to . . . actually make my job easier. . . . It was really . . . a matter of my own survival as much as it was for the kids. . . . If I didn't have a place to keep the kids . . . I felt an obligation to put them somewhere. I would take them home with me, or I would actually call my [own] parents up. One time I . . . put [a kid] in a van next to the building, because he wasn't allowed in the building, and I put an extension cord right out the window and gave him a heater. He stayed in the van . . . until the landlord said he wasn't allowed to park there any more at night. . . .

". . . That [was] the basic way to serve these kids who [didn't] have a place to live. . . . Put them up in various places. . . . And it just wasn't Paul [Lowry] and myself. . . . There was [Bill] Nash who did the same thing . . . and there were a lot of people [volunteers] whom we could use for temporary housing as a means to serve these kids. So it wasn't . . . that [the] idea was new at all. That's . . . common sense. . . . You find a kid a place to live. . . ."

Given the practice of recruiting volunteer foster homes for runaways, the next step was to attempt to have these homes officially sanctioned. Although this task was not accomplished until 1976, with the successful proposal to U.S. H.E.W., the process was begun by Jim Novotny. After engaging in the practice for some time, Jim began to realize the hazards: "I realized it was illegal . . . the [volunteer parents] . . . were not legally allowed to house a kid who was a runaway. . . . [Furthermore], let's say the kid had drugs on him, and he was taking drugs in that house. Well, it really wasn't fair to the people who would put him up for the night. [Or] let's say the kid was hurt at the house. Those people were not covered. There was no insurance or anything. . . ."

Given these problems and misgivings, Jim Novotny, under auspices of the YDA in Northport, began to investigate certification of the homes. The specific impetus, which gave Jim the idea for certification, was the case of a particular teenage girl who was living in a foster home under the nominal supervision of the State Division for Youth: ". . . The DFY had only one worker for all of Suffolk County. . . . Basically the foster care unit [of DFY] was confined to the city, and the woman who was the worker . . . called up on the phone once or twice a month. . . . And this [particular] kid [was living in a] foster care home which . . . was [also] her boyfriend's [home]. . . . I had handled . . . two abortions for the kid and then [with] the third one . . . I grew out of patience. . . . The kid . . . shouldn't [have been] staying [in that home]. There was no supervision. Her [foster] mother was never home so she usually lived with her boyfriend, but she was only 15. And she was in foster care. . . . [DFY] had an obligation to her, and her foster . . . mother . . . had an obligation, [but] nobody was picking it up. [However, what] the foster care worker did was to allow me to find her [another] home. . . . She said 'Okay, if you find a home, I'll certify [it]' and she wrote me a letter to that effect. . . . I don't think . . . we [ever] got the kid a home . . . but what that [experience] did was [make] . . . me think in terms of another way to deal with kids [and that] people [would] . . . delegate me things. [Now] the

DFY was the funding agency for the youth bureau so . . . I decided to research . . . what the law was. . . . I [was] thinking [that] . . . putting up kids . . . could be more formalized and would [make it] easier for me to serve these kids who were runaways who had problems at home. . . . So I researched things . . . went to the library and . . . looked at the state laws . . . on foster care. I realized that kids could be placed in foster care [and that] parents may give the kid permission to stay with a stranger. . . . That it was legally all right . . . and . . . also . . . there were certain [authorized] agencies which were legally allowed to place kids in foster care and to deal with a runaway situation. . . . And I guess that from that experience I had with the DFY, I realized that an agency could probably delegate the power to do it. . . ."

Novotny's efforts progressed through discussions with officials of DFY and other agencies, and ultimately to the writing, with Paul Lowry (then coordinator of the Northport YDA), of a program proposal on behalf of the YDAs in Northport and Half Hollow Hills. The proposal called for an experimental program, with procedures for screening and certifying volunteer homes, and providing ancillary counseling services to children and their families, although it made no specific mention of funding. In any case, this local YDA effort was short-lived—technically quashed by Andy Casazza on grounds that the YDAs were attempting to go over his head to the State DFY. In addition, substantive issues arose over what children would be eligible for service by locally recruited homes. Novotny, for example, preferred local access only, while Casazza was worried about access to the homes for minority group kids. In any case, the Novotny initiative did serve to engage the central youth bureau in serious discussions regarding the development of a network of certified homes for runaways. In summary, Novotny recalls, ". . . I should have gone through the youth bureau, and the youth bureau should have checked the program . . . and then [gone] to DFY. What eventually happened is that the youth bureau picked up the program. I couldn't get anywhere with it myself."

By 1974, the central youth bureau began writing a series of proposals which, by 1976, would succeed in funding a Sanctuary program. In 1974, a comprehensive service proposal was sent to the Law Enforcement Assistance Administration (LEAA) of the U.S. Justice Department. It failed. Early in 1975, the coordinators of the eight YDAs began discussing an integrated Sanctuary effort, focused on centralized youth bureau coordination. In May 1975 funds for Sanctuary were sought by the Youth Bureau from H.E.W. under the new runaway legislation. It, too, failed. Early in 1976 CETA allocations were secured by the bureau, and Sandy Booth was assigned to plan and coordinate a Sanctuary program. Late, in May, 1976, a successful proposal for Sanctuary was sent to H.E.W.

There seem to have been two sources of impetus for this spate of grant-seeking activity. One source was simply the general entrepreneurial mode of the bureau in seeking to expand and diversify its programming for the town. The second was pressure from the YDAs for the youth bureau to provide help and support for their informal volunteer programs—some of the problems of which the Novotny proposal had sought to address. As the (1977) Youth Bureau Annual Report summarizes it: "What was clearly needed was a more formal program in which a greater number of carefully screened homes could be recruited. . . . In addition, these volunteers' homes could be properly certified, by the New York State Division for Youth, and volunteer parents could be carefully trained and professional staff support could be provided during this period of crisis intervention."

And there were other good reasons for seeking central youth bureau involvement. Paul Lowry reviews a number of such reasons, beginning with easing of the load on youth workers: "When you work with runaways, it just takes so much of your time. . . . One case can wipe out a whole 40-hour week. . . . It is a crisis situation [that] needs your support. . . . At the same time, as a youth worker you have other things to do . . . counseling cases . . . supervision [etc.]. . . . You need someone who can really coordinate the services, who would have the time to deal with just runaways. . . . The [Sanctuary] coordinator [and her] two case managers are very important.

"The other major difference is that the only way for a runaway, two [o'clock] in the morning to get [help was] to get in touch with the worker [by calling] their home phone number. . . . [We] now have a 24-hour hotline . . . 24 hours, 7 days a week . . . so there is no problem. If you call the hotline number . . . at 4 in the morning . . . the [operator] that answers . . . will refer it [appropriately]. . . . So we increased the possibility of a real quick response . . . not leaving the kid on the street. . . ."

There was also the matter of providing more comprehensive therapeutic services, via a central program. According to Lowry: ". . . What was needed [was] to make sure every runaway had the potential of coming here and getting the services that [he] wanted. . . . Someone [who] can really devote the time that the runaway needs . . . [and] what the family needs . . . [as opposed to] the youth workers [who] have to do everything. . . ."

Finally, there is the question of coordinating the capacity of the volunteer homes themselves. Despite a preference for keeping the use of volunteer homes confined to youth from the local YDA districts, the YDAs still needed flexibility in particular cases. As Sandy Booth explains: "If a YDA had a runaway . . .I could tell them where [someone] had a home. . . . It would still be very decentralized . . . except for information and referral purposes. . . ."

The precise design of Sanctuary, in terms of what was sought by the youth bureau through grant proposals, went through a number of phases. At first, Casazza sought to make Sanctuary part of a comprehensive proposal to LEAA in 1974, as such funding would accomplish a variety of service needs. According to Casazza: "It was a very extensive proposal, which to this day I think was a fantastic proposal. It called for what we know now as . . . Sanctuary; it called for . . . actually a runaway house to be called Harbor House as an interim placement which we [still] don't have . . . and it also called for FACILE [a supportive services component]. . . ."

The "Harbor House" proposal failed, for political reasons according to Casazza because approval through the Republican-dominated County was required for LEAA projects [see "Constraints" below]. When the H.E.W. legislation was passed, the youth bureau's response was more modest. The YDAs had already begun to mobilize themselves around the voluntary homes network, and Casazza had decided by that time to drop the Harbor House facility, and to break off and fund FACILE on its own. What was left was an innovative proposal, submitted in May, 1975, more closely resembling the original YDA volunteer home system, and more in tune with the spirit (and funding capacity) of the new legislation. The fact that FACILE was already operating to provide ancillary services to the families of runaway youth appeared to strengthen the proposal.

The first H.E.W. proposal also failed for a variety of reasons connected with the urban, facility-oriented "mind-set" of H.E.W., and the lack of political leverage [see "Constraints" below]. Also, while the proposal was well written, it did not marshall the facts on the runaway problem, nor provide other necessary documentation. This failure plus the continued pressure from the local YDAs set the stage for the next key decision—the use of CETA to underwrite a Sanctuary coordinator at the youth bureau. CETA allocations were available from the U.S. Department of Labor, and the youth bureau would naturally respond to this opportunity to supplement its staff. And for two reasons, assignment of a CETA worker to Sanctuary made good sense. First, that worker could directly undertake some of the coordination functions. As Sandy Booth saw it: "I was to pursue certification [of the homes] and to coordinate and maybe recruit homes . . . making a central service for runaway kids with what was available."

Second, the CETA person could do the leg work required to pull together a successful proposal. As Casazza puts it: ". . . CETA came down the pike and we decided to use somebody to . . . keep on top of this [Sanctuary] thing. Sandy was a facilitator . . . able to pull in the little things that had to be done on that [proposal]. . . ."

The youth bureau might have been content to run Sanctuary at a rudimentary level—a CETA worker providing whatever coordination she could. But this would have been uncharacteristic of the Huntington Youth

Bureau especially in view of the recurring proposal solicitations of H.E.W. As Sandy Booth puts it: ". . . The government sends out every year guidelines for that year's funding, so we just made another stab at it. . . ."

Moreover, as Paul Lowry notes, reliance on CETA would have been unstable: "We [might] get a few more CETA people . . . and let them be the Sanctuary staff. But that would have been a fairly unstable sort of situation. The turnover at CETA would have [been too rapid]. . . . It's much better to go for funding since it was available. . . ."

By 1976, with Sandy Booth on board, the lessons required for funding the proposal were well learned. According to Andy Casazza: ". . . Sandy's job was to put in place some of the things that we needed to sell this to . . . H.E.W. We worked out the whole certification [problem] of foster homes through the Division for Youth. We rewrote the project . . . Mary [Boyle] doing most of the rewriting . . . and we made lots of phone calls to Congressman Ambro and his staff. And lo and behold, we were funded. . . . If you look at it from a business standpoint . . . we took what we saw was a market here, we packaged it correctly, and then did an aggressive sales job using the one contact that we had, [Congressman] Jerry Ambro, and it worked."

RISKS AND CONSTRAINTS

Significant risks were taken by youth workers and volunteer foster parents in the early days of development of the Sanctuary program. The youth workers, and the YDAs with whom they were affiliated, were aware, for example, of the potential liabilities they faced if a runaway was maltreated in the home of a volunteer or if a runaway caused harm to the volunteer. Furthermore, the informal arrangements themselves were probably illegal. The state law, as reviewed in the first proposal to H.E.W. in 1975, requires that ". . . no person may provide board for children without a certificate to do so" and that the placing agency "inform parents and receive their permission to place their runaway child in an emergency placement." Neither requirement was fulfilled by the informal Sanctuary system prior to 1976.

The risks to the youth workers and YDAs were mitigated by the fact that volunteer homes were recruited on an informal, personal basis. Thus, there was reasonable assurance that volunteers were trustworthy and sincere. Seemingly greater risks were taken by the volunteer parents themselves, not only because they weren't legally certified to board children, but because they opened themselves to unknown hazards associated with the runaways. Drug usage and the possibility of accidents or destructive behavior are two contingencies that Jim Novotny worried about, for example.

Even later as the program became officially sanctioned, some risks remained. As Sandy Booth puts it: ". . . To house runaways in volunteer families is risky business. . . . If one person got hurt, either the kid . . . or the family who was the host . . . it would not only [have] destroyed this project, but [would have] really been very harmful to the youth bureau."

As the realization of the risks led to efforts to formalize the volunteer home system, and ultimately to coordinate and support it through centralized funding, the entrepreneurs were both inhibited and channelled by various institutional constraints. These constraints can be roughly divided into two types—bureaucratic and political.

The early efforts of Jim Novotny to explore certification of the volunteer homes tested some of the bureaucratic waters. Novotny found, for example, that if the State DFY were to certify the volunteer homes that these homes would be subject to general usage for placement of juvenile offenders by DFY. As Paul Lowry notes, this problem was not solved until much later: ". . . We wanted [DFY] . . . not [to] use those homes for anybody else. . . . I think [DFY] looked more positively on the program once the federal government sanctioned it by giving it money. . . . [Then] it [became] a lot easier to work out the mechanics of home studies and . . . certifying the homes. . . ."

Another option Novotny explored was to have his YDA qualify as an "authorized" child care agency. This would permit it to receive foster children and place them out in its own (certified) homes. But such an option would have entailed a multitude of difficulties including departure from the principle of volunteer homes, in favor of per diem reimbursements, and (as with DFY) opening the YDA to a range of placement demands by the County Department of Social Services. More to the point, however, the possibility of mounting the considerable effort for YDAs to become incorporated as child care agencies, within any reasonable period of time, seemed remote.

Once the Sanctuary initiative was picked up by the central youth bureau, the constraints exhibited more of a political flavor. Indeed, underlying the rationale for squelching the independent YDA initiative was the notion that the youth bureau was there to serve the whole town and that major new services ought to be available townwide. As Paul Lowry puts it: "One of the main thrusts of this system [is to] have equal access to the basic services that people need. . . ." It is part of Casazza's notion of "something for everyone": "Not just [in] suburbia [but] maybe everywhere. . . . Everyone wants a piece of the action. . . ."

At the county level, politics was a clear constraining factor on the youth bureau's Sanctuary-related efforts. Huntington is a Democratic town in a Republican County. This fact of political life appears to reflect itself generally in the share of county services Huntington receives, and it is blamed for the failure of the Harbor House proposal to LEAA in 1974, which required the blessing of the Suffolk County Youth Bureau. Indeed, the political roadblock here helped induce the youth bureau to look elsewhere for funds.

Elsewhere meant H.E.W. Here, however, there was a bureaucratic "mindset" that had to be overcome. For one thing, runaways were conceived as an "urban problem," so it would take some convincing to fund a program in suburban Huntington. As Andy Casazza describes it, this stance seems both politically and dogmatically based: ". . . It came back that, well, the county and Long Island were, you know, not priorities [for] the federal government and [for] runaway projects. . . ."

Another apparent bias of H.E.W. was toward residential programming, where "beds" could be counted and credited to the funding program. The most clear (hardest) manifestations of "beds" would, of course, be the development of new residential facilities. Sanctuary, on the other hand, was based on "soft" beds in the homes of volunteers, and on preventative programming through ancillary counseling to minimize actual residential care. As Paul Lowry indicates ". . . H.E.W. . . . would like to see a lot more housing. . . ." Casazza elaborates that: ". . . We were very lucky . . . that we were one of the few [early] grants that didn't have . . . what I call the traditional type of runaway program—a runaway house. We didn't have a building attached to this [proposal]."

Ultimately, Casazza recognized the semi-political nature of the grant process through H.E.W. And he skillfully remedied the situation through the office of local Congressman Joseph Ambro, a former Huntington Town supervisor: ". . . I learned that congressmen do have . . . certain inputs into decisions . . . so I went through Jerry. A lot [was] done through that congressional office."

OUTCOMES

By several measures, the Huntington Sanctuary program can be regarded as a success. Starting with five active volunteer homes prior to the grant in 1976, it has generated more than thirty certified homes in the town, exceeding the goal of 25 set in the 1976 proposal. By 1979, Sanctuary reported a 95 percent return rate of boarded runaways to their own homes, somewhat higher than the 90 percent reported rate from volunteer homes prior to the grant.

The crisis aspects of the runaway problem were also moderated in Huntington. For example, between 1976 and 1977 there was a 38 percent decline in the number of Huntington youths reported to the police as missing compared to an 8 percent increase in such reports for the county as a whole. Furthermore, the recruiting of volunteer homes has leveled off. Thus, Sanctuary was seen to be working in a preventative as well as crisis mode. According to Paul Lowry: ". . . They stopped recruiting [homes] because they couldn't use any more. . . . The major difference that we found over the two and half years [since 1976] with the grant has been the number of cases that we house. We found in the beginning that there was [relatively] more housing. . . . We . . . now often get to a case before it's a real home crisis. Kids will call. Parents will call. . . . It's more preventive [now]. . . ."

Clearly one reason for this outcome is that Sanctuary was accepted by the local residents of the town. According to Lowry: "My feeling is now that if someone runs away, and you were a parent, you would just as likely pick up the phone and call the [central] Sanctuary or [the] YDA [as] you would . . . call the police. It would be more likely [that] the Sanctuary [coordinator] or case manager, or YDA youth worker [would] know about the runaway and [have] already met with him. . . ."

On a regional basis, the Huntington Sanctuary program became the model for youth bureaus in other towns in Suffolk County, especially since 1978 when New York State passed its own legislation funding runaway programs. Sandy Booth and her staff have provided technical assistance, for example, to nearby Islip, Babylon, and Brookhaven towns.

Nationwide, Huntington Sanctuary has been cited as an exemplary project by H.E.W. According to the youth bureau's 1977 Annual Report: "The program has been selected as an exemplary model for aftercare services as among the five best in the country and as among 20 runaway programs of all types selected for a special study. Visitors from as far away as California have come to inspect the program first hand."

The spate of publicity and attention came unexpectedly to the Sanctuary staff. But as Paul Lowry notes, Sanctuary's uniqueness was recognized: "Of the 20 [exemplary] projects that I know of . . . there were none very much like this. [For example], none . . . were part of a comprehensive youth system plan . . . [which] had somebody . . . [with] the power to coordinate and make things work. . . . There are other systems . . . that provide just as good youth services, I am sure . . . [but] I think there are very few superb runaway programs. . . ."

ANALYSIS

Several crucial factors were responsible for the successful evolution of the Sanctuary program in Huntington. At the outset, the idea of a volunteer foster home network was born out of the empathy and pressing circumstances of a handful of dedicated youth workers. These workers acted out of conscience and expediency, and perhaps out of some predilection for community organizing and career ambition in administration.

The relatively free-wheeling context of the local nonprofit YDAs seems to have encouraged enterprising behavior by the youth workers. Not only were informal home networks developed by individual workers, but the structure allowed for someone like Jim Novotny to explore on his own program arrangements for official certification and supportive services. The motivation for that exploratory effort was again, a mix of problem-solving addressed to the risks and burdens of dealing with runaways, and an adventurous (perhaps naive) personal determination to see what could be organized or put together.

The structure of the Huntington Youth Bureau system, created by the 1972 Comprehensive Plan, was another key factor in allowing Sanctuary to develop into a mature and stable program. Although the youth bureau restrained Novotny and the Northport YDA from pursuing the original initiative, the youth bureau was structured to be receptive to local YDA needs and to the development on a townwide basis, of ideas that percolated up from below. Another characteristic of the youth bureau, its aggressive grant-seeking posture, was also an essential ingredient. Under Casazza, the youth bureau became attuned and prepared to respond to external grant opportunities appropriate to its program.

The program ideas of the YDAs and the channeling of these ideas into the central bureau structure, still required catalysts. One catalyst was Sandy Booth. With Mary Boyle's guidance, Sandy marshalled the facts, drawing on the materials gathered by Novotny and others, to develop a successful, high-quality proposal. In addition, she put into practice the first coordinative efforts of the central youth bureau runaway program. With someone like Sandy being given specific and primary responsibility for coordination and development of Sanctuary, this project would no longer risk falling through the cracks of the decentralized youth bureau–YDA structure. Another catalyst was Casazza's own behind-the-scenes efforts in support of the latter proposal. Casazza pressed the right political buttons to smooth the way for proposal acceptance.

The case of the Huntington Sanctuary program provides an interesting perspective on the interplay between government and nonprofit agencies. As private, nonprofit community-based agencies, the YDAs had the autonomy and mandate to explore in relatively uninhibited fashion new programmatic mechanisms. But as contractors almost exclusively dependent on government (youth bureau) funds, their wings were clipped, limiting their ability to go beyond local matters without great risk.

The Sanctuary case demonstrates how government can both inhibit the flexibility of nonprofits, through fiscal reliance, but also build upon nonprofit initiatives. Here the youth bureau was able to take an essentially good idea (volunteer homes) which probably could not have been effectively marketed by the individual YDAs, and provide the coordination and resource development to make it work. In the process, the original YDA considerations became transformed from essentially programmatic concerns (how to cope with regulations and resource requirements) into more political questions (how to distribute benefits and satisfy alternate constituencies).

More fundamentally, however, the relationships of the YDAs to the central youth bureau constituted a study in maintenance of organizational vitality. As chief executive, Andy Casazza seemed to have extracted the benefits of both decentralized activity and centralized services and controls. In particular, the youth bureau managed to give the YDAs sufficient autonomy, encouragement, support, and credit for what they were doing, so as to foster innovation and development of new programs and concepts. Yet the bureau also exploited economies of scales in resource development (e.g., grant-writing) and coordination (the hotline, facilitating resource exchanges among YDAs, etc.). Moreover, the central bureau candidly policed and harvested YDA service programs once they were ready for town-wide application. Clearly a delicate balance was maintained between too much control, which might have discouraged innovation, and too much autonomy, which would have led to inefficient and poorly distributed services.

Outpatient Clinic
(Sagamore Children's Center)

PRÉCIS

Sagamore Children's Center is one of five psychiatric children's hospitals operated by the New York State Department of Mental Hygiene. In 1974, under the leadership of its director, Dr. Mary Hagamen, Sagamore received a three year hospital improvement grant from U.S. H.E.W. to establish an outpatient program. Over the period of the grant, a comprehensive program of outpatient and parent-training services was developed, moving the emphasis of Sagamore's overall program from inpatient to outpatient care. Following expiration of the grant and the departure of Dr. Hagamen, this emphasis was largely dissipated, although some of the new services have been continued.

THE ENTREPRENEUR

Establishing Sagamore's outpatient department involved the efforts of a number of key people. Staff of the central office of the New York State Department of Mental Hygiene originally alerted Dr. Hagamen to the opportunity and assisted the negotiations with personnel at U.S. H.E.W. Staff of the Suffolk County Department of Health, including Dr. Lewis Kurke and Oliver Shepers, collaborated on development of the plans and proposal. Aileen Townsend, a social worker picked by Dr. Hagamen as director of the new department, was largely responsible with others like Jeff Hammerman for putting the plans into practice, while Ken Kaufman, a staff psychologist at Sagamore, deserves primary credit for developing the parent-training components of the program.

The central character, however, was Dr. Mary B. Hagamen, the director of the Sagamore Children's Center. Dr. Hagamen, who generated the idea, took major responsibility for writing the proposal and hiring and overseeing the staff that would implement the venture. As Dr. Hagamen deprecatingly saw her role: ". . . [the] guy from Albany said . . . 'You want to write a letter to Santa Claus?' and I said 'yes' and I wrote it." Nonetheless, while the grant opportunity may have been fortuitous, and probably crucial in permitting the development of the outpatient department, it represented a logical extension of Dr. Hagamen's own professional thinking and development of programs already underway under her leadership at Sagamore (see "Organization" below).

THE ORGANIZATION

Sagamore Children's Center was the first of five state psychiatric hospitals for children in New York State to open in the early 1970s. The hospitals culminated a movement begun in the 1930s to separate child from adult institutional programs in mental health. In the 1930s, Rockland State Hospital was built as a special hospital for children, under WPA. In the 1940s, Rockland became overcrowded with children having emotional problems. In the early 1950s, a state-sponsored committee with prominent clinicians such as Lauretta Bender developed a plan for children's psychiatric facilities. Twelve new units were envisioned. In the interim, however, temporary facilities for children were opened at King's Park and Central Islip hospitals on Long Island. In the 1960s, Governor Rockefeller became interested in the plans, expressing his own predilection for interesting architecture. Ultimately, five new hospitals, each of approximately 200 bed capacity and 300 to 400 staff, were authorized and built. Sagamore's mandate was to serve the Long Island region —Nassau and Suffolk counties.

As Dr. Hagamen explains, the initial conditions and environment under which each of the hospitals opened influenced the nature and flexibility of their operation. The children's hospital in the Bronx, for example, opened empty, and was able to give more emphasis to outpatient services from the start. Sagamore, on the other hand, inherited the child patient load from King's Park and Central Islip and opened with a nearly full inpatient registration. Still, the children's hospitals were all basically designed as inpatient facilities. As Dr. Hagamen notes: ". . . I would say that the goals of all these places were pretty much the same—to provide the best possible psychiatric service, with a priority for inpatient service. In other words, nobody else did the inpatient service to the degree that the state facilities did. And, therefore, you had to take care of all the inpatients before you could do anything else."

In most respects, Sagamore is a prototypical state operation. Expenditure and policy decisions have to be cleared through the central office in Albany. Employees are civil servants, with appointments drawn from lists determined by performance on civil service tests.

During Dr. Hagamen's tenure as director at Sagamore there were some anomalies in her accountability structure, leaving her a considerable degree of autonomy. Dr. Hagamen recalls: ". . . The director historically had total accountability to the commissioner [of mental hygiene]. Then Albany began to interject a series of associate commissioners. Where there had been six associate commissioners . . . in 1960, there were over 50 in 1975. . . . We started out reporting to the Deputy Commissioner for Mental Health. Then . . . about 1971, we were changed over . . . to the Deputy Commissioner for Mental Retardation. . . . Around 1976 . . . they created an office for children, and . . . we were supposed to report to [the director of that] but he didn't have any authority over us because he was a staff . . . person. . . . Then they made these regional offices, where they put a whole new group of people . . . hoping to decentralize. . . . They did that to a degree, but they didn't take out many of the people in the central office. So then you had two systems. And you know, when you have that, nobody has a line on you. . . ."

The speed with which the proposal for the outpatient department was approved (see "Chronology"), including its clear intent to shift state supported staff from inpatient to outpatient coverage, attests to Dr. Hagamen's relatively free hand at the time.

In addition to the formal bureaucratic hierarchy within the Department of Mental Hygiene, the Director of Sagamore also reports to a Board of Visitors. This is a group of gubernatorially appointed citizens that serves essentially as a sounding board for the director, although it is required to make periodic investigations of conditions, and file a report with the governor. Dr. Hagamen found her board helpful and supportive: "Our Board of Visitors was a watch-dog board, an advisory board, a sounding board for the director. . . . I think any director likes to have someone to tell what he is doing . . . to talk . . . to bounce off ideas. . . . We had a magnificent Board of Visitors. . . ."

"It is a thankless job to be on the Board of Visitors. You have to go to meetings every month. You have to do investigations.

". . . Four of the seven people were parents [of current or former patients]. And the ones that were not were very good people . . . [including] . . . the wife of one of the state representatives . . . [and] a man who was active in one of the . . . church establishments. . . .

"I'll tell you, I thought that they were behind me 100 percent. And you know, there was considerable hardship for themselves, too. . . . They spent hours and hours. . . . They were by far, in my estimation, the best informed and the most active Board of Visitors in the state. And they were called all sorts of names by people who were jealous of their position. . . ."

Internally to Sagamore, Dr. Hagamen says that authority was delegated to deputies, under her watchful eye and within established regulations: ". . . Most authority was delegated to division heads but I knew most everything that was going on, and I didn't like it if I didn't. . . . I didn't [restrict] what people did, but I had to know it . . . and in a . . . facility where you are dealing with a lot of people that work over a 24-hour period with the same clients, you have to have dependence on rules of procedure. Otherwise, it would be chaos. . . . You have to have some guidelines. You can't be loose and informal. . . . You must draw up things so people know what to expect. . . ."

Given her accountability structure, service mandates, and available resources, Dr. Hagamen made the most of the discretion at her disposal to deemphasize institutional (inpatient) care in favor of preventative and commuity-based alternatives, well before the opportunity of the grant from U.S. H.E.W. In a paper published in the *Journal of Child Psychiatry*, Dr. Hagamen explains the situation faced by Sagamore, early in her tenure as director: "In 1971 we were concerned when it was realized that although the Center had been conceived and designed as a facility for children of average intelligence, our energies and resources were being increasingly utilized by the autistic mentally retarded. It was obvious that unless ways could be found to decrease the need for 24-hour care . . . it was only a matter of time until the very retarded youngsters would be utilizing all of our resources to the exclusion of the brighter children. Thus we looked to means of secondary prevention and alternatives to long term hospitalization.

". . . Gradually, over a period of five years, a variety of programs was developed that focused on the management and treatment of the child in the context of family at home. . . . The family support services that evolved . . . can be divided into two major groups—home support systems and parent training programs."[1]

Thus thinking about outpatient-related services and some program developments were already underway at Sagamore by 1974 when the H.E.W. grant opportunity arose. It was a direction in which Dr. Hagamen's professional thinking had already been engaged.

CHRONOLOGY OF EVENTS

January, 1970—Sagamore Children's Center is opened. Dr. Mary Hagamen is appointed as its first director.

1970–1974—Sagamore evolves a series of "home support" programs to reduce dependence on institutional care of low-functioning (retarded and autistic) youngsters.

Early 1974—Dr. Hagamen becomes aware, through an office of the New York State Department of Mental Hygiene, of the possibility of applying for a Hospital Improvement Grant from U.S. H.E.W.

March 1, 1974—Sagamore submits the grant application for an outpatient program.

July 1, 1974—U.S. H.E.W. approves the three-year grant.

---

[1]Hagamen, M. (1977). Family support systems. *Journal of Child Psychiatry*, 53–66.

September 1, 1974—Expenditures on the grant officially begin. Ailene Townsend is appointed as Director of Outpatient Services (a new department).

October 1, 1974—The Sagamore Outpatient Clinic is opened. Development of an array of outpatient and parent training services is begun.

1976—Allegations of abuse and neglect in Sagamore's inpatient program appear in the press. Ultimately, Sagamore is engulfed in controversy and involved in official child abuse proceedings.

May, 1977—Dr. Ken Kaufman is appointed as Director of Outpatient Services, replacing Ailene Townsend who leaves Sagamore for another job.

June, 1977—Dr. Mary Hagamen leaves Sagamore to become Director of Child Psychiatry Clinic of Nassau County Medical Center. Robert Evans is appointed as the new director.

August 31, 1977—The Hospital Improvement Grant officially terminates.

January, 1978—The Sagamore outpatient unit is eliminated as a distinct organizational unit. Dr. Kaufman is made Director of Treatment Services, which encompasses both in and out patient care. Some outpatient services continue. Some are spun-off to external agencies.

CONTEXT

The fact that the Sagamore Outpatient Department was funded by the last grant under H.E.W.'s Hospital Improvement Program was symbolic of the juncture in social programming generally evident in the country and in New York State in the early 1970s. As Dr. Hagamen observes: "This was the last hospital improvement grant. . . . Hospital improvement plans were very big items in the '60s and this was the absolute bottom of the barrel. We drained the pot. . . . The '60s . . . were a splurging time for social and economic programs . . . [a] release of energies into the War on Poverty . . . that carried with it programs of building hospitals like Sagamore Children's Center [and] . . . Headstart, Title I Education [etc.]. . . . All kinds of social and economic programs focused on kids and particularly underprivileged kids. [Then came] the first [New York State] budget crises of 1972. . . . So in 1974 we were beginning to feel poor. . . ."

In certain ways, the Sagamore outpatient project represented the thinking of the 1960s. For example, the clinic idea was consistent with the objective of expanding government services to fill existing lacuna. As Dr. Hagamen notes: "[It was] the first psychiatric clinic for children in Suffolk County. . . . It seemed most important to have some kind of an outpatient unit because children would come to us and maybe not need inpatient care, yet that was the only thing we had to offer. . . . In Suffolk County in 1974 . . . there were no specific units for children. There were units for the developmentally disabled run by pediatricians at Suffolk State School. There were adult psychiatric county services, but there was no specific link with specialists trained in child psychiatry, geared to serving children exclusively. . . ."

There was even an anti-poverty flavor to the clinic idea. As Dr. Hagamen explains: "[Just as] education had its problems with segregated schools, health services had problems in that rich people went to private outpatient care and poor people went to inpatient care. And inpatient [care] was always kind of the end of the road. . . . So when you were designated as an inpatient facility, you just caught what was thrown to you. . . . We were conceived of as kind of the last place, and when I went to Sagamore it was my goal to make hospitalization treatment of choice rather than last resort. . . ."

The outpatient project was also consistent with emerging trends of the 1970s. New York State as well as other jurisdictions in the country had already begun to embark on "deinstitutionalization" of mental hospitals in favor of community-based care, and while there was no specific intent to apply this policy to the recently opened children's hospitals, the outpatient program was certainly consistent with that general policy.

Furthermore, professional thinking about autism and retardation was progressing to the point where institutional programs were being severely questioned. The Willowbrook state institution for the retarded in New York City was soon to come under heavy fire and forced to reduce its population in favor of community-based care. And as Dr. Hagamen explains, autism was beginning to be understood: ". . . [There was] a lot of pressure . . . put on us to take all kinds of youngsters . . . particularly those very low-functioning youngsters whose families did not want to put them into the facilities for the retarded. . . . [You see] in the 1960s there was a great confusion that gradually resulted [over] the difference between an autistic youngster and a retarded youngster. At that time, particularly the people in retardation were saying that autism is a psychiatric disorder and therefore . . . if you just do the right psychiatric treatment, up would pop a normal child. Well, that was a lot of magic thinking. . . . Gradually [we found] that 75 percent of autistic children are retarded and . . . were appropriately placed with other children with developmental disabilities and ones who need life long care. But [still] there was great argument as to where they belonged. Many of the other children's hospitals declined to admit them, but it seemed to me that there was a need for this service. We were there and if they were going to come in, the only thing for us to do was to develop services for them. Not to say 'we don't have a program.'"

CHOICES

Development of the Sagamore outpatient program exhibited a combination of fortuitous, evolutionary, and purposeful modes of decision making. The grant opportunity itself, rather than being deliberately sought out, was a bolt from the blue. A concerted effort to develop and fund a coherent outpatient program might never have emerged without this unexpected opportunity.

Yet in a real sense, Dr. Hagamen and her staff were "ready" for this choice. There was not much debate over what kind of proposal to prepare. The notion of an outpatient service was a logical extension to the home-support programs already developed at Sagamore for low-functioning children, and a reasonable response to local service demands. As Dr. Hagamen explains: "If you saw Sagamore as a bright and shiny . . . new place with lots of dedication, lots of young staff, you would get very excited . . . if you . . . had a [low-functioning] youngster and were having troubles with him. . . . It would be much easier to apply for a place here than it would be to apply to a place like Central Islip where [special children] had been. So, we rapidly became a place with these low-functioning youngsters . . . [who] are poorly understood and . . . are excluded from many services. Gradually . . . we . . . developed . . . programs that began to . . . work with these youngsters long before the family became burned out. . . . We could [then] make sure that they got into appropriate day programs. . . . [Sometimes] we felt it was better for the child and better for the family if we only took the child for the weekend, rather than have them living in an institution full-time, or at home full-time and exhausting their family [or] distorting their family interaction. So . . . we developed a variety of ways to help families . . . [i.e.,] family-support services. . . . And a natural extension of that . . . [because] we came to look at all children earlier, was to do outpatient work. . . . And we found that many of the things that we developed for our low-functioning youngsters, were also helpful to parents who had hyperactive kids. . . ."

As envisioned in the proposal, the outpatient department would provide a potpourri of services, roughly divisible into three categories of psychological and psychiatric treatment and evaluation; behavior management and social casework including family therapy and parent training; and physical treatment and evaluation including pediatric and neurological diagnosis, and speech and learning therapy. To a large extent the proposed array of services represented special interests of core Sagamore staff. For example, parent training for the care of handicapped children was a particular specialty of Dr. Ken Kaufman, while the concept of diagnostic and evaluation services was modeled somewhat on Columbia

Presbyterian where Dr. Hagamen had been a resident. Nonetheless, the services of the outpatient department were not rigidly defined at the outset; rather they were adapted to operational needs as the clinic began to function. Dr. Hagamen describes some of the evolution (and broadening of function) that took place: ". . . We began to develop classes for all kinds of parents. Having started out working with the parents of the retarded, we then began to work with the parents of the hyperactive youngster. . . . The parents began to come to us to understand their children better and to know . . . how to raise kids. . . . So we had some very wonderful people with some very normal, healthy children come to us like they might go to adult education. And we felt that that would be a very good thing . . . [because] it was . . . helpful to people who had disturbed children to see parents of healthy children there. . . . I have always felt that as far as 'mainstreaming' is concerned it is just as important to bring normal kids and normal people into the activities of the more disturbed [as] it is to get the more disturbed into [normal settings]. . . ."

A similar evolution took place in the diagnostic component of the outpatient program. Dr. Hagamen continues: ". . . There are many twists of the rope that you don't foresee. . . . [For example] we found that it took more time to do evaluations. . . . Initially we planned to be able to do treatment without doing evaluations and we found very quickly that we could not do treatment on other people's assessments. . . . We had to do our own assessments. . . . Putting people into treatment using outside referral information . . . we found was . . . not a good idea because we had such a great demand for treatment from the people that we had already diagnosed. . . . So . . . our treatment programs were largely done with the people that we diagnosed ourselves. . . . For instance, [if] a school program worked up a kid and said 'go there for treatment,' we still had to do an evaluation and assessment."

As befit the concept of the clinic, admission policy gradually broadened not only to include a wide variety of mental disabilities, but also to permit earlier intervention in children's and families' problems rather than have Sagamore serve solely as a last resort. In contrast, however, the geographic catchment area for the clinic was to be substantially narrower than that of Sagamore as a whole. Still a gradual broadening was anticipated here too. As Dr. Hagamen explains: "It was a new activity for us, so it seemed to me that we needed to develop expertise. . . . It was easier to start with a tiny core and then work with that, and develop our expertise as we went along. . . . Hopefully we would be able to transfer it out of the catchment area . . . once . . . we understood what needed to be done and how to do it. . . . We focused on a particular area surrounding the Sagamore Children's Center . . . in Babylon Township. . . . It seemed appropriate that we should be focusing on that as our target population but that we would not exclude anyone that came from another area. . . ."

If program and client policy decisions were developed gradually and adaptively over the period of the grant, certain strategic organizational decisions were clearly specified at the outset. A twin rationale underlied these organizational decisions: (1) Dr. Hagamen's desire to maximize the mileage she could get out of whatever (limited) grant funds were available from H.E.W., and (2) her intention to turn Sagamore "inside out," i.e., to shift its emphasis from inpatient to outpatient service.

A key decision was to staff the clinic largely with "per diem" people rather than full-time career employees. This would minimize fringe benefit costs associated with permanent employees and it would avoid long term commitments to people before their performance in the program could be properly assessed. Dr. Hagamen elaborates: "It was a very small grant—a hundred thousand dollars a year for three years. . . . What I did was to take the basic Sagamore staff and use them as senior people . . . but I hired per diem psychiatrists, per diem psychologists [etc.]. . . . The idea was to use the core personnel from the Center, and then let them pick whom they [wished]. . . . The people would come in from the outside . . . an afternoon a week and work in the outpatient clinic. And that meant that I really didn't have to pay that 33⅓% fringe. . . . [Another] reason for hiring people on a per diem basis . . . was . . . that we could decide whether we ever wanted them in a civil service position. . . . You really can't tell from a curriculum vitae or an interview what a person is going to be like. . . . Even with extensive recommendations you need to know how that person fits into your system, and this was an ideal way to find out whether anyone fit into our system."

As Dr. Hagamen observed, $100,000 a year wasn't very much money, but what she managed to do was to leverage this money with state funds, at an increasing rate over time so that more and more resources were devoted to the clinic operation. It was all part of her "inside-out" strategy to deemphasize inpatient care: ". . . This is another reason that it might have been attractive to H.E.W. . . . [In the] first year I put in 100 thousand dollars of state funds with a 100 thousand dollars of federal funds. The [second] year, I added enough staff from the State, so it was $200,000 of state funds and $100,000 of federal funds. . . . The next year we made it $300,000 of state funds. . . . You see, so as you close down the hospital [inpatient wards . . . you build up the clinic]. . . . I thought it was a very neat thing."

All this was consistent, of course, with Dr. Hagamen's general ideas on how to improve patient care: "We wanted . . . not . . . just to . . . lower inpatient care . . . we wanted to provide the services needed . . . and we felt that we could do that by offering alternatives to inpatient care

. . . with a better assessment of the youngsters who would be referred to us, particularly from Suffolk County [where outpatient services for children were meager]. . . ."

Over the period of Dr. Hagamen's tenure, the inpatient census of Sagamore was reduced from approximately 190 to 70, while the number of outpatients rose from approximately 50 in 1971 to 250 in 1977. The bulk of these changes were effected during the 1974–1977 grant period. One aspect of the "inside-out" decision was that Sagamore became bifurcated into two separate departments, a shrinking inpatient department and a growing outpatient department, with staff assigned to one or the other, and with the momentum of excitement (and possibly morale) favoring the latter. It was a situation that seems to have had serious long term implications. (see "Risks and Constraints" below.)

RISKS AND CONSTRAINTS

Turning a hospital "inside-out" would appear to be a rather radical venture, entailing concomitant, risks and resistance. But Dr. Hagamen seems to have had a fairly free hand until late into the grant period, when some of the risk factors began to materialize.

One of the risks was that Sagamore would be penalized financially by the State for having reduced its bed capacity, the traditional "hard" indicator of hospital workload. Initially Dr. Hagamen was assured that this would not be the case, but with the onset of the State's fiscal crisis the assurance became less meaningful. Dr. Hagamen recalls: ". . . There were problems because we were given cutbacks continuously from Albany because the census was going down and they began to allot staff based on increase in census, which was just the opposite of what they had told [us]."

A more serious source of risk was not specifically associated with the outpatient project so much as with the general tenuousness of the director's position. Running an institution for troubled children provides ample oportunities for incidents to occur that can be exploited by opponents of the director's policies or by the media, seriously hampering the director's effectiveness. Of more specific relevance to the outpatient venture, it was possible, although apparently unanticipated at the time, that phasing down the inpatient program would decrease the effectiveness of supervision in that area, hence increasing the chance of an incident. In any case, such an incident did occur in 1976, causing Dr. Hagamen to reflect on the risks: ". . . We went through some pretty hairy times based on some distortion of . . . minor incidents that were blown way out of proportion. . . . And because of the rapidity by which our communication system works now, there is always something on television, or a [newspaper] headline going into every home. So the life span of an administrator is cut down enormously compared to years ago. . . . You can't tolerate too many of these [incidents]. . . ."

In terms of actually implementing the outpatient program, Dr. Hagamen faced a number of conventional constraints associated with state government operations. For example, as noted earlier, funding for the program would not have been possible without the external grant: "[If the grant] hadn't come through . . . I don't think I could have done it. . . . I probably would have fought [for it] . . . but I think the time was not right for me to get any money [from the State] to do anything. It was also likely that 'bottom line' resistance would develop to a complete phase out of the inpatient program."

Dr. Hagamen feels this is endemic to any effort to eliminate a government program: ". . . I'm sure that on the part of some people . . . there was a worry that as we decreased the inpatient beds that we would be working ourselves out of existence. . . . And that is kind of hard for people [in] civil service to accept. . . . When the thing worked and we got the inpatient population . . . down to about 75 . . . people began to think 'Gosh, we need more patients.' . . . It's something to think about. . . . In the large state governments where in the past 15 years [there] have been a tremendous number of innovations, what you find in . . . [when] a program . . . comes that replaces [another] . . . nobody will have the guts to cut [the latter program] out."

Despite a generally effective, cooperative relationship that Dr. Hagamen enjoyed with officials of the State Department of Mental Hygiene in developing and processing the grant proposal, she still complained about the cumbersomeness of working administrative matters through the central office in the state capital. For example, the grant called for a subcontract for computer services: "[One problem was] . . . being able to develop contracts. . . . you know as a state agency, having to follow their contract protocol and getting approvals in Albany. [Things] would come through two or three weeks later. . . ."

Of all constraining factors, the civil service appointment system gave Dr. Hagamen the most grief in implementing the grant, although she got what she wanted after long hours of interviewing and processing candidates on civil service lists: ". . . You are very hampered in government operations by having to deal with civil service lists. . . . Some of the problems [with] civil service . . . were overcome by our stamina and knowledge. . . . I think we went down several dozen people on the list to get [the outpatient director]. . . . Civil service is a cumbersome method of hiring, and we followed the rules to the nth degree. But it is an exhausting procedure. Many people on the list have no idea of what the job is about and are really not interested, but to protect their standing on the list they respond to the canvass letter. This means hours of interviews. . . . I had interviews on my free days. . . . I worked on Sunday and . . . I had people come from out of state for 8 o'clock appointments on Sunday morning, because I had to start early to finish the interviewing. . . . [This] is why people don't do it. It just takes so much out of you."

OUTCOMES

During the period of the grant (1974)–1977) Sagamore Children's Center was rather dramatically turned "inside-out," exhibiting a major reduction of its inpatient beds and a build up to about 250 outpatients and 180 parent-training participants. Yet following 1977 the enterprise began to unravel. In January of 1978 the outpatient department was eliminated as a separate organizational unit, by Sagamore's new director, and staff members were no longer exclusively assigned to outpatient care. By 1979 the outpatient case load had dropped to 140 and the parent training enrollment to about 50. In contrast, the inpatient census rose from about 60 in 1977 to 130 in 1979.

There was also a change in the nature of outpatient care. Rather than serve children with a broad spectrum and varying levels of disability in a preventive orientation, Sagamore now confined its outpatient service to cases which would otherwise require immediate inpatient care. Similarly, parent training services were tied more closely to the needs of the inpatient population.

To a degree these changes were hedged by the spin-off of services from the outpatient department to other agencies in Suffolk County. For example, developmental pediatric services was still funded by Sagamore but administered by the Psychiatry Department at the State University at Stony Brook. And training for parents of autistic children was turned over to the Suffolk Child Development Center, with Sagamore staff (Ken Kaufman) in consultation.

It is difficult to pinpoint what caused the demise of the Sagamore outpatient program, but two factors are obviously involved—the departure of Mary Hagamen from Sagamore, and the expiration of the H.E.W. grant, both in the summer of 1977.

Although Dr. Hagamen took a relatively back-seat role in actually running the clinic, it was her sponsorship and support that enabled it to grow. It was "her baby." Anything that hampered her effectiveness would be likely to reduce the viability of the embryonic new department. The events of 1976—allegations of child abuse, child protective hearings, and adverse media coverage in connection with incidents in Sagamore's inpatient section—apparently took their toll. Although she rode out the storm, Dr. Hagamen had lost considerable strength. It became inevitable that she would leave, and that her pioneering programs would be jeopardized: "It was futile . . . to do anything. I waited until the whole thing was over . . . but I didn't want to [leave] . . . in the middle of that mish-mash. . . ."

"[In any case] I had to finish the job I started. I did everything that I felt I could do within the state system. . . . By the time I had the outpatient department done, by the time I had turned this hospital inside-out, I had done everything . . . that could be done in a state hospital. . . . I was ready to go on. . . ."

Even if Dr. Hagamen had not left, or if the adverse publicity had not marred her tenure, it is very possible that the outpatient program might have been phased down anyway. Without its external touchstone of support from the expiring grant, a renewed state endorsement and additional funds for the program would have to be sought. And it was becoming clear that the times were not right for this. Indeed, as Dr. Hagamen observes, it seemed more logical to disperse Sagamore's outpatient work throughout the county: ". . . We had arrived at the next chapter in the delivery of health services in the Department of Mental Hygiene. . . . Many things were changing rapidly. . . . Funds were changing from the state to the county [level]. . . . Population was moving eastward [on Long Island], away from the Center. . . . The [State] University [Health Sci ences Center at Stony Brook] was beginning to develop. A lot of things were happening. . . There was [also] an increased need for inpatient care for adolescents. Therefore, as the outpatient department evolved, so did the recognition that here was a building that was empty in terms of what it was designed for. . . . For Nassau and Suffolk Counties . . . therefore, would it not be appropriate to put those youngsters in that empty space that was now occupied by more preventive [services] and . . . to have the prevention programs move out to the community?

"[So] . . . it depends on where you take your photograph. . . . [Up to] 1976 there was a very optimistic outlook. Things were moving [toward outpatient emphasis]. If you take a photograph at the end of 1978, looking at the outpatient department, you see that the regional office had said 'Look, we built this as a hospital. The outpatient department should be in the community. Therefore, we want you to . . . do what needs to be done first. . . . Do what this hospital was built to do . . .'"

ANALYSIS

The Sagamore outpatient program was an opportunistic response to an RFP (request for proposal) by an energetic, idealist psychiatric professional committed to principles of good clinical practice, and to leadership in the world of professional ideas.

The venture took place in the public sector simply by circumstance.

The grant opportunity was noticed by someone in the State Department of Mental Hygiene and found fertile soil in Dr. Hagamen's administration of Sagamore. It is perhaps more germane to ask why Dr. Hagamen became a public sector administrator to begin with. Certainly she chafed constantly against the bureaucratic environment of the state system. But it was basically a physician's career ladder—specifically that of a child psychiatric professional—that Dr. Hagamen had followed. As such she had worked in both the nonprofit and public sectors. But it was the State, in recognition of her service as supervising psychiatrist at Central Islip State Hospital, that gave Dr. Hagamen the first major opportunity to shape her own program, as director of a new children's hospital. It was in this context that the outpatient program took root.

The clinic represented a natural extension of Dr. Hagamen's beliefs in early intervention and prevention-focused care, and parent-oriented training and support systems. It also provided a context for her involvement at the crossroads of psychiatric, pediatric, and obstetric disciplines. More than this, the outpatient department was an experiment—a model of the "inside-out" concept which Dr. Hagamen sought to demonstrate to her professional colleagues in other psychiatric hospitals.

The Sagamore outpatient program demonstrated both the skills and limits of Dr. Hagamen as a manager and administrator. Primarily a physician, and unused to the grantsmanship·game or other aspects of entrepreneurship, she might never have organized such a project if others had not made her aware of the opportunity. As an idealist, she is impatient with the administrative mentality, viewing bureaucracy as an obstacle to be overcome rather than to be indulged. Nonetheless, as an energetic, tenacious, competitive, and achievement-oriented person, she acquired considerable strategic skill in overcoming civil service constraints to staff the clinic by her own standards. And as a respected physician with adequate support at the top, and good standing among professional colleagues, she was able to indulge a relatively free hand to reorganize Sagamore Children's Center as she wished.

In 1974–1975, Dr. Hagamen was riding high. Hard work and good fortune had produced federal money to organize a pet program. She enjoyed not only a good personal reputation, but savored the image of Sagamore as a bright new children's psychiatric facility, with enthusiastic young staff. And her outpatient program, while somewhat inconsistent with Sagamore's original design parameters, was consistent with the State's new emphasis on deinstitutionalization of mental health. She succeeded in turning Sagamore inside-out although she may have erred strategically in departmentalizing inpatient and outpatient programs in a manner that might have demoralized the former.

In 1976 things began to change. Bad publicity emanating from incidents in the inpatient department undercut Dr. Hagamen's base of support. In 1977 the H.E.W. grant ran out, removing a strong reason for continued state commitment to the outpatient program. More conventional bureaucratic and political forces began to reclaim lost ground. Sagamore workload and budgeting requirements were still seen from above in terms of inpatient beds and Sagamore's institutional space began to be coveted to satisfy new demands for adolescent inpatient care. State budget crises reinforced these pressures to consolidate around old lines of defense and to allow local communities to pick up outpatient programs. Dr. Hagamen was no longer in the driver's seat. In better times, she might not only have completed the "inside-out" strategy, but found a way to maintain it on a more permanent basis.

Index